FOUR PILGRIMS

FOUR PILGRIMS

BY
WILLIAM BOULTING

Author of
Giordano Bruno : his Life, Thought, and Martyrdom;
Woman in Italy, 1100-1600 A. D. etc.

GYAN

Published by

GYAN

Gyan Publishing House
5, Ansari Road
Daryaganj, New Delhi-110002
Phone: 011-47034999, 9811692060
E-mail: books@gyanbooks.com

Distribution Network
gyanbooks.com
India, USA, Canada, UK, Australia, France

ISBN: 9788121234054 (PB)
First Published, 1920

2nd Impression 2020

Printed at: Gyan Press, Delhi.

Four Pilgrims
Author: William Boulting

FOUR PILGRIMS

BY

WILLIAM BOULTING

Author of

Giordano Bruno: his Life, Thought, and Martyrdom;
Woman in Italy, 1100-1600 A.D., etc.

LONDON:
KEGAN PAUL, TRENCH, TRUBNER & CO., LTD.,
NEW YORK: E. P. DUTTON & CO.

ERRATA.

Page 84, Line 2. For "a little before" read "some time after."

CONTENTS

I: HIUEN-TSIANG

Master of the Law: and his Perilous Journey to the Sacred Land of Buddha, A.D. 627-643.

II: SÆWULF, AN ENGLISH PILGRIM TO PALESTINE

III: MOHAMMED IBN ABD ALLAH,

Better known as Ibn Batuta, the Greatest of Moslem Travellers, A.D. 1304-77.

IV: LUDOVICO VARTHEMA OF BOLOGNA,

Renegade Pilgrim to Mecca, Foremost of Italian Travellers.

PREFACE

PILGRIMAGE has been popular in all countries and at all times. For what could be happier than an agreeable change which should contribute at once to welfare of soul, refreshment of spirit, and vigour of body? Adventures on the way gave zest to the enterprise. If the more timid or feeble were content to visit neighbouring shrines, those of hardier mould, like the Wife of Bath, took more formidable journeys.

> "Thries hadde she been at Jerusálem;
> She hadde passed many a straunge strem;
> At Rome she hadde been, and at Boloigne,
> In Galice at Seint Jame, and at Cologne,
> She koude muchel of wandrynge by the weye."

Some of the boldest and bravest of ancient travellers were pilgrims, and we have their records of wide wandering But their style is archaic, has at best little purely literary merit, and is usually forbidding. They are little known. except to the special student.

The footprints then are scanty, and all the worse for time, which testify to ardent spirits that once inhabited the warm vesture of flesh, but have long, long ago been laid to rest. I have tried to set forth certain of these dead and half-forgotten worthies as with "organs, dimensions, senses, affections, passions," even as we. Four have been chosen. Three of these were shrewd, fearless, observant men, who overcame surpassing obstacles and met with adventure almost unparalleled. The first of my bundle of four was a Chinaman, a Buddhist monk of the early Seventh Century, who started alone on an almost impossible quest. My second was an Englishman of the earliest years of the Twelfth Century, who gives us some notion of what the ordinary palmer was like who got to Jerusalem,

> "e qui devoto
> Il gran sepolchro adora e scioglie il voto"

("and venerates the Holy Sepulchre and discharges his vow"). My third was a Mohammedan, who, in the first half of the Fourteenth Century, made several pilgrimages to Mecca and ran over the world from Tangier to Pekin and from Turkestan to Timbuktu. My fourth was a very son of the glowing age of Julius II, the first European Christian on record to reach Mecca, one who outstripped the Portuguese in reaching the aromatic islands of the Banda Sea. In each case, there is a brief historical foreword to give the pilgrim due introduction into his proper setting.

WILLIAM BOULTING.

I.—HIUEN-TSIANG.

"MASTER OF THE LAW; AND HIS PERILOUS JOURNEY TO THE SACRED LAND OF BUDDHA, A.D. 627—643.

CHAPTER I. THE ISOLATION OF CHINA

FOR thousands of years China was a world to itself, cut off from the races of men. The main causes of this singular seclusion are simple:—

China was protected from serious invasion by her geographical position. Northward, it was no easy business for the barbarous intruder to find a way into China from the Manchurian plain, or for a Chinaman to find a way out; and it was still more difficult to effect a passage by force. To the North-West rose the forbidding walls of the Altai Mountains; and, between them and China, a broad and demon-haunted waste of sand blocked the way. Westward, huge interlocked ranges of Central Asia—the Thian Shan and Pamirs—mountains which o'er top Alp or Caucasus, which rival the loftiest Andes, and which are inferior only to Himalaya, presented perils in abundance. These difficulties surmounted, the vast, trackless sands of Gobi formed a second barrier; and the steep rocks of Ala-Shan and In-Shan were a third. To the South-West rose the plateau of Thibet, interlocking with the Pamirs—a plateau with a mean level of more than 12,000 feet, terminating southward in Himalaya, that highest and broadest of mountain-walls. To the South of China were the dense forests, deep valleys, and rapid rivers of Burma and Tonquin. Eastward the Celestial Empire was guarded by the sea: to reach China from India was a long and perilous voyage; and the boldest navigator might hesitate to entrust his clumsy craft to the caprice of the Indian Ocean, to thread his way through the tortuous straits of Malaysia, and to chance an encounter with the fierce islanders who lined them, only in the end to reach a jealous shore. The unwieldly Chinese junk—a town afloat—did, however, make a periodic and prolonged voyage—at least in later days—to India ; and a few bands of bold, hardy traders were wont to cross over the formidable passes of Central Asia on horses, mules, or asses, and to traverse vast, trackless wastes on camels. They exchanged the products of India, Persia, and those States which were watered by the classic streams of Oxus and Jaxartes, for the silks and manufactures of Cathay. Chinese porcelain has been found in Egyptian tombs.

China enjoyed a soil so productive of every kind of wealth that she was independent of commercial intercourse with other lands. Secure from all invaders but the scattered hordes of Mongolia, she developed a high and distinctive civilization, which became more and more fixed and rigid, but was superior in many respects to that of other Eastern States. By the Seventh Century of our Era, good roads, good inns, and an admirable system of canals rendered internal communication easy ; the heavens had been surveyed by astronomical instruments of some precision ; and the art of printing, which had not then been discovered long, was in use ; although to this day the Chinese do without the valuable economy of an alphabet.

Moreover the Chinese People preferred to be undisturbed by stimulus from without. Yet China transmitted her culture to her near and less civilized neighbours—Japan and the Indo-Chinese peninsula—and claimed a precarious overlordship of semi-barbarous Manchuria, Mongolia, Eastern Turkestan and Thibet. During a long stretch of time, the powerful and jealous Persian Empire was a bar to intercourse with the far West ; because it tried to preserve a monopoly of its own products.

The records of early intercourse with other countries are few ; and those few are meagre. Thirteen centuries before the age in which Hiuen-Tsiang lived, Embassies from distant nations would seem to have reached China. Marcus Aurelius despatched a mission (A.D. 166) to establish direct relations; it travelled by way of India; and failed. Carus sent another (A.D. 284). At the close of the fourth century, Ammianus Marcellinus knew of the Chinese as a people dwelling on fertile plains enclosed by protecting mountains: "a frugal folk, studying to live peacefully and shunning intercourse with the rest of mankind." Half a century later, Moses the Armenian spoke of them as "dwelling in wealth and civility at the end of the earth; a people worthy to be called not merely the friends of peace but of life." Until the Great Age of Discovery arrived as a novel development of the Great Age of the Renaissance to derange and remodel the earth, Cathay was little more than a name to European ears: before the Nineteenth Century, the Celestial Empire remained undisturbed by the Modern World.

Although the Chinese Government was always persistently obstructive to foreign intercourse, it took an interest in foreign religions. This seeming paradox was due to the fact that Confucianism, the official Faith, was essentially a body of moral precepts, as was Taoism, (albeit Taoism had stronger pretension to metaphysic), and both people and rulers were eager to receive any moral doctrine which might strengthen that love of peace and orderly conduct which would seem to be inborn in the Chinese breast. There was no *odium theologicum* in China. Now, Buddhism was essentially an ethical system, and had much in common with Taoism. On the whole, the Chinese were eager to adopt it; especially as becoming a good Buddhist did not disallow of one's remaining a good Confucian, or of reconciling Buddhistic and Taoistic speculation. The Chinese government naturally sanctioned a creed fitted to keep a people quiet and submissive; and Buddhism proved to be peculiarly suited to the Chinese mind: it touched the Chinese heart and left a profound effect on Chinese character.

It had to compete with other religions. For with the caravan of the trader came many religious Zealots, such as the Fire-Worshippers of Persia. At the very beginning of Mohammedanism, Wahd-Abi-Kabha, the maternal uncle of the Prophet, reached China, bearing presents to the Emperor; and Mohammedans were to be found there in the third decade of Hiuen-Tsiang's life; while, in the following decade, Nestorian missionaries introduced Christianity, which, after due examination, an Imperial Decree declared to be a satisfactory and permissible faith. Buddhist missionaries carried the teaching of Gautama to China at a period not yet ascertained; but it must have lost much of its early purity by whatever time that may have been.

CHAPTER II.

BUDDHA AND BUDDHISM.

GAUTAMA was the son of a petty chieftain, who exercised limited authority in a district which lay north of Faîzâbâd. He lived about 600 years before the beginning of the Christian era—about the time when Jerusalem fell to Nebuchadnezzar and Assyria to the Medes. The evils of disease, old age, and death weighed on the melancholy mind of the young princelet: he sought for some way of escape from the curse of craving flesh and the wild delirium of desire. He abandoned wife and family; and dwelt, at first, in the solitude of a jungle. At this time, his life was one of pure contemplation. Then a wave of love for humanity and profound grief at human suffering swept over him. He resumed the active life, preaching a pure religion of duty and affection along the valley of the Ganges; for his soul, like the soul of Plato's poet, "was no longer within him." He had learned and he taught that the misery of Being is mitigated by strict obedience to the Law of human kindness and duty. He made stirring appeals to heart and conscience, and supported his mission by the ancient doctrine of Kharma, which Brâhmans had taught him—the doctrine that the action of the evil will, barren as its fruits invariably prove for the living agent, is delayed, but not destroyed, by death, and builds up a new body and mind, which reap the bitter harvest of former transgression and also the weal which results from former well-doing. The heart achieves blessedness in proportion to its purification; a good life acquires merit, by means of which relative freedom is obtained from the mournful, malevolent turnings of the "wheel of things." Completely purified, Nirvâna (which is sometimes interpreted as nescience, sometimes as the supra-conscious), peace in the very heart of things, is obtained. All men may be touched by love ; but only rare intelligencies will seek Nirvâna. For the way to the Blessed Life is steep and beset with thorns ; but the resolute spirit may achieve increasing and even perfect tranquillity by up-rooting every germ of ill-will and trampling down every one of those passions of mind or body the results of which are as futile as their origin is senseless. Gautama accepted the institution of the cloister then, for such men of high intelligence as sought the truly spiritual. In time Buddhistic monasticism became divided into the system of the "Lesser Vehicle"—an ascetic scheme of discipline,— and that of the "Greater Vehicle" for richer and more metaphysical minds. The first aimed at restraint ; the second, at contemplation. Buddha had no regard for caste ; and this brought his teaching into conflict with that of the Brâhmans ; he promised no endless personal life in heaven—only progressive release from the evils of temporal existence ; he did not interfere with the popular worship of gods. His doctrine was an appeal to our more spiritual nature, and closely resembles the Sermon on the Mount. It awakened a people bound by a system of lifeless forms framed by a priestly caste, yet who were all athirst for living waters.

But Buddhism speedily became metaphysical in the metaphysical East. Some of the convents grew into abodes of speculation and seminaries of learning. It was held that Gautama was the latest of those Buddhas, those "redeemers" of the world, into whose mother's womb Bôdhissatva, the spirit about to become a Buddha, descended spiritually. Yet the purest teaching of the Spirit contains within itself the seeds of its own decay : the germ of fulfilment is also the germ of dissolution. The history of Buddhism strikingly illustrates the truth of this, its own tenet. Before long the new Faith, like unto Brahmanism, became half-throttled by formalism and encrusted by all manner of ridiculous legend and vulgar superstition. And Asôka, who usurped a throne and established an Empire at Magadha, near Behar (in the 3rd century before Christ ?) embodied the ethics of Buddhism in formal ordinances. The letter and not the spirit, of the Law prevailed. But Asôka sent forth missionaries, East and West and North and South, and they reached far distant lands.

Probably imperfect and infrequent relations between Chinese Buddhists and Indian priests were maintained through the medium of caravans of trade. These have left no record ; but in A.D. 65, the Chinese Authorities sent envoys to Sind by the long, painful, and perilous overland route. They returned with an Indian priest, sacred writings, and sacred images of Buddha. After this, an occasional embassy from India arrived ; but such missions soon came to an end, although a little intercourse was kept up with Ceylon by means of an arduous and dangerous voyage. Not until the fourth century were Chinamen allowed to become Buddhist priests. Then, at once, monasteries sprang up all over the country. About the year 400 Fa-Hian and others with him were sent on an embassy to secure religious writings. They made their difficult way through Central Asia. Fa-Hian alone returned, after 14 years absence, by way of Ceylon, bearing authentic scripture with him. A hundred years later Sung-Yun became a pilgrim to the same end and was successful in securing a hundred and seventy volumes. Gautama, like Jesus, had taught by word of mouth only. His manner was to utter some pithy precept, and then to develop it in a running commentary. But his disciples recorded these precious words ; and, from time to time, expositions and doctrinal developments and marvellous fables were added. Of these, the earlier were written in Pali ; the later in Sanskrit, even then a dead tongue, knowledge of which was the privilege of a small learned class. These Buddhistic writings, made on prepared palm-leaves, were regarded by the faithful with superstituous reverence; and Chinese Buddhists were anxious to obtain complete and accurate copies of them, as well as sacred images and relics of Buddha, which might serve as the objects of deep veneration.

At no period has the disordered tragedy of human history been more cataclysmic than in the early part of the Seventh Century after Christ. The whole world was then a theatre of wild unrest and stupendous change, little as one fragment of the human race might know of aught but its own disasters or triumphs. The shattered edifice of the Roman Empire of the West was run over by Lombard, Frank and Goth and races still more barbarous than these. From Cheviot to Illyricum, all was confused, bloody, and unceasing riot. The exceptional vigour of Heraclius alone saved the Roman Empire of the East from the ever-watchful and now advancing hosts of Persia; while a new and wholly unexpected menace arose in the Arabian desert: there a peril burst forth as abrupt, fierce and overwhelming as a sandstorm of that rocky waste. For Mohammed and his followers advanced thence with fiery and resistless speed to offer the nations choice between the Koran, tribute, and the sword. Even distant, tranquil China, the land cut off from the rest of mankind was parturient: the Empire had broken up, and was contended for by vulturine feudatories, who fought together for sole possession of its bleeding carcase. A new and strong dynasty arose amid slaughter and desolation. But, for a time, Central China was hell let loose. The adolescence of Hiuen-Tsiang was passed amid scenes of death and dismay.

CHAPTER III.

AN ADVENTUROUS JOURNEY.

THIS boldest of pilgrims, greatest of Chinese travellers, came into the world A.D. 603—nearly twelve hundred years after the founder of his faith. He was the fourth son of a Chinese Professor in the Province of Ho-nan, in Central China. Probably he shewed mental ability and a devotional spirit early; for the second of his elder brethren took him into his own monastery at Lo-Yang, the Eastern Capital, to supervise his education. The boy is said to have evinced such brilliant parts and such a spiritual mind that he became a novice at what would seem, at that time, to have been the exceptionally early age of thirteen years; although, two centuries before, Fa-Hian was a novice at three! It was soon after this event that revolution shook the ancient Empire, and came near to disrupt it. China became a slaughter-house, and Buddhist priests were murdered as well as Government Officials.

As certain saints bear witness, the passion that wings its flight towards no earthly home is occasionally combined with bold and efficient direction of mundane life. It was so combined in Hiuen-Tsiang. The monk of perfervid faith gave early proof that he was a lad of mettle as well as an enthusiast for the Greater Vehicle. In resolution and spirit, he dominated his elder brother, and insisted on their both setting off, in the teeth of peril, for a safer place in the Eastern province of Sz-chuen; and here he ended his novitiate and was fully ordained at the age of twenty.

At last, chaos within the Chinese frontier and warfare along it began to yield to the military genius and statecraft of T'ai-Tsung, the greatest of Chinese warriors and rulers. Hiuen-Tsiang was not slow to avail himself of the return of some measure of tranquillity to the State. He disobeyed monastic authority, joined a band of nomadic traders, and visited convent after convent of the wide Empire, with the purpose of clearing his mind, in debate with their inmates, concerning difficult problems in scriptural scholarship and the precise import of certain tenets of his faith. There was full scope for speculative discussion, since Chinese Buddhists did not yet possess a complete set of the Sacred Writings or of the Buddhist Fathers and workers in that kind of suggestive fiction which is so often taken to be veritable history and which becomes the wardrobe of moral truth. Much was, as yet, unsettled by authority and lay open to dispute.

Dissatisfied by the indefinite results of controversy, and fired by the records of previous pilgrims, the young monk resolved to make for the cradle and sanctuary of Buddhism and to seek there for the books which his countrymen lacked. He and a few ardent monks applied to the newly-established Emperor for permission to do this. The monarch was Kao-T'sou, first of the T'ang dynasty—that most famous of the many Imperial lines of China—the glory of having founded which rests with his son, the redoubtable T'ai-Tsung, whom, later on, we shall find seated on his father's throne. The request was made at an inopportune time, and was refused. For monkdom did not stand in court-favour just then; monks were ordered to marry; possibly, because recent internecine strife had thinned the population; possibly, also, because the new government was jealous, in a perilous time, of the power of growing sacerdotalism. This prohibition put an end to the hope of Hiuen-Tsiang's coadjutors: it only increased his own ardour and hardened his own resolve. He was now 24 years of age; therefore in the full vigour of early manhood; he cared nothing for obedience to constituted authority when constituted authority stood in the way of spiritual enlightenment. And he was not merely filled with religious enthusiasm: the restless force and curiosity of youth were his; there were shrewd, observant eyes in his head as well as disciplined wits. Here was a man anxious and fitted to observe the physical features, governments, productions, and peculiarities of unknown countries and to record them. Westward, beyond the setting sun, lay mysterious lands, vague as a dream, yet to be found a reality in this so wondrous world. There was a call from afar. When the spirit of one born for action is all a-fire with enthusiasm begotten of idea, let the world keep watch!

It would appear from Tao-Sun, a Chinese author contemporary with Hiuen-Tsiang, that there were three routes from China to India—the one which our traveller took; the one by which he returned; and a third from Lake Lob-nor, over the thousand miles of terrible plateau in Thibet and the Himalayas to Nepal. Before long Hiuen Tsiang was at Liang-chau, the capital of the province of Lan-su, far beyond the upper reaches of the great Yellow River, and nearly at the extreme north-western limit of China Proper. Here were gathered merchants from Thibet and other far-distant lands; and these were so impressed by Hiuen-Tsiang's fervour and the grandeur of his project that they are said to have cast themselves at his feet. They provided him with ample means to go on. Now, Chinese administration in the province of Lan-su had only been established recently, and remained insecure; no inhabitant was allowed to cross the frontier; and the Governor was a strong man who rigorously enforced his regulations. But what are the strongest bonds of any mere narrow national group against the conflicting obligation of Moral or Ideal impulse? How can usage and prescription and enactment prevail against more spiritual forces? Our would-be pilgrim secured the aid of a friendly monk, and stole out of the city by night, accompanied by two young novices. The trio stealthily, yet rapidly, pursued their course each night; they crept furtively into some hiding place before each dawn. By the time this evasive noctambulation had brought them to Kwa-chau, more than a hundred miles north-east of Liang-chau, Hiuen-Tsiang's horse was dead. There was small comfort in learning that he would have to cross a river so turbulent that no boat could live on it; that, beyond the river, was an entrenchment which he must contrive to get over; and that, even should he overcome this obstacle, the frontier was closed by rings of forts; beyond the forts there was a vast stretch of herbless, waterless waste; and beyond this desert lay the land of a Turkish people—those Uïghurs, who appear in European folk-lore as the terrible Ogres.

His heart sank within him; the melancholy which seized him lasted a whole month, and his taciturnity made it apparent. The Imperial Veto arrived at Kwa-chau; the Governor of the city sent him a summons to appear. But this new blow roused his failing courage; he pulled himself together; personality and enthusiasm prevailed at the interview; the Governor was won over; Authority gave the pilgrim a hint to lose no time in making off; and closed its official eye to his departure.

Now, one of the novices was faint-hearted; the other sickly. Hiuen-Tsiang sent them back. He was anxious to get on his solitary way as fast as he could; so he bought a new horse; but he lacked a guide. By a lucky accident he fell in with a "barbarian," who expressed a desire to become a monk, and who offered to guide him past the five successive forts which lay ahead, and which he must somehow contrive to dodge. The "barbarian" also took him to see an ancient trader who had been to the land of the Uïghurs over thirty times. This old gentleman made no attempt at reassuring him. "The routes of the West are rough and dangerous," he said, "now, one is stopped by shifting sands; now, by demons and scorching winds. Even big caravans are liable to lose their way and come to a miserable end. How, then, can you hope to make the journey all by yourself?

Be wise, I entreat you, and do not play with your life." But the monk answered that he held his life as nothing when set against his holy quest. The old trader then dropped vain arguments and proposed a deal which should be mutually profitable: he would take the horse which Hiuen-Tsiang had bought, and would give him his own Rosinante, which had made the journey so often, and therefore must remember the road. The pilgrim, when he saw the beast, recalled how one skilled in occult science had once spoken to him of an ancient steed, reddish of colour, with a varnished saddle and an iron framework to it; and lo! was not the very steed before him? He closed the bargain; and he and the barbarian set forth together, each on his "mount."

The twain came up to the river (the Bulunghir) and found a place where there were narrows. The guide proved himself to be resourceful: he made a sort of bridge of boughs, covered them with sand, and belaboured the horses until they dashed across the frail structure. A strange way of crossing an unfordable stream! but by no means so improbable as it sounds. It is said to be still used in Central Asia.

Night drew on. Both men were weary, and spread their mats for sleep. But Hiuen-Tsiang placed small confidence in his guide. They lay fifty paces apart. And, before long, our hero heard a stealthy footfall and saw the dim outline of the half-savage stalking up to him. With drawn sword, too! He sprang up, and breathed a prayer; whereupon the guide returned to his own mat, stretched himself out, and straightway fell asleep. Had he meant evil? or did he wish to make off if he found the pilgrim asleep? or was his desire to frighten him from pursuing a journey so perilous to them both?

Next morning, being already within the verge of the desert, they ate sparingly, but were lucky enough to find water. No more water would be found until they reached close up to the first fort; and they must steal this by night;

for, once espied by the garrison, they might count themselves dead men. The guide tried to work on our pilgrim to give up such a mad enterprise. But Hiuen-Tsiang knew no shadow of turning; so the twain, ears and eyes wide open, wormed they way over the rough tackless waste. Suddenly the guide tightened his bow and bade Hiuen-Tsiang go on in front. Our pilgrim was far too wary a person to do anything of the kind; he was by no means satisfied as to the designs of the half-civilized stranger. However, the barbarian quietly resumed his duty as scout; but he displayed such a desire to be out of it all, and his fears were so obviously growing, that Hiuen-Tsiang dismissed him with a present of the horse he rode.

Behold our traveller, then, solitary on the unending, pathless desert of Gobi—one of the most immense of Earth's waste places,—eagerly on the look out for such heaps of bleached bones as might mark the track of some caravan. After some time of slow, painful progress, he beheld a band of men wearing glittering armour and bearing their banners unfurled; they were making for him, but vanished as suddenly as they appeared. It was the mirage come to perplex and delude him. One illusion followed another in rapid succession; fleeting, dissolving scenes which were the works of the Devil. But a voice said to him: "Fear not." This brought comfort, and his fear departed. He pushed on, and in the end he sighted the watch-tower. He hid in a sand-hollow until night closed round, and then he crept up to the wall of the fort and found the hoped-for water. He was busy filling his leathern-bottle, when an arrow whizzed by and very nearly hit him; and a second arrow followed. He shouted out: "Stop your shooting. I am a monk from the Capital." Soldiers ran up, dragged him into the fort, and took him before their captain. He produced papers which proved his identity, and was treated with the respect due to a priest of Buddha; yet the Captain urged him to return home. Finding the pilgrim to be a man of heroic piety and inflexible will, he set out with him and guided him some distance along the way to the next fort. He even gave Hiuen-Tsiang a message to its captain, recommending the pilgrim to his favour and assistance. But the message was a verbal one only. And Hiuen-Tsiang was not sure that he might not find more rigour and less charity at the next watch-tower; so, when he came up to it, he crept furtively towards its base, in search of water as before. The dispatch of an arrow was sufficient warning; he came into the open, and the scene at the first fort was re-enacted. He repeated the message to its Captain; and this second officer gave him hospitable entertainment and better advice. For he urged him to avoid the third fort, which was held by rough soldiery, who would not be nice in making delicate distinctions and might easily become violent. And he directed him to take a route which avoided this fort altogether, and along which, at ten leagues distance, he would come across sweet water.

He set off across the arid plain, where was neither beast nor bird to be seen, nor blade of grass, nor any sign of moisture—only mirage. A pandemonium of fantastic forms encircled him; forms begotten of the Power of Evil. But he felt secure in the midst of devils; for did he not bear, folded in his bosom, a sure talisman—none other than a Sacred Manuscript, the gift of a grateful leper to whom he had stood as a friend?

Illusory peril was followed by solid disaster: he dropped his water-bottle and spilled its precious contents. Next, his horse lost its way, and made the same long circuit again and again. For a moment, he was tempted to assay a return to the fort: he brushed the thought aside, turned his horse's head to the North-West, and pushed on.

Night came on. Evil spirits seized on the opportunity to close in on him. Every demon bore a burning torch. They were more in multitude than the stars of heaven.

Four horrid nights, filled with hallucination, wore away. Four days he struggled on, tortured by thirst, his body one ache. At last horse and rider fell to the ground, worn out. Death was close at hand when a refreshing night-breeze swept over the desert, and horse and rider renewed the struggle. Suddenly, the horse insisted on taking his own way: he had scented water; and soon a little oasis was reached. It was uninhabited; but a day's rest there refreshed man and beast; and, on the third day, the traveller saw the last of the shifting sands of Shamo and came to the pastures of the Uïghurs.

In the capital, probably identical with the town now known as Hâmî, he found a Buddhist monastery, wherein dwelt three Chinese monks. He had already made fully 600 miles from Liang-chau; but that was as nothing to the journey which lay before him; and from this he was compelled to digress. For he was in a region tributary to the ruler of Kau-chang (Turfan) and this monarch, having heard of his arrival, ordered that he should be sent on to him. Six days of travel to the West, through a desert, brought him to Turfan. The Lord-paramount of the Uïghurs received him with all honour and much state-ceremony. He sat under a "canopy of precious stuffs" pitched in the courtyard of a palace. Soon after the pilgrim's arrival, the queen, accompanied by her suite, appeared; but Hiuen-Tsiang being fatigued, their Majesties retired to the "palace," and he was conducted to his chamber, where eunuchs served and guarded him. Next day he was taken to a Buddhist convent, still in the custody of the eunuchs. For the monarch had resolved to keep such a holy person for the better instruction of his subjects.

Hiuen-Tsiang incurred the royal displeasure by stoutly refusing to do as he was bid and stay on. Then ensued, in that far-away time and half barbaric land, the ancient and ever recurrent struggle which history so copiously illustrates—the contest between regnant authority and the claims of religion. At one time the despot tried to brow-beat; at another time, to cajole; he even put aside his dignity and offered to serve the monk at table. Both men were equally resolute; and the situation seemed hopeless, when Hiuen-Tsiang bethought him of an expedient with which we moderns became familiar at no very recent date. He started to hunger-strike. In four days the result of this policy alarmed the King. The queen-mother declared herself for the holy pilgrim, and the monarch gave in. He begged that Hiuen-Tsiang would at least stay in the country during one short month. The monk accepted the compromise; and in that single month his unaffected piety, passionate singleness of aim and personal attraction did the work they never failed to accomplish everywhere and on every occasion. Moral intensity was the secret of his success.

And so we see the poor wanderer who came to Uïghur-land alone, famished, and half dead, leaving the land under the protection of an armed escort, and provided, not merely with an ample supply of warm clothing for the heights he must cross, but with 100 ounces of gold, 30,000 pieces of silver and 500 pieces of satin for the presents which were necessary and to pay his way. He was also given letters of recommendation to the Princes of the West. Monks and the population of the city followed him beyond its gates; and the despot, having sent the queen and people back, conducted him surrounded by his whole court, some miles on his journey.

The route lay westward, over a difficult, mountainous land. Southward lay the Tarim, a considerable river, which discharges itself into Lob-nor, one of the numerous inland salt-seas of Asia, for ever rising and falling and shifting its boundaries. It was well that the pilgrim had a military escort; for a band of brigands lurked among the mountains. They were probably quite as strong as the Uïghur soldiery; for negotiations were entered into, and ended in their being bought off.

A little farther on there was ghastly evidence that these ruffians had recently attacked and destroyed a caravan of traders: a few score corpses lay stretched out on the ground.

When Kara-shahr (Karshâr) was reached, its King behaved courteously, but refused to grant fresh horses, by reason of the frequent raiding of his domain by the Uïghurs. He was disquieted by the presence of Uïghur soldiery. Hiuen-Tsiang tells us, among much else that is interesting, that the coinage here was of gold, silver and copper,— that there were ten Buddhist monasteries of the Lesser Vehicle; that these were properly kept, but that the country "had no annals" and that "the laws were not settled. The people clothe themselves in cotton or wool, and go about with their scalps shorn and uncovered."

The separate account of each country the pilgrim visited or concerning which he believed he had credible information—his great monumental work—the *Si-yu-ki* —begins with Kara-shahr which he calls Akni or Agni. One is at once struck with the exactness of the author's observation, the orderliness of his mind, and the minute precision of his statement. One is equally astounded at his oriental love of the marvellous and his eager haste to record every grotesque and absurd legend. There is before us a man as full as any modern explorer of ardent zeal for travel, eager curiosity, keen eye, and quick interest in all that is novel and peculiar. There is the same intellectual grasp of the natural features, products and government of strange countries. But Hiuen-Tsiang's inmost, burning passion is revealed both in this book and in the biography compiled from his documents and discourse by two pupils and intimate friends Hwui-Lih and Yen-Tsong[1]: it was for all that appertained to his

[1] *Mémoires sur les contrées occidentales*, par Hiouen-Thoang, tr. du chinois par S. Julien, 2 t., 1857–8.

Si-yu-ki. Tr. from the Chinese of Hieuen Tsiang by S.

religion, whether sacred writing or Buddhist monuments or the relics of saints. When he deals with mundane matters he rarely goes astray. And, from his earliest years, he bore a sacred flame, a consuming fire in his breast, fed by the highest and holiest emotions and aspirations of man. But, although he breathed the breath of life, the purest atmosphere of the East in his century was tainted by superstition. The mental disposition for the marvellous, implanted in him at a tender age, and sustained by precept and example, waxed with the years. The absurdest legends became credible if they bore the name of his faith. This close observer, this clear minded man became passionate for prodigies, had a Gargantuan swallow for the superstituous-grotesque. Brought up on legend, he soon found himself in a home of fable. He records every marvellous tale which is told him, and worships at every shrine which guards any relic of wonder. And this although he was not wanting in passion for orderly thinking.

News from Kara-shahr that a holy pilgrim, bound for India, might be expected reached the next Kingdom, and he found monks standing to greet him at the gate of Kutchê, its capital. Feelings of simple grace and beauty dwelt in those Eastern hearts; they welcomed him with a gift of flowers. But the strict laws of his order did not permit of his accepting these for himself. He placed them before an image of Buddha, Teacher of the Law. Kutchê was a land of music, its people

Beal. 2 v. (Trübner s Oriental Series) 1884.

Hist. de la vie de Hiouen Thsang et de ses voyages dans l'Inde A.D. 629–45, par Hoei-Li et Yen-Thsong. Tr. du Chinois par S. Julien. Imprim. Impér. 1853.

The Life of Hiuen-Tsiang. Tr. by S. Beal. (Trübner's Oriental Series) 1878.

The spelling of Oriental names of persons and places varies widely in English, as well as in other European languages, according to the system of transliteration employed.

excelling all others on the lute and pipe. They were a wholly honest folk, with an incompetent ruler. "The King's wisdom being small," says our Chinaman, "he is ruled by a private minister. The heads of children of the humbler order are flattened by the pressure of a wooden board"; which recalls the custom of certain North American Indians. The King had ordered a banquet to honour his visitor; but the strictness of the rule which Hiuen-Tsiang followed forbade him to be present. This cast the potentate into a mighty rage; but once again the simplicity and sincerity of the pilgrim's character, which glowed in his countenance, disarmed wrath. He was retained at Kutchê, an honoured guest, until such time as the snows should melt. He spent two months there, chiefly occupied in religious discussion with the monks. He tells us that the monarch and his ministers met together once a month to discuss matters of state, and consulted the priests before publishing their decrees.

When the season ripened and the ways became open once more, he was sent forth in magnificent pomp and protection; he was accompanied by an armed escort and a staff of servants, all mounted on camels and horses. The escort was very necessary; for a great horde of Turkish robbers were passed on the way, quarrelling about the booty of a caravan which they had stopped and plundered. A march of about 120 miles brought our party to a small desert which they crossed over, and so entered the domain of another Khân. A single night was spent at what is now Bai, where he found Buddhist monasteries, and the party pushed across another small desert. The towering and forbidding ranges of Thian-shan were before them, "very dangerous and reaching up to the sky." Indeed Khân Tengri, the highest mountain of the range, has an elevation of 24,000 feet. The imposing features of the mountain-masses and the horror of the passes across them left indelible marks on Hiuen-Tsiang's memory. "Since the creation of the world," he says, " the snow has gathered there and become frozen blocks, which spring and summer cannot melt. Shining sheets of solid ice spread before one, and there is, as it were, no end to them ; they blend with the clouds. Frozen splinters have become detached and have fallen ; some of these are an hundred feet high ; others measure some dozens of feet athwart, and they bar the way. You attempt to climb over the former kind at your peril ; you get across the latter with pain. And all the time tempest assails you with gusts of wind and whirling drifts of snow ; so that double soles to your foot-gear and fur garments to your body fail to keep out the cold. Of dry shelter there is none, either to feed or sleep in. You have to sling up your cooking-pot and lay your sleeping mat on the frozen ground." Mountain-staves were used, and we learn from the *Si-yu-ki* (the "Record of Western Countries") that mountaineers were accustomed to cut steps in the ice. But to climb uncharted hills, among the highest of the world, led by guides of no great experience ; to make one's way over rock and glacier unroped and unprovided with specially constructed boots ; to sleep in the open in rarified and arctic air ; to live on poor food, and often to lack it, was to loathe the mountain-pass. And this Hiuen-Tsiang did, heartily.

It cost the caravan seven dolorous days to cross the higher ranges, and, by the time the western uplands were reached, 13 or 14 strong men had been lost through cold and hunger, and more than double that number of beasts of burthen.

Beyond the mountains, the uplands of Western Turkestan lie at a higher level than that reached by Ben Nevis, and they embosom a great inland sea—the Issyk-Kul, which lies nearly 5,000 feet up. Wending their way along its southern shore, our travellers ran into a hunting party of the Khân of the Turks. Only half a century had then passed since nomadic Turkish tribes possessed themselves of the "thousand sources" of those two great rivers which lose themselves in the Aral Sea, which are known to modern geographers as Amu Daria and Syr Daria, and which readers of the classics know as Oxus and Jaxartes. The Turks speedily became masters of the fertile plains of Sogdiana and Bactria, subdued the tribes that occupied the region we call Bokhâra, and extended thei. sway into the very heart of the Hindû Kûsh, reaching as far south as the Kapiśa of the Greeks—that is to say, within a few miles of Kâbul.

We have an interesting account of how the Nomadic Ruler gave the travellers a gracious reception within a great tent, resplendent with cloth of gold. Two long rows of dignitaries, clad in figured silks of many colours, squatted on mats before the Khân; behind him stood the royal guard. He wore a cloak of green satin; his long hair was bound over the forehead by several folds of silk, the ends whereof fell over his back. When on horseback, two hundred captains, gay in brocade and riding horses with plaited tails, and an army with banners, spears and long bows accompanied him. This was not foot soldiery; horses or camels were ridden, and the men were clad in furs and fine wool. One could see no end to the army, it was such a multitude. Our author tells us that the Turk of his day worshipped fire, and sat on mats, since wooden chairs contain the quality of fire. Ten centuries later Sir Thomas Browne, in his "Urn-Burial" refers to the Parsees of India "which expose their bodies unto vultures and endure not so much as *feretra* or biers of wood, the proper fuel of fire." A huge arm-chair, made of iron and covered with a mat was brought in for the use of Hiuen-Tsiang. The whole party was invited to sit, Turkish fashion; wine was brought in, cups clinked, and everybody drank, turn and turn about; while music, which to Chinese ears was barbaric yet not unpleasing, came from strange instruments. After the wine, legs and shoulders of boiled mutton and veal were brought in; but the Buddhist was separately served with "pure food"—rice-cake, cream, milk, crystallized sugar, honeycomb and grapes. Of course the divine gadfly which pursued our hero stung him to testify on this occasion, as on all other opportunities, whether in season or out of season. But his personality stood him in good stead; moreover, to this day, a holy man is respected throughout the pagan East, no matter what his faith may be. The Khân was interested and attentive; even impressed. He raised his hands towards heaven, cast himself on the ground, kept Hiuen-Tsiang about his person for some days, and earnestly besought him to give up his project. "You must not go," he said. "The country is a very hot one. You look too frail a man to give hope of your success. The natives are black; they go about naked; they have no modesty; they are unworthy of your presence among them." "Whatever I may be," replied the Master of the Law, "I burn with longing to seek for the commands of Buddha, to inspect the ancient monuments, and to follow lovingly the track of our Lord's footpath on earth." What followed marks yet once more the personal ascendency of our hero in every situation. This half-savage head of wild Mongolian hordes sought straightway for some one who knew Chinese and could also interpret the confusion of tongues in his own subject-lands to the south. Such a man was speedily picked out of the Khân's army; for Chinese had been carried off by the Turkish Hiung-nu (a people possibly, though by no means certainly, identical with the terrible Huns whom Attila led to devastate Europe) and had settled down in towns, deserted when Hiuen-Tsiang arrived in the district, but where they had kept up their native tongue, although they had adopted Turkish dress and ways. With true Eastern courtesy to a guest, the great Khân accompanied our traveller some little way on his journey.

At first the route lay westward towards the "Land of the Thousand Sources"—a region of lakes and pools, great trees, much vegetation, and a sweet and wooing air. Hither the Khân was wont to repair in summer. Still travelling westward, Talas was reached, and then, by bending round to the South-West and South, Samarkand, the "storehouse of precious merchandise from many foreign countries." Our traveller found the ruler "full of courage, and controlling neighbouring countries" with his fierce soldiery. He received the pilgrim with an air of lofty disdain; but Hiuen-Tsiang was not a man to be daunted, and, next day, when he boldly set forth his faith, contempt became respect. Buddhism was practically dead in Samarkand. The monasteries were empty. Two young monks who were with Hiuen-Tsiang sought to pass the night in one of these vacant buildings; but the populace threw burning brands at them and drove them out. The King condemned the offenders to decapitation; but Hiuen-Tsiang pleaded for mercy; so they were merely beaten and expelled from the city. His successful intercession increased the fervour of his missionary zeal; nor did he toil in vain; the monasteries were re-opened; and he ordained priests to fill them.

Leaving Samarkand, about 90 miles off, he entered a pass bordered by mountains "of prodigious heighth, with a narrow road" to add "to the difficulty and danger." The pass was closed by double wooden doors, studded with iron, and hung with bells. The pass owed its name—The Iron Gates—to these strong defences.

The Oxus was reached and crossed, and our pilgrim now deviates considerably from the direct route to fulfil a promise which he had made to the Khân of the Uïghurs to visit his son-in-law, the son of the great Khân of the Turks, who ruled over a little Khânate, called Hwo, and probably identical with the district which lies east of the Surkh-âb. When he arrived, he found the monarch on his death-bed; and was obliged to wait two months until the funeral ceremonies were done with. During this time a tragedy took place which casts a lurid light on court-life in Central Asia during the Seventh Century, and which reminds us of the Italian tragedies during the High Renaissance. The wife of the Khân had died, and the Khân replaced her by marrying her young sister. At the instigation of a son by the first marriage, the bride murders her husband. "The serpent that did sting his father's life now wears his crown," and marries his aunt-step-mother. A similar atrocity is recorded of the Chinese Imperial family in Hiuen-Tsiang's time. In A.D. 655 the Emperor, Kao-Tsung, deposed the Empress and married one of his father's widows, who wholly ruled him, cut off the feet of the Empress, and of another queen, and then had these unfortunate ladies drowned "like Clarence in his Malmsey-butt," in a vat of wine.

Hiuen-Tsiang was fortunate in finding a monk who had dwelt in India and had studied the Scriptures there; and the twain set forth for Balkh in some sort of waggon. At Balkh, he found no fewer than a hundred Buddhist monasteries, three thousand monks, and sacred memorials and relics beyond count. He might have become very rich; for the Kinglets around Balkh were eager to secure a visit from such a holy being, and offered to load him with gold and jewels. But he was not the man to depart from the straight and narrow path he had chosen. He refused them one and all, and set forth for ways "even more difficult and dangerous than the deserts of ice. Every moment one is at battle there with frozen cloud or snow-whirlwind. Sometimes one is faced with worse than this, even, namely, morasses of mud, dozens of feet wide. Ice, pile on pile, rises into mountain masses, snow-blasts dash on for a hundred leagues." "The raging spirits and demons of the mountains send every kind of calamity; and there are murderous robbers to be met with." Thus does Hiuen Tsiang describe the passage of the Hindû Kûsh.

At Bâmiyân, in the heart of Afghanistan, a great centre of Buddhism after the model of the Little Vehicle, he was honourably received by its ruler and rested five days in his palace. He visited the great Buddhist images, hewn out of the solid rock (which our soldiers saw in the Afghan Campaign of 1843) and other remarkable monuments. On the second day after leaving Bâmiyân, he was caught in a blinding snowstorm, lost his way, and was like to perish, when mountaineers who were out hunting came across him and put him on the right track. A mountain pass brought him to the Kapiśa of Ptolemy and Pliny. It was situated a little to the north of the present Kâbul. Here "the people were fierce and cruel speaking a rude tongue, their marriage a mere intermingling of the sexes." The monarch, shrewd, brave, firm and sagacious, had established a little empire by bringing ten neighbouring States under his overlordship, and had won the love of his subjects. Hearing of the approach of the pilgrim, this potentate set out to meet him, accompanied by a procession of monks. These pietists of various monasteries of the Great and Little Vehicle remained sufficiently human to quarrel as to which house should shelter so rare a guest. Now the King was an enthusiastic supporter of the more rigid Order; and Hiuen-Tsiang would naturally have prepared to take up his abode in a convent of the Great Vehicle. But the appeal of the monks of a convent following the Little Vehicle, an appeal made on historic grounds, touched him; yet one of the monks who had accompanied him showed strong repugnance to sleep in a house of Hiuen-Tsiang's rival and stricter sect. Our Chinese was neither a Courtier nor a Pharisee; he could "suffer fools gladly," and took up his abode with the weaker brethren. Then the rivals had but one voice in entreating him to uncover a treasure, which had been set aside for the repair of some religious house, and which lay buried beneath the foot of an image of Buddha.

CHAPTER IV.

THROUGH INDIA IN THE SEVENTH CENTURY.

HE passed the wet season at Kapiśa, and then, protected by the King's envoys, went along the North bank of the Kâbul river and through districts memorable in the record of the Indian expedition of Alexander the Great. Again and again do we come across the names of places familiar to the reader of Arrian and Strabo. He visited Peshâwar and Attock; he travelled through many a little Kingdom of what is now North-Eastern Afghanistan and the North-West Provinces of India, by zig-zag and perplexing routes. Here was the classic soil of ancient Brahmanism; here was to be found many a Buddhist record of the great days of Aśôka. It was a land of monasteries and monuments, of countless *stûpas* (monuments containing relics) and sculptured stones, of ancient tradition and extravagant myth. The recording carvings of ages still stood thick on the ground or lay there in ruin. He saw every one of them, traversing perilous ravines by the help of chains affixed to the rocks; crossing frail swaying bridges made of rope. He got as far north as Baltistân, or Little Thibet, "in the midst of the Great Snowy Mountains." More than six centuries later, Marco Polo refers to the inhabitants as "an evil race of savage idolaters," and Hiuen-Tsiang found their forefathers "fierce, passionate folk, ill-mannered, and of uncouth speech." "Strictly speaking, they do not belong to India, but are rude frontier-folk." Sometimes the ways were deserted; for brigands were abroad. Almost everywhere Brahmanism was in the ascendent; Buddhism in decay; but, as yet, the rivalry of the two creeds had nowhere become acute; rival religionists behaved kindly and courteously one to another; and Brâhmans received the traveller with generous hospitality. Yet the careful student will not fail to observe that the antagonism between Brâhman and Buddhist, which is evident in the pages of Fa-Hien, had not decreased in the two centuries since his time. For Exoteric Brahmanism, with its clever adaptation of the ancient gods of India; its appeal to the imagination of the vulgar, always concrete in character and incapable of comprehending an abstract proposition; its deities, embodying human passion and evoking human sympathies; its support of human pride in the institution of caste; its intercessory priesthood and vicarious sacrifice; and its supple manipulation of men to obtain power, was on the high road to revival. But there is an esoteric Brahmanism, as Macaulay found out, always the lofty, pure creed of the educated Hindu.

Hiuen-Tsiang went up and down and to and fro in these frontier-states, threading many a delicious valley which nestled among the mountains and was overlooked by the snows of Himalaya; and returning from time to time to the more enervating atmosphere of the valley of the Indus. The King of Kaśmîr (Cashmir) visited him at a monastery where he was stayimg, preceded by a brilliant procession. "The roadway was covered with umbrellas and banners; it was carpeted with flowers, and the air was filled with sweet scents. The monarch was full of compliment and shows of respect, and scattered a great quantity of flowers in Hiuen-Tsiang's honour. Then he begged him to take his seat on a great elephant. And he walked behind him. The pilgrim remained two years in Kasmîr, sitting at the feet of a sage, studying Sanskrit and the Buddhist scriptures. Indeed, throughout all his travels, he was forever studying or collecting or transcribing manuscripts, when he was not visiting and venerating relics.

Now near Nagarahâra, in the district of Jalâlâbâd, there was a certain cavern, where, peradventure, the pious might behold the shadow which Buddha had cast on its walls. It had been granted to Sung-Yun to see it, when the Empress Dowager of a Tartar dynasty which ruled in Northern China sent him and another on an embassy to obtain Buddhist books (A.D. 518); and Hiuen-Tsiang was consumed by desire to see it also. His escort from Kapiśa earnestly begged him not to make the attempt; it was a rash and perilous project; brigands were abroad; and few indeed were those who might see the holy vision. They could not dissuade him; so they left him and went home, and he took an old man as guide. When he got near the cavern five brigands pounced upon him. He pointed to his monks' robe and told them that, if they were brigands, they were none the less men, and he had no fear of men, or even of wild beasts, when sacred duty called him. He touched their hearts, and they let him go.

Although a man visited by visions and a dreamer of significant dreams, he spent a long time in the cave and saw nothing. Prostrations and convictions of sin were in vain. Then, quite suddenly, came a flash of light; thereupon he vowed that he would not quit the spot until he should behold the veritable shade. In the end the reward of such persistent enthusiasm was bestowed: he beheld the Buddha, attended by his sacred court, in all their heavenly splendour. But, just then, torch-bearers came into the cave, intending to burn perfumes in the holy place, and the glory disappeared. Hiuen-Tsiang ordered them to put out their lights, and lo! there was the vision as before. Five of the six torch-bearers declared that they beheld the shadow. It is characteristic of our pilgrim that he is careful to tell us that the sixth man saw nothing whatever. Never a shadow of doubt arises as to his good faith. Sung-Yun the Chinese ambassador and pilgrim, writing an account of his journey a hundred years before Hiuen-Tsiang, tells us how, "Entering the mountain cavern fifteen feet and looking for a long time (or, at a long distance?) at the western side of it, opposite the entrance, at length, the figure, with its characteristic marks, appears; on going nearer to look at it, it gradually grows fainter, and then disappears. On touching the place where it was with the hand, there is nothing but the bare wall. Gradually retreating, the figure begins to come into view again, and foremost is conspicuous that peculiar mark between the eyebrows, which is so rare among men." And Hiuen-Tsiang tells us, in his "Records of Western Lands," that in later days the shadow has faded to a feeble likeness, although, by fervent prayer, it may be clearly seen, "though not for long."

Leaving the North-Western corner of India, he now proceeded through the Punjâb. Many a city he names has perished, and not a stone thereof is left; of others a few stones mark the seat of departed greatness; but often the names recall the Embassy of Megasthenes and differ but little from those by which they were known to the Greeks of a yet earlier age.

He had left certain rude tribes behind him, yet he found particular districts by no means free from murderous gangs; and he had to traverse many a forest inhabited by wild elephants and great beasts of prey. In one forest, he and fellow-monks who accompanied him found themselves at the mercy of half a hundred armed brigands, who chased them into the bed of a pond which had run dry. Hiuen-Tsiang and some others contrived to hide among thorny bushes and coarse growth; but some of the company were caught and bound. Happily a hollow, scooped out by escaping waters, was hit upon; and our pilgrim and some who were in hiding contrived to make their way out. About half a mile off they came across a Brâhman ploughing with oxen; and he took them to a village hard by. He blew a conch and beat a drum, and soon 80 men of the village snatched up their arms and gathered together to attack the robbers. These latter, seeing so many bounding towards them, made off with all speed; the villagers found and released their captives, who lay bound, stripped, and quite helples , groaning and weeping many tears. The good people of the village covered their nakedness and took them to their homes for food and shelter. "Master," said one of the monks, to Hiuen-Tsiang, "all that we had has been taken by the thieves, and we have barely got off with our lives. How is it you can smile and look so cheerful!" "Because life is man's greatest boon," was the reply. "When that has been saved, why vex one's self over clothes and food?"

Soon we are with Hiuen-Tsiang at a centre of Brahmanism which was probably Lâhôr (Lahore). Everywhere he is received with courtesy; usually welcomed with procession and pageantry. Before very long, we find him making a long détour to the cold upper valley of the Bujas river, under the Himalayas, and among a rude, hard, fierce race, but one that had a regard for justice as well as for courage.

He returns to a warmer latitude, and reaches Mathurâ, or Muttra, on the River Jumna; a place once famous for the relics stored in its *stûpas*. Here, different convents followed different authorities; but once a year they gathered together, and each sect made offering before the relics of its chosen saint. A little later, after traversing several small States, it would seem that he visited the source of the Ganges, although, in spite of explicit statement, this has been doubted. He speaks of the river as being $\frac{3}{4}$ mile wide at its source! May he not mean that the end of its parent glacier is of that width?[1]

[1] The Author possesses a picture of the source of the Ganges, painted on panel, on the spot, by the late W. Simpson. Fakirs, at least in his time, were wont, when the end of life drew near, to ascend the glacier, and terminate the illusions of existence on the snow-mountains above it. Simpson saw a Fakir climbing up a snow-slope for this purpose. Now, as well as one can judge from this panel, the lower end of the glacier from which the infant Ganges is seen flowing would be about as broad as Hiuen-Tsiang states the source of the river to be.

A little later on, we are told of the softness of Ganges water; of how multitudes of bathers assemble on its sandy banks to cleanse them of sin; and how a mere rinsing of the mouth with its water will avert every calamity and secure future blessedness. "But there is no truth in this universal belief, which is wholly the invention of heresy," adds our traveller, critical of everything but the superstitions which had encrusted his own faith. And he is of opinion that this special form of false belief is on the wane among the Indian people!

We find him before long in Western Rohilkand, and then again in an icy Himalayan valley, where "for ages a woman has ruled; wherefore it is called the Kingdom of the Eastern Women." It corresponds to what is now British Garwal and Kumain. As then, so is it to-day: relics of the matriarchate and polyandry are to be found among the Himalayan ranges.

He returns to the Ganges, and, passing through several small States, arrives at Kanauj. He is for ever visiting scholars, and sits for months at the feet of every famous sage. He does so at Kanauj, which he tells us is a city measuring four miles in length and one in breadth. He is now in an Empire recently established by Sîlâditya, a warrior of the Vaiśya, or trading, class, who had forced a number of petty Kinglets to become his tributaries. Sîlâditya would seem to have been a devout Buddhist, favouring the Greater Vehicle, and, really devoting himself to the prosperity of the Empire he ruled.

He now enters Ayôdhyâ—Oude—the same name that, eleven centuries later, rang so compellingly in the ears of Clive and Warren Hastings. Here Brâhmanism was getting the upper hand. And there was not merely much lawlessness but a terrible perversion of religious worship abroad in this land, which reminds one of modern Thuggee. A boat with Hiuen-Tsiang and eighty others on board was gliding peacefully down the Ganges, when a whole little navy of pirates, which had lain concealed under the dense foliage of the river-bank, shot out into mid-stream, and surrounded the pilgrim's vessel. Some of the passengers leaped into the river ; those who remained in the vessel were towed ashore and robbed. Now these water-thieves were devotees of the goddess Durgâ, the wife of Siva, and were wont to offer at her altar a yearly sacrifice of some unblemished human victim, selected from their captives. They carefully examined Hiuen-Tsiang, and pronounced him fit for this purpose. Some of his companions generously offered to take his place ; but the pirates would have none of them—Hiuen-Tsiang and he alone was the goddess' chosen prey. He, of all the company, remained calm amd undismayed. " Let me enter Nirvâna tranquil and happy," he said, his mind wholly occupied with some future incarnation wherein he might turn such cruel hearts as those of the pirates. These, amazed, and even touched, by his meek and compassionate fortitude, granted him a few more minutes of life. Just at this moment, a squall came on, so fierce that it terrified the pirates, even. Hiuen-Tsiang's companions were loud in exclaiming that it was heaven's warning of the awful vengeance which would ensue on the murder of a saint. The hearts of the homicides were stricken by fear. One of them took the pilgrim's hand. He only felt the pressure ; for his eyes were closed and he was wrapt in some celestial vision. He asked if the fatal moment had come ; and when he learned that the mind of the robbers was changed, he began to unfold " the Law " to them with such persuasive power that they cast their instruments of sacrifice into the river, restored what they had stolen, and quietly went their way.

He visited Prayâga (Allahabad), near the confluence of the Ganges and Jumna, and then took a dangerous course, south west, through a forest infested with wild elephants and beasts of prey, to Kosâmbi-nagar, now a mere village on the Jumna, only to find ten Buddhist monasteries ruined and deserted and fifty temples of flourishing Brahmanism, frequented by an enormous number of "heretics." Thence he travelled northwards, and came to Gautama's birth place, Kapila. It was a waste. Almost everywhere Brahmanism was quietly triumphing and Buddhism in gentle decay; although it was not until the following century that this shrivelling process became rapid, and four or five centuries had yet to pass before new dynasties sacked monasteries and burned their inmates or expelled them from India in such wise that Buddhism became extinct throughout the Great Peninsula.

At Bânâras (Benares) he saw Brahman asceties who shaved the head, or went about naked, or covered themselves with ashes, and "by all manner of austerity sought to escape from any more births and deaths." He tells us of the blueness of the sacred river and its rolling waves; of the sweet taste of its waters and the fineness of its sands; of how numbers of people, in order to wash away the pollution of sin, "would abstain from eating for seven days, and then drown themselves in the sacred stream. Daily, towards sunset, ascetics would climb up a pillar set in the middle of the river, cling to it by one hand and one foot in a marvellous manner, and gaze at the sun until he went down, when they would descend. Thereby they hoped to escape from re-incarnation." "If the body of a dead man be cast into the stream, he cannot fall into an evil way. Swept on by its waters and forgotten by men, he is safe on the other side."

It was at Bânâras that Gautama began his evangel, and the vast district between Jumna and the mountains of Nepal was the main scene of his labours. In the Kingdom of Magadha, which, like Kanduj, was under the rule of Sîlâditya, he found an area of fourteen miles covered with the ruins of a city which was flourishing when Fa-Hien visited India. The stones of *stûpas*, monasteries, pagodas and hospitals for men and beasts cumbered the ground.

While Hiuen-Tsiang was staying at the place where Gautama "Sâkyamûni" as he was called during the ascetic portion of his career—that is to say, "the sage of the family of the Sâkyas—became "Buddha," or "the Enlightener of men," a deputation of four of the most distinguished monks of the great Sarighârâma of Nâlanda —the greatest scholastic and monastic institution in the world—came to him bearing an invitation to stay there. When he arrived he was welcomed with much state and ceremony. Two hundred monks and crowds of people greeted him, singing songs in his praise, bearing standards and umbrellas, and scattering flowers and scent. They raised him to a seat of honour, and then the sub-director sounded a gong and repeated the invitation. Twenty grave and reverend seniors of the monastery presented him to the Father Superior, who was no other than the famous scholar Sîlabhadra, a dignitary so exalted that no one dared name him except by his title of "Treasury of the Righteous Law." Hiuen-Tsiang had to drag himself towards this sage on knees and elbows, clacking his heels together, and striking the ground with his brow. This done, seats were brought forward, compliments were interchanged, and the pilgrim was made free of the institution. The best rooms were given up to him; ten servants were allotted to him, and, daily he was furnished with an ample supply of food at the cost of the monks and the Râja. A Buddhist monk and a Brâhman, dwelling in peace together, took him abroad from time to time and shewed him the holy sights of the neighbourhood, seated in state on an elephant or carried in a palanquin; but when he was in the convent the "Treasury of the Righteous Law" devoted no small measure of his time to his instruction in the higher learning.

In the Seventh Century there was not, in the whole world a seat of learning which might compare with the splendid establishment at Nâlanda. It had been magnificently endowed by a succession of monarchs and still enjoyed the royal favour as much as ever. There were open courts and secluded gardens; splendid trees, casting a grateful shade, under which the monks and novices might meditate; cool fountains of fresh water that gurgled delightfully in the hot season. Ten thousand inmates dwelt in six blocks of buildings four stories high, which looked out on large courts. There were a hundred rooms set apart for lectures on religion and on all the science and literature of the time. There were halls wherein disputations frequently took place; and in these Hiuen-Tsiang took a distinguished part. The monks impressed him favourably: he found them sincere, and living in the strict observance of severe rules. He says: "from morning to night, young and old help each other in discussions, for which they find the day too short." The mental power and learning of the monks were as renowned as the towers, the pavilions, and the cool retreats of the convent-university in which they dwelt. The study of medicine and natural history and useful and useless branches of mundane research was by no means cast aside for speculation. But the latter was of so subtle a character that, while ten hundred might be found capable of expounding twenty books of the Sâtras and Sâstras, only five hundred could deal with thirty books, and only ten with fifty; although students were not admitted until they had proved themselves men of parts, and well-read in books, old and new, by hard public discussion; and of ten candidates for admission, seven or eight were rejected. Altogether, Hiuen-Tsiang spent five years in study here; and he became one of the ten who could expound fifty sacred books. But Sîlabhadra, the Father Superior, who was his tutor, had left no sacred book unstudied.

From Nâlanda, our pilgrim proceeded to Patna, and crossing the Ganges, visited Gayâ. He saw everything worth seeing in the country about Bhagalpur, and found there a monastery of the first order, the origin of which was a curious history. A "heretic" from South India had marched into the country, staff in hand, with stately step and pompous mien, beating " the drum of discussion." On his head, he bore a lighted torch, and his belly was encased in plates of shining copper. When asked the reason for such strange attire, he replied that the torch was to enlighten the ignorant multitude, who dwelt in darkness, and the belt was for self-preservation, since he was so filled with wisdom that he feared his belly would burst. In spite of this mummery, he proved himself so well instructed and persuasive that all the learned men in the Kingdom were unable to controvert his arguments. At last, a Buddhist from Southern India was sent for and reduced him to silence. The Râja was so impressed by the victory that he founded the monastery.

Our traveller now came to the land of the sugar-cane. His account of the Kingdoms he visited after leaving the chief scenes of Gautama's missionary zeal, and the history of his wanderings, put together from his notes and conversations with his pupils, become less full than before; but it is clear that he made his way to " the shore-country " of the Bay of Bengal, which would seem to be the Sunderbans, between the rivers Ganges and Hûgli—afterwards a name of horror, as the lair of infamous Portuguese pirates. At all events, he crossed the great Delta of the Ganges, intending to embark for Ceylon at Tamluk on the Selai, just where that river joins the Hûgli. Fa-Hian had done so, and had seen Ceylon and its monuments; but Hiuen-Tsiang was given such accounts of the perils of the long voyage that anxiety for the safety of the treasures he had collected induced him to travel by land to South India, and he determined to sail thence across the narrow Palk Strait. So he returned inland, nearly as far back as Bhagalpur again, and proceeded thence to Orissa. Thence he travelled south-westward to the district watered by the upper tributaries of the Mahanadi and Godavari in Central India; penetrating many a pestiferous marsh and perilous jungle, deep and dangerous forest and scorching desert-plain, before he arrived at Congeveram, the Dravidian capital, a little south-west of Madras and north-west of Pondicherri. Here he learned that Ceylon had become the theatre of a bloody war and that it would be impossible to reach it. So he turned his reluctant steps to the north.

He tells of the courage, honesty and love of truth of the Dravidian race, and of the heat and fruitfulness of the land they inhabited. He speaks of his return-journey as being partly through "a wild forest and many deserted villages where bands of brigands attack travellers." Then, going north-west, he came to the country of the Mahrattas—not the modern race which goes by that name, but a people who apparently were Rajpoots, the old military Aryan aristocracy of India, whose widows, following a Scythian custom, cast themselves on the funeral pyre of their husbands to be worthy of their chivalry and to rejoin them in the next life. Hiuen-Tsiang describes the Mahrattas as being tall of stature, honest and simple; grateful to friends, relentless to enemies. They avenged an insult at the risk of life; they would forget all about themselves in their haste to give aid. They always gave due warning to a foe before attacking him, and spared the enemy who should yield. A commander who lost a battle was not directly punished; but he received a present of women's clothes, and this was enough: it drove him to suicide. The army was of several hundred chosen men, who went into battle drunk, and made their elephants drunk also. Then they would rush forward in close array, bearing everything before them and trampling on the foe. Nothing could withstand such an onset. And one man all alone, with his lance in hand, was always quite ready to challenge and fight ten thousand. These champions had drums beaten before them every time they went abroad; and should one of them come across a man and slay him no notice of the offence was taken.

Passing through Western India and States which bordered on the Arabian Sea, we find our traveller in Southern Malwa and Rajputana and, later, in Sind. Twice in his account of Southern and Western India and once in the *Life and Journeyings of Hiuen-Tsiang*, we are told that he heard of a " Land of Western Women." While on the Coromandel Coast, he heard of an island inhabited by women who bore female children only to Persian demons. Of old time, they were wont to allure sailors and traders by signals. If successful, they changed themselves into beautiful women, holding flowers and dispersing sweet scents. They went forth to meet voyagers to the sound of sweet music, and, having inveigled them into their City, which was built of iron, and having solaced them with their society, they would cast them into an iron prison and devour them at leisure. On the Western Coast, he is told that the island is rich in gems and lies to the south-west of the Byzantine Empire, to which it is tributary, and where its precious stones are exchanged. It is inhabited by women only. Once a year, the Emperor of Byzantium sends them male partners; and, if boys are born of the union, the laws forbid their being brought up on the island. Marco Polo also speaks of a Kingdom of Western Women. Ferdusi, the Persian Poet, makes Alexander the Great visit an island-city of women where no man was allowed to dwell. In the early art and literature of Buddhism the legend is to be found. It reached Malaya. It made its way into Chinese literature, too, some generations before the time of Hiuen-Tsiang. But the locality given to the island varies with the legend.

Here, surely, are our Homeric friends, the Sirens—the daughters of Achelous, serpent and ox, and the Muse Calliope—whose " shrill music reached Ulysses on the middle sea " from a little island off Sicily. Can these Western and Eastern legends have come from a common source; or, did they travel overland with trader or missionary;

or was some faint echo of the golden harp of Hellas wafted by the breezes which bore the trader across the Arabian Sea to Sind and Southern India? Possibly the latter; for our author speaks of the island as lying to the west, beyond the great sea which laves the shores of Kutch. It is perplexing to find what would seem to be the same story told by the natives of Martinique to Columbus during his second voyage.

From Sind beyond the Indus, Hiuen-Tsiang proceeded to Multân in the Punjâb, and saw the majestic temple of the Sun-dêva, whose image was cast in gold and set with rare gems. Crowds of worshippers flocked hither from other Kingdoms; and women did honour to the god with music and torches and offerings of blossoms and perfumes. The temple was surrounded with water-tanks and flowery groves; and near it was a "House of Happiness," which was a hospital for the poor and sick.

He visited this temple on his way back to the sacred land where Gautama had assumed his mission of teacher of mankind; for he felt that he must return thither. So he made a thousand miles eastward and arrived at Magadha in time to see the grand procession of the ashes of Buddha. He thought the remains too large to be genuine; so did an Indian sage of great reputation, and it would seem that the crowd of spectators were also in doubt. Some time afterwards, suddenly, the relics could not be found; the *stûpa* in which they were kept was a sheet of light, and flames, in five different colours shot up to the sky. This brilliant phenomenon was witnessed by a wondering multitude; it gradually passed away; and so did incredulity.

Hiuen-Tsiang passed his time in the monasteries of Magadha, partly in study, partly in refuting Brâhmans and the followers of the Little Vehicle. To refute the latter could not have been a difficult task: simple monks, only instructed in practical ethics, would stand no chance against an erudite monk trained in subtle speculation and fine distinctions. As in European Universities of the Middle Ages, the thesis to be disputed was hung up by its supporter; and whatever wrangler chose to deny it would take it down. Then a contest ensued; and, at Nâlanda, its learned Head, the "Treasury of the Law," was wont to preside at great discussions. In some of these, our Chinaman took a triumphant part.

On one occasion, a certain Brâhman had hung up a challenge to the Buddhists, which consisted of 40 articles, and, according to custom, he wagered his head to maintain them; possibly perfectly well aware that, in the unexpected event of defeat, the forfeit would not be exacted. For some days, no one would come forward to oppose him. Then Hiuen-Tsiang sent a monk to take up the insolent challenge in his name: it was torn into shreds, and trampled under foot. At the solemn discussion which ensued, he held forth at portentous length, and dumbfounded the Brâhman. Hiuen-Tsiang then told him he had suffered humiliation enough: he was free to go.

The defeated wrangler went to Kâmarûpa, a Kingdom which extended from west of the Brahmaputra to Manipur, on the borders of Burmah. The eloquence and learning of our Chinaman would appear to have converted the Brâhman, who was generous enough to tell the Râja of his defeat. The tale so impressed that monarch that he sent an invitation to Hiuen-Tsiang to pay him a visit; but our pilgrim, having fully accomplished the purpose for which he had travelled so far, was eager to return to China. The Râja waxed wroth at his disobedience to a royal command, and warned the "Treasury of the Law" that, little as he cared for the religion of Buddha, he would come with a vast army and level with the dust the famous building over which he presided if Hiuen-Tsiang were not forwarded without delay. It was evident that the Râja, a powerful ally or tributary of Sîlâditya, whose loyalty to that great monarch was not too assured, might conceivably let loose the hounds of uncertain war. Here, a gleam of enlightenment is thrown on the attitude of Râjas tributary to Sîlâditya, who had won his empire by the sword and who had made Kanouj and Allahabad his capital cities. Hiuen-Tsiang was despatched by Silabhadra to far-off Kâmarûpa; He had been at the Râja's court a whole month, when Sîlâditya returned from the chastisement of a rebellious feudatory and learned whither he had gone. Sîlâditya had urged the pilgrim to visit him in vain; now he finds him at the court of a rival. Here is the making of a very pretty quarrel. Sîlâditya sends to the Râja, saying that he wants the Chinese. "My head first!" replies that monarch. Then Sîlâditya waxed wrath; and his wrath is terrible. "Since I have power to cut off your head, it may be given straightway to my ambassador," is the message he returns. The Râja of Kâmarûpa now begins to reflect. He orders his court-barge and sets off with Hiuen-Tsiang in it to make amends to Sîlâditya.

But he took the precaution to be accompanied by a great army. The Ganges was crowded with boats filled with troops, and, as these were rowed up the stream, other soldiery mounted on war-elephants marched slowly along the banks. On their arrival at the court of Sîlâditya he commanded that Hiuen-Tsiang should be presented to him. The Râja of Kâmarûpa saw at once that here was an opportunity of quietly humiliating Sîlâditya in his turn—a monarch who, from conviction or by policy, professed the deepest reverence for the Greater Vehicle and was the munificent patron of Buddhist institutions. He suggested to Sîlâditya that it would be unworthy of a monarch so renowned for cherishing sages and saints to do otherwise than pay the holy and learned Chinese pilgrim the compliment of visiting him first. Sîlâditya fell in with the proposal; and the Râja at once went back to Hiuen-Tsiang and persuaded him, "for the honour of the law of Buddha," to consent. Thus, should his enemy, or anyone, never be sensible of so subtle a revenge, the secret of it was sweet in the heart of the Eastern King; a psychological peculiarity by no means confined to the ruler of Kâmarûpa.

Next evening, shortly after sunset, the Ganges was ablaze with torches; the air resounded with the noise of tom-toms, for Sîlâditya was about to pay his visit with Generals and Ministers of State. It was the distinction of the Lord-paramount that the beating of a hundred gongs heralded his approach and gave step to his guards. The haughty despot, who determined the fate of thousands by a gesture, cast himself on the ground at the feet of the humble monk, and kissed them. Next day, the Master of the Law returned the visit. Now, a sister of the great monarch, an enthusiast for high doctrine, who was seated behind the throne, entreated that a great assembly of all the sages of the Empire should be convoked at Kanouj to give Hiuen-Tsiang an opportunity of setting out the beauty of the Greater Vehicle. So, at the beginning of the cold season, the sages assembled at Kanouj, mounted on elephants or carried in palanquins, surrounded by banners and accompanied by an immense multitude. An elephant bore a golden statue of Buddha on his back, and this was solemnly erected on a daïs. To the right of the elephant, marched Sîlâditya, dressed as Indra and carrying a white fly-flap in his hand; to the left was Kumâra, monarch of Kâmarûpa, in the gârb of Brâhm, and carrying a parasol of precious silk. Both monarchs wore magnificent tiaras, from which garlands of flowers and ribbands set with jewels hung down. Following the golden image and the two Râjas came our Master of the Law, seated on a big elephant, and then the officials and monks of the two Kingdoms, also on elephants. Eighteen tributary princes were drawn up on either side, also riding elephants, and these fell into the procession as the great Râjas and Hiuen-Tsiang passed on.

Food was provided for everybody, without distinction of rank, and rich gifts were bestowed on all the monks. Hiuen-Tsiang ordered his thesis to be hung up; but eighteen days passed, and no one attempted to controvert it. But the followers of the Little Vehicle were so mortified that some of them conspired against Hiuen-Tsiang's life. The plot was detected, and a severe edict was issued that even the very smallest slander against him would be punished by loss of tongue; while any attempt to injure him bodily would be followed by decapitation. At the end of the eighteen days, following ancient usage, the victorious pilgrim was mounted on a richly-caparisoned elephant and taken a tour round the crowd, in the company of the dignitaries of the Empire and with full state-honours. Rich presents were offered him; but these he refused; and then Sîlâditya dissolved the assembly; and the eighteen kings, the monks, and the crowd returned every man to his own abode.

Now, it was the custom of Sîlâditya, as it had been that of his predecessors, to distribute all their accumulated wealth at the end of every five years. But they were careful to keep their war-elephants, war-horses and weapons of war; for on these their power rested. The practice kept the people submissive and contented, while effective force remained with the Râja. The distribution was made on a plain at the confluence of Ganges and Jumna, three miles from Prayâga, and not far from the existing city of Allahabad. When the time for it arrived, Sîlâditya took the Master of the Law with him. He observed that gold and silver, silk and cotton, and much else were stored up in temporary buildings within an enclosure, and arrangements were made for seating a thousand persons at a time. The eighteen tributary Kings and a vast crowd of monks and laity were summoned to be present, and did not fail to arrive. It is significant that each tributary prince brought his army with him: it throws light on the character of Sîlâditya's empire.

On the first day, the statue of Buddha was installed in a temple and adorned with jewels. A great feast followed on this ceremony; it was accompanied by music and the scattering of blossoms; and then rich gifts were distributed among the more important of the guests. On the second day, the image of the Sun-god was honoured, and presents of magnificence were made. The third day, the god Siva received honours, and a similar distribution was made. The fourth day, every one of about 10,000 monks was given a hundred pieces of gold and a cotton garment. The fifth day, distribution to the Brâhmans was begun; but it is worthy of note that the awards to them took up three weeks all but a day. On the sixth day, and for 9 days following, alms were given to "heretics"; on the eighth, and for the next nine days, to naked medicants from distant Kingdoms. Lastly, it took a whole month to give to the poor, to orphans, and to poor men who had no family to fall back upon. Finally Sîlâditya took off and gave up his tiara and necklace, exclaiming that he had exchanged them for incorruptible riches. And now, the tributary Râjas surrendered their robes and jewels to their Lord-paramount. What with this ordinance and the retention of the sinews of war, Sîlâditya remained no less powerful than before.

Our pilgrim now obtains permission to set forth on his return-journey. He is offered an escort to China should he choose to return by sea; but he has precious manucripts to preserve, the rich harvest of his labours, and he prefers to take the smaller risk of desert and icy mountains to that of pirates and of frail, clumsy craft, breasting "the feasted waters of the sea stretched out In lazy gluttony, expecting prey." Moreover, whether T'ai Tsung, now Emperor of China, would welcome a foreign Embassy, may have been in his mind. He refused all gifts from the Râja of Kâmarûpa, save a warm garment needful for the high passes.

Now, the Master of the Law had been wont, if he had no escort to protect him, to send an attendant monk ahead, and, should his fore-runner meet with wayside thieves, he would announce the character of Hiuen-Tsiang's mission. The explanation had been made more than once, and prevailed. But many a Râja was now eager to give him a warm welcome and send soldiery to see him safe in the next Kingdom. And, Sîlâditya, not merely went with him some small part of the long way, but charged a tributary prince of the North to accompany and protect him through the Punjâb. He also presented the pilgrim with a big elephant, horses and chariots to convey the manuscripts and images he had collected, and 3000 pieces of gold and 10,000 pieces of silver to defray the expenses of the journey. He also provided him with letters to various princes whose territories he would have to cross, ordering or recommending them to expedite his journey. These documents were written on rolls of cotton and sealed with red wax. Sîlâditya and his tributary Râjas even rode out again to catch the pilgrim up and bid him a second farewell.

Easy progress was made across North-West India; and native rulers vied with each other in doing honour to the traveller from afar. Now, at the best of times, to cross the Indus is perilous; and this time it was not effected without mishap. The "Master of the Law" rode on the elephant; but the manuscripts, images, relics, and a precious collection of seeds, which he had made during his travels, and which he hoped might grow in China, were placed in a boat under the care of a special custodian. When the middle of the current was reached, a storm-gust swept over the river, and the boat was well nigh sunk by tossing waves. The custodian was rescued with great difficulty; but half a hundred manuscripts and the valuable collection of seeds which might have done so much service, were lost. Only by the very greatest exertion was anything at all saved.

CHAPTER V.

INDIAN SOCIAL LIFE IN THE SEVENTH CENTURY.

ONCE more we find Hiuen-Tsiang by the Kâbul river. Many years had passed since he rested on its banks and and entered India. Since that time he had made himself a finished Sanskrit scholar; he had visited three and a half score of States; he had traversed the whole breadth and well-nigh the whole length of the great Peninsula; he had debated the subtlest questions with the profoundest scholars and acutest minds in India; he had been entertained by powerful princes as their venerated guest. In every corner of a vast territory, he had met with large hospitality at the hands of men of differing creeds; he had seen many new things, strange and wonderful; more than once, his life had been in jeopardy, and narrow indeed had been his escape; he had visited every spot connected with the life of Gautama, from the scene where Bôdhisattva "descended spiritually into the womb of his mother" to the place where he became Buddha, and to the place of his death. He had visited every spot sacred to Asôka-râja, the great promulgator of the faith. It had been granted him to see the shadow of Buddha. And, above all, he had not failed in his quest. Written on prepared palm-leaves and carefully packed, were the so much lacking sacred scriptures; much of them tales of the absurdest fantasy and most extravagant romance, it is true; but the sympathetic eye can still discover in the fable the mild and sweet moral teaching of the Buddhist faith.

In the *Si-yu-ki* (Observations on Western Lands) there is a very full account of India in the early Seventh Century. So long a residence in that land, and such a wide knowledge of its various peoples as the Master of the Law had acquired in personal intercourse with them makes this invaluable. The work is preceded by a general description of the Great Peninsula, which applies more particularly to that land, so sacred to a Buddhist, which lies between the Jumna and the lower slopes of the Himalayas. And, now that Hiuen-Tsiang is leaving India, it will be well to know what he has to tell us concerning that vast region.

He begins by discussing the various names given to In-tu (India); for each district is differently called. He gives its shape, extent and climate. "The north is a continuation of mountains and hills, the ground being dry and salt. On the east, there are valleys and plains, which, being well-watered and cultivated, are fruitful and productive. The southern district is wooded and herbaceous; the western parts are stony and barren."[1]

Indian measures of length and the Indian Calendar and seasons are next described, and the author then goes on to treat of towns and buildings, seats and clothing, dress and habits, ablutions, language and literature, schools, castes, marriages, kings, troops, weapons, manners and customs, administration of laws, ceremonial observances, revenues, natural products, and commercial dealings—all in systematized order. The lapse of thirteen centuries; conquest by Mohammedan and European invaders; and Mohammedan and Brahmanistic oppression would appear to have altered but little the ways and external appearance of Indian life since Hiuen-Tsiang's time. He tells us that "the walls of towns are wide and high; the streets and lanes, tortuous; the roads, winding, ; the thoroughfares, dirty; the stalls, arranged on both sides of the road and furnished with appropriate signs. Butchers, fishermen, dancers, executioners, scavengers and their like dwell outside the city. Coming and going these people must keep to the left side of the

[1] Beal's translation of *Si-yu-ki* vol. i., p. 70.

road." The city-walls are of brick, but their towers are made of wood or bamboo; the houses are plastered with cob, "mixed with cow-dung for purity"; they are provided with wooden balconies, coated with mortar and shaded by tiles. The roofs are of rushes, branches, tiles, or boards. It is a habit to scatter flowers before the house. The *sanghârâmas*, or monasteries, are very cleverly built in quadrangles, ornamented with dome-shaped buildings of two or three stories at the corners of each quadrangle, and joists and beams are adorned with carving; there is much decoration and mural painting; the cells being plain on the outside only.

Everybody takes his rest on a mat of one uniform size, but of various degrees of ornamentation; but the Râja has an imposing throne, studded with gems, and nobles use painted and enriched seats. The garb is of pure white silk or cotton or hemp or goat's hair, uncut to fit the body and wound round the waist, gathered up under the armpits, and then slung across the body to the right. There is quaint humour in our pilgrim's observation that "some of the men shave their moustaches and have other odd customs": one thinks of the strange appearance of some of our long-shore men.

Women keep their shoulders covered, and their robes reach the ground. Their hair is knotted up on the crown; otherwise it hangs loose. They wear crowns and caps and flower-wreaths on the head, and necklaces of jewels.

In North India, where the climate is colder, close-fitting garments are worn. Some non-believers wear peacock-feathers, or necklaces made of the bones of the skull; some cover their nakedness with leaf or bark, or go bare. Some pull out the hair; others wear their whiskers bushy and braid their hair.

The monks wear three different kinds of dress, either red or yellow in colour. Merchants, for the most part, go bare-footed, stain the teeth red or black, bind up the hair, and pierce the nose for the wearing of ornaments there. Everybody is very cleanly, washing before eating, never eating of a dish served twice over, never passing the dish on. Wooden and stone vessels are destroyed after use; metal ones are polished. The teeth are cleansed with a willow-stick after eating; the hands and mouth are washed; and folk do not touch one another until these duties are carried out. The body is washed after attending to the calls of nature, and then perfumes are used. The bath is taken before religious functions, and also at the time when the King washes himself. Each province keeps its own record of events. Education is begun early. Young Buddhists are put to the study of the five Vidyâs, or treatises on grammar, progressively; first come the principles of mechanics; then elements of medicine and drugs and the use of charms; then the principles of right-doing and the distinction between the true and the false; and, finally, the various "vehicles" of the faith. Brâhmans are trained on similar lines by skilled teachers. Some "rise above mundane rewards, and are as insensible to renown as to contempt of the world. . . . . . Rulers value men of reputation highly; but are unable to draw them to court." But the thirst of others for honour leads them on in the search for wisdom, and, if they finish their education at thirty, they seek for occupation. Some Brâhmans are devoid of virtuous principles, and waste their substance in riotous excess. Unhappily the Buddhist schools are not without reproach: "they are constantly at variance, and their contentious utterances swell like the waves of an angry sea"; yet, "in various directions, they do aim at one end." Knowledge of sacred books and successful exegesis are rewarded by successive grades of distinction, beginning with exemption from control and leading up to the possession of "an elephant-carriage," and even to a "surrounding escort." A successful disputant, like Hiuen-Tsiang, is mounted on an elephant (as he was), the animal is completely covered over with precious ornaments, and the rider is conducted by a numerous suite to the gates of the convent." But woe betide the unhappy wretch who proves himself a fool at these mental wrestling bouts; "his face is painted red and white; he is bedaubed with dust and dirt, and then borne off to some deserted spot, or cast into a ditch!" For slight faults a monk is only reprimanded; for graver offences, silence is enforced; for a great fault, he is cast out of the convent to find a home for himself and take up some kind of work, or he may wander about the roads.

We are told next about the four great castes, The Brâhman, or heriditary priest takes precedence of the Kshattriya or military descendents of the Aryan conquerors, a caste which rules, and observes human kindliness. Next come the traders (Vaiśyas); fourth is the Sûdra, the caste of tillers of the soil. When one marries, he takes social position according as he preserves or impairs purity of caste. Widows may not marry again.

"The succession of Râjas is confined to the Kshattriya caste, who have from time to time achieved power by means of usurpation and bloodshed." The army of the Râja is one of the many separate hereditary castes of India. In times of peace, it is garrisoned around the Râja's palace. In each Indian army are elephants, protected by strong armour, and the tusks capped with sharp metal. A general issues his command from a car, driven by two attendants, between whom he sits, and is drawn by four horses abreast. The generals of the foot soldiers also ride in cars and are protected by a guard. An attack is met by the cavalry, who also carry orders. The infantry is very brave. It is armed with spear and shield, bows and arrows, swords, axes, slings and many other weapons of ancient usage.

Hiuen-Tsiang speaks of the common people in the highest terms. As Wheeler remarks they "would almost appear to have been a different race from the modern Hindus. They had not yet been moulded into existing forms by ages of Brahmanical repression and Musselman tyranny; and they bore a stronger resemblance to the unsophisticated Buddhists of modern Burma than to the worshippers of Vishnu and Siva."[1] Our traveller admits that they are volatile, but "gentle and sweet, straightforward, honourable, keeping their word, with no fraud, treachery or deceit about them." Criminals are rare, and these few are not even beaten, and are never put to death, but cast into prison and left to live or die, "not being counted among men." A small payment is exacted for a small offence; but those who seriously offend the moral sense of the community are mutilated in various ways, or expelled from it. Frank confession is followed by punishment proportioned to the offence; but denial, or attempt to wriggle out, is met by trial by ordeal. Of this there are four kinds:—1, The accused person is put into one sack and a stone into another; both sacks are tied together and thrown into deep water: If the man sinks lowest, he is deemed guilty. 2, The accused has to stand or sit on red pot iron, or to handle it, or have it applied to his tongue: If no scars result, he is deemed innocent. 3, He is weighed against a stone: If he weighs it down, he is innocent. 4, An incision is made in the right thigh of a ram, and all manner of poisons and some food of the accused are put into the wound. Should the ram survive, the man is innocent. "The way of crime is blocked by these four methods." It is obvious to us that the issue of every one of these ordeals could be manipulated in the interests of justice, or against them.

We are next told of etiquette, and are informed that no less than nine ways of being polite are employed. Of these, the most respectful is to cast one's self on the ground, and then to kneel "and laud the virtues of the one you address." When one of inferior rank receives orders, he lifts the skirt of his superior, and casts himself on the

[1] J. Talboy Wheeler, "*History of India*," London, 1874, vol. iii, p. 261,

ground. The "honourable person thus reverenced must speak gently to the inferior, and touch his head, or pat him on the back, and give him kindly orders or good advice, in order to show affection."

When ill, there is no rush to the physic-bottle. "Everyone who falls sick, fasts for seven days. Should he not get well in the course of this period, he takes medicine." Hiuen-Tsiang causes us no surprise when he informs us that "doctors differ in their modes of treatment."

At funerals there are weepings and lamentable cries, rending of garments and beatings of head and breast. No one takes food in a house where someone has died until after the funeral; and all who have been at the death-bed are unclean until they have bathed outside the town. Those who desire release from life "receive a farewell meal at the hands of relatives or friends," and then are put into a boat amid strains of music; and this is shot into mid-Ganges, "where such persons drown themselves." Sometimes, but rarely, one of these may be seen on the banks, not yet quite dead.

Hiuen-Tsiang speaks of the civil administration as being mild and benevolent. Officials have "a portion of land assigned to them for their personal support." There is neither registration of families nor forced labour. Râjas possess their own private domains, divided into four portions; whereof one provides for state-matters and the cost of sacrifices; one, for salaries; one, for rewarding men of exceptional talent; and the fourth affords charity to religious bodies. By this arrangement taxation is light, and the personal service required is moderate, labour at public works being paid for. "Everyone keeps his own belongings in tranquillity; and all till the ground for food. Those who cultivate the royal estate pay a sixth part of the produce as tribute." There is a light tax payable on travel by river and at barriers across the roadways.

Such people as smell of onion and garlic are thrust out of the town. The usual food is simple, consisting of milk, cream, butter, sugar-candy, corn cakes and mustard. Fish, mutton and venison are eaten; other flesh is prohibited. Brâhmans and warriors drink unfermented syrup of the grape; but the trading caste indulges in strong drink. Rich and poor eat precisely the same food, but out of very different vessels, both as to material and cost. They eat with the fingers, and have no spoon, cup, or chopstick.

Hiuen-Tsiang tells us that he found India divided into 70 Kingdoms. Nine centuries before his time Megasthenes the Greek Ambassador, found twice as many. In spite of the many political settlements which have had their day and vanished, some of the territories described by Hiuen-Tsiang are divisions corresponding to natural features, race, language, and religious customs, and remain distinct districts, each of them with its idiosyncracies, to-day. Consolidation by successive conquests has taken place, it is true, but the village persists. The village-settlements were there before the Aryan conquest; they have survived the long passage of time; they carry on their ancient tradition, and have maintained provincial characteristics against the pressure of the Mohammedan, the Mahrattan, and all other attempts at organic Empire.

CHAPTER VI.

THE JOURNEY HOME BY A NEW AND PERILOUS ROUTE.

We left our hero on the Kâbul river, beyond the boundaries of India: a royal reception awaited him at Kapiśa, and a hundred experienced men were chosen to conduct and protect him in the passage across the Hindû Kûsh. The shortest, but most difficult of the passes—probably the Khawak, which reaches 13,000 feet, was selected. Seven days of travel brought the party to those snow-mountains of which Hiuen-Tsiang always speaks with mingled wonder, fear and dislike. Born and brought up in a mild climate, and having now spent many years in a hot one, he describes the discomforts and dangers of every high pass at length. He tells us how wild and perilous are the precipices; how fearsome, contorted, and difficult the path. Of the Hindû Kûsh he writes: "Now the traveller is in a profound valley; now aloft on a high peak, with its burthen of ice in full summertide. One gets along by cutting steps in the ice, and, in three days one reaches the summit of the pass. There, a furious icy blast, cold beyond measure, sweeps on; the valleys are laden with accumulated snow. The traveller pushes on; for he dares not pause. Soaring birds must needs alight; it is impossible for them to fly; and they have to cross afoot. One gazes down on mountains that look like hillocks." The whole cavalcade had to dismount and clamber up with the aid of mountain-staves. One wonders how the guides got the elephant over such ridges; but they did. "Great men lived before Agamemnon"; Hannibal solved the same problem two hundred years before Christ.

At the end of the second week a large village of a hundred families was reached, the inhabitants of which lived by rearing a very big variety of sheep, which is said still to be found in this district. Here the "Master of the Law" secured the services of a local guide, and took a whole day's rest. His escort now returned; and he set forth in the middle of the night, mounted on a camel accustomed to the hills, and attended by seven priests, twenty servants, the elephant which Sîlâditya had given him, six asses, and four horses. Next morning the bottom of the pass was reached; but there still lay before them what, in the distance, looked like a snow-peak. But when they had ascended a long zig-zag path and come up to it, it turned out to be mere white rock. None the less, it towered far above the clouds, and the icy wind there blew so hard and cutting that headway could hardly be made.

The descent of the range occupied five or six days. The route now lay north-westward to the Upper Oxus. Hiuen-Tsiang rested a month in the camp of a petty Khân,—and then joined a caravan of traders who were eastward bound. The caravan took a meandering course through several little Khânates; and in one of them the Master of the Law was struck by the singular headgear of the women. They wore caps three feet high, topped by two peaks of unequal length, if both father-in-law and mother-in-law were living. The higher and lower respectively represented these relatives. But, when one of them died, the corresponding peak was removed; should both of them be dead, no peaks were worn. This region was mountainous, and its inhabitants were remarkable for their surpassing ugliness. They differed from all other peoples in the peculiar blue-green of the iris. They were innocent of all manners, and knew no law of justice; the horse was their study and care, and they reared a breed of sturdy little ponies.

The caravan now followed the narrowing stream of Oxus, and, after a time, ascended to the great plateau of the Pamirs, no less lofty than the topmost Pyrenees.

"There even in summer" says the Pilgrim "one suffers from squalls and eddies of snow-storm. Just a few wretched plants manage to root in ground that is almost always frozen. No grain will sprout and no trace of man is to be found in all this vast solitude." But he came across a species of ostrich, a bird "ten feet high," of which he had previously been shown the eggs which were "as big as small pitchers."

The central valley of the Pamirs along which the caravan advanced, led to difficult snow-passes of the Kizil Yart range, the highest peak of which soars to 26,000 feet. Having forced a way over ice and through snow, the long descent of the Eastern slopes was nearly at an end when a band of brigands was observed to be on the look out for prey, The traders fled, helter skelter, up the hill-side; and the robbers charged furiously at their laden elephants, several of which they killed, while others were drowned in trying to get across the torrents from the mountains. It was probably at this time that Hiuen-Tsiang lost his elephant. The thieves were soon fully occupied with their booty; the traders seized the opportunity, drew together again, and proceeded, with what goods they had been able to save, towards Kâshgar.

At Kâshgar the same custom obtained as at Kutchê: "When a child is born the head is compressed by a wooden board." The people are "fierce and impetuous and most of them are deceitful and indifferent to polite manners and learning. They paint their bodies and eyelids." But they show real skill in the making of hair-cloth and finely woven carpets. More than six hundred years later, Marco Polo travelled along the caravan route through Kâshgar and by Lob-Nor to China.

At Yârkand he was told that Arhats, (very purified and wise men), "those who had obtained the holy fruit and were no longer bound by worldly influences" "displaying their spiritual power, coming from afar (that is, from India), abode here at rest."

Arrived at Khotan, he found it a land of song and dance. Fa-Hian also describes the inhabitants as being, in his time, "lovers of religious music."

It would seem that the caravan in which Hiuen-Tsiang travelled was bound for Kau-chang, that land of the Uïgurs whose Khân-paramount had tried to detain him "for the better instruction of his subjects." Now Khotan was tributary to this despot; and as the Master of the Law had no desire to go out of his direct way home, or to be detained again, not to speak of another hunger-strike, he wrote the Khân a politic letter, wherein he recounted the perils he had undergone and the successful issue of his sacred mission. Yet, an elephant which bore the burthen of many scriptures had been drowned on the way home; but the writings were saved. Would the Great Khân grant him a convoy?

It took six or seven months for a reply to arrive; and Hiuen-Tsiang filled up the time in expounding sacred writings to the Khân of Khotan and his subjects. When the answer came from Kau-chang, it was favourable; the Khân of Khotan was permitted to furnish the Master of the Law with transport for his treasures.

Fully a thousand miles still lay before him, and the painful desert known to modern geographers as the Takla Makan must be crossed. The route pursued was a very tortuous one, south of the great lake Lob-nor (which lies between 2,000 and 3,000 feet above the sea-level), and north of the Altyn-Tag mountains, which are the northern buttresses of the great plateau of Thibet. He passed by ancient cities of Eastern Khotan, once flourishing, now buried by drifting sands. Mere mounds marked their sites.[1] Going East "we enter a great desert of shifting sands, which are as a vast flood, driven hither and thither by the wind. There is no track; and, without guide

[1] W. H. Johnson, who was the first European to visit Khotan for 260 years, heard of these cities buried in the sand (1865).

or indication, travellers get bewildered and are lost. So the bones of beasts (which have perished) are piled up to serve as beacons. Neither water nor herb is to be found, and hot winds, which are frequent, befog the mind and muddle the memory of man and beast, and make them ill and feeble. Sometimes one hears plaintive notes and piteous lamentations, and men get confused and know not whither they are going. Hence, many a life is lost. And all is the work of demons and evil spirits." All travellers in deserts speak of the weird noises, which we now know to be due to the shifting of the sand-ridges.[1]

And now, after sixteen years of pilgrim travel, after visiting a hundred and ten different States, and journeying some twenty thousand miles, Hiuen-Tsiang is drawing near his native land. He bears with him five hundred grains of relics, reputed to belong to the body of Tathâgarta (Gautama Buddha); one hundred and twenty-four works of the Great Vehicle; five hundred and twenty other volumes, borne by twenty-two horses; and six images of Buddha, in gold or silver or sandal-wood. In the appeal for transport sent to Kau-chang, he had written: "Notwithstanding differences in climate and mode of life; and notwithstanding perils beyond count which have menaced me in my journeying, I thank Heaven that nowhere did I come to harm. Reverence, beyond all limit, has been done to me; my body has suffered no ill; and I have fulfilled all that I vowed to accomplish."

But his body *had* suffered ill. The terrible ordeal of crossing ice-bound ranges left its mark: it weakened his robust constitution and shortened his life.

At the Chinese frontier, waggons and men were obtained, and the escort from Khotan returned. T'ai Tsung, the great warrior-statesman, now sat on the throne he had won for his father, and to him "The Master of the Law"

[1] For recent travels in Eastern Turkestan, see Prjevalsky, N. From *Kulja across the Thian Shan to Lob-Nor*, tr. E. D. Morgan, 1879.

announced his return. Emperor, Mandarins, Priests, and People made ready to receive the great pilgrim with plaudit and parade such as Western reserve bestows only on the victor in some scene of slaughter, or on the inheritor of some soiled circlet and blood-stained robe.

The great day arrived. It was as if all China were present, so crushing were the crowds. The Sacred Writings were taken in state to the "Convent of the Great Bliss." (Later they were transferred to a "Convent of Beneficence," specially constructed to contain them.) High dignitaries led the way; marvellous wind-instruments discoursed astounding music; priests in thousands chanted hymns; banners and brilliantly-coloured rugs floated in the wind. A procession of the most varied character, miles long, passed through the narrow, crowded streets, which were lined by rows of flower-scatterers and less poetic, but even more desirable, perfume burners. To the irreverent European mind, the record of this Eastern parade in the Seventh Century suggests a highly variegated travelling-circus; and the brow is involuntarily raised when we come to the royal harem and its enthusiastic ladies welcoming the return of the monk and the arrival of yet more ascetic doctrine. The best of us is but human, and it is evident from the narrative that, true saint as he was, the "Master of the Law" none the less thoroughly enjoyed the recognition of his great merits, and made little objection to the honours he received.

CHAPTER VII.

PEACEFUL DAYS.

At intervals an order came from T'ai-Tsung and his successor to appear within the green enclosure which surrounded the Imperial Throne. It was by Imperial command that the world possesses Hiuen-Tsiang's report of the States he had visited and of eighteen other States of which he believed himself to have gathered authentic information. The work, as already stated, is full of the absurd, fantastic fables of corrupted Buddhism, related at full length and with perfervid unction ; but it is also a record of observation so close, systematic, and even scientific, and of a will so firm-set and bold, that it is surpassed in no age by any record of travel whatsoever. But there is little of personal narrative in it. Now, Hiuen-Tsiang had lost full command of his native language during so many years of residence among alien peoples, and it was found necessary to get a Chinese stylist to redact his "Account of Western Countries" ("*Si-yu-ki*") This was done, in the main, from notes which the pilgrim had brought back with him.

When the "Master of the Law" had finished this big undertaking, he returned to work that had been interrupted by it—the collating, translating and editing of the books he had brought with him. He was accustomed to eat a slight breakfast at dawn, and to lecture to the monks (*Sramans*) of his convent during the next four hours on some canonical book or religious treatise. When this task was done, he would go on with translation, marking out a certain portion for the day's task ; but, if he had not finished this by night-fall, he usually sat on until it was ended. He was scrupulous in his efforts to restore corrupt text to its pristine purity ; and one would always find him fully occupied. Yet he always made time to discuss religious matters with the sages who visited him. "When he had penetrated some profundity, got light on some obscure passage, or amended some corrupt reading, it seemed as if some divine being had come to his aid. . . . . . When expounding, he was wont to become impassioned and his voice swelled out." He had the great gift of a convincing manner.

One is glad that his biographers did not neglect to describe his personal appearance and other details of a similar kind. "His face," they say, "had a little colour to it; it was radiant and gracious; his bearing, grave and stately. His voice was clear and penetrating; and one never got weary of listening to him; for his words were noble, elegant, and congenial. Often a distinguished guest would listen to him for half a day with rapt attention. He liked to wear a garment of fine cotton, of a length suited to his height, which was 7 *tchi*.[1] He walked with even steps, and as one at ease. He looked you straight in the face; there was never a hint of side-glance. He kept strict rule and was always the same man. Nobody could rival him for warmth and kindness of heart and gentle pity, ardour, and inviolate observance of the Law. He was slow in making friends, and reserved in intercourse with those that he made. Once within the gates of his monastery, nothing but an Imperial decree could make him budge."

Yet, on one occasion, he paid a visit to his native village. Only one feeble old sister was left of all his family. He went with her to the graves of their parents; it is said to clear them of weeds which had overgrown them; but probably also to restore the few bones he had taken with him on his pilgrimage. His parents perished during the time of bloody civil strife, and their remains were hastily buried in a mean grave; so he obtained Imperial permission to carry them to a better resting-place. Thousands

[1] A measure which varies in different provinces. It is the Chinese foot-measure, always shorter than ours.

of monks and laity came to honour the father and mother of the "Master of the Law."

When Hiuen-Tsiang was a little more than 60, the hardships of travel and the intense application of his latter years told on him; health rapidly failed him. "I have come to the end of my work on this sacred book,', said he to a disciple, "and also I have come near to the end of my life. Bury me in a simple, quiet way. Wrap my body in a mat and bear it to some lonely, hushful valley, far from any palace (*sic*) or convent; for so impure a carcass as mine should not be near either." His disciples were disturbed at his condition and wept bitterly; they tried to persuade him that he was mistaken as to the approach of death. "I know myself," he replied; "How can you enter into my intuition?" The weakness increased, "The moment of departure is at hand," he told them. "Already my soul gives way and seems to leave me. Sell my clothes and belongings without delay, and turn the money into images (of Buddha), and tell the monks to pray." He lay stiff and still for days, taking no food. At last, when asked if he felt sure of reaching the goal of his desires, he answered "Yes" in a weak voice. In a few moments he was dead; yet his face retained its rosy colour and suggested supreme happiness. He was 65 years of age.

He had begged for a simple funeral. He was buried in pomp; and there was an immense giving of alms at his grave-side. His wish was so far respected, however, that his remains were ultimately carried to a reposeful spot in a tranquil valley.

Hwui-Lih, one of Hiuen-Tsiang's disciples, whom he had employed in translation, had gone far in writing a biography of the Master from his notes and conversation, when his labours were interrupted by death. Yen-Tsong, another devoted disciple took up the uncompleted work; he collected and put the manuscripts of Hiuen-Tsiang and Hwui-Lih in order, corrected the blunders and imperfections of Hwui-Lih's five volumes, and expanded them into ten volumes; which Monsieur Julien translated into French many years ago. M. Julien condensed the later and less interesting part of the biography, for the complete work was too voluminous and too full of flowery periods to be worth the labour of full translation; and even with this abridgement, much of the work, like the *Si-yu-ki*, remains tedious reading. There is also a much abbreviated translation into English by Dr. Samuel Beal.

Yet, the work is an imperishable monument to a great mind. When, here and there, one suspects a little of that chastened self-inflation from which few, if any, saints have been exempt; and when one has made due allowance for the natural desire of two enthusiastic disciples to offer innumerable flowers of Chinese rhetoric at the tomb of a beloved Master, the fact remains that his lofty mind and gentle, yet ardent, character, secured their deep reverence and commanded their devotion. This affords further evidence of that personal attraction, the effects of which we have so often observed in the record of his pilgrimage. We may justly apply to this ancient Chinaman the happy phrase of John Lyly, the Euphuist, and say of him that his soul was "stitched to the starres."

II.—SÆWULF, AN ENGLISH PILGRIM TO PALESTINE.

A.D. 1102

CHAPTER I.

EARLY PILGRIMAGE TO PALESTINE.

VERY soon after Hiuen-Tsiang set forth on his arduous enterprise, Jerusalem witnessed a remarkable scene (A.D. 629). Heraclius, Emperor of New Rome, had overthrown the hosts of Chosroes II, the Persian, and now he marched on foot through streets which that monarch had so lately ravaged and shorn of half their population. A spirit of devout and humble thankfulness possessed Heraclius and his chastened people. The imperial feet were naked; the imperial shoulders bore the weight of that True Cross which the aged Helena, mother of Constantine the Great, had so significantly discovered, and which Chosroes had carried away from the Church of the Holy Sepulchre.

Long before the True Cross was miraculously found, pious Christians were wont to visit the sacred scenes of their Faith; but, after that event, Pilgrimage became fashionable. Not the devout only thronged to the Holy Land, and crowded all its many sanctified spots. The inhabitants of Palestine were not slow to provide for the satisfaction of the pilgrim; whether he were of the eager faithful, burning to behold the burial places of Patriarchs and the very spot associated with some scene of the Gospels; or were one moved by a love of novelty and excitement. Tradition was revived, or legend invented; a vast number of sacred relics was hit upon and produced; hostelries became scenes of piety, and, alas! often of dissipation.

Many, if not most, of the travellers were undoubtedly impelled by a genuine spirit of reverence; but pilgrimages have always been popular because, under the sanction of Religion, they afforded the excitement of mild adventure and the physical and mental exhilaration which accompanies change of scene. As is always the case when men gather together from many lands and find themselves released from the restraints of home and the specified conventions of country, many were pliant to the allurements of pleasure. Indeed, Jerusalem was soon turned into a theatre of the passions, a centre of wild dissipation, and even of serious crime. Gregory of Nyssa, St. Jerome, and St. Augustine, set themselves against the fashionable craze, and told would-be pilgrims that they might do far better by remaining at home and praising God in whatsoever station he had assigned to them.

When Jerusalem fell to the onrush ot the Arabs (A.D. 637), the Moslem conquerors regarded it as a sacred city; for they believed Mohammed to have been transported thence to visit Paradise. Christian subjects and Christian pilgrims added to Mohammedan wealth; and they were allowed, under restrictions, to dwell in or to visit the Holy Land. Haroun-Al-Raschid, Caliph of Bagdad, and Charlemagne, Emperor of the West, were drawn together by the political antagonism of Constantinople alike to the Saracen and to an upstart Empire. They exchanged gifts; and the traveller may still see some of those sent by Haroun-Al-Raschid, as well as much else that is curious or beautiful, in the Treasury of the great Church which Charlemagne built at Aix-la-Chapelle. Bernard, one of three Benedictine monks who visited the Holy Land A.D. 870, says that Christians there enjoyed such security that if, by some accident, a traveller should lose a beast of burden on the road, he might leave his belongings where they lay, proceed to the nearest city for assistance, and find them untouched on his return.

When the great Empire of the Abassides crumbled and fell, the Fatimite Caliphs of Cairo were usually tolerant of infidels, who increased their wealth and power. Commercial relations with the Christian West continued; and pilgrims flocked to the Holy Land. In the tenth century, that darkest of the Dark Ages, John of Parma visited Palestine no fewer than seven times; and even far-off Iceland sent its pilgrims.

But in the eleventh century (A.D. 1074) the Seljuk Turk swept down from the Oxus, and, aided by Emirs in revolt, took Jerusalem. The main body of the Turkish army retained the barbarous habits of a nomadic people; they lusted for battle; they were drunk with blood. Palestine became the scene of exaction, of debauchery, and of every kind of licence and excess. Churches were ransacked for spoil; the rich pilgrim was subject to threat and compelled to disgorge much of his wealth before he was allowed to see Jerusalem; the poor pilgrim, already worn down by privation and suffering in some diminutive crazy craft, met, on landing, with insult and outrage. Neither Mohammedan Cairo nor Christian Constantinople were strong enough to deal with the Turk: he exhibited Moslem fanaticism at its worst. The Scimitar had indeed displaced the Cross.

CHAPTER II. "DIEU LE VEULT."

One of the eye-witnesses of the wretchedness of Christians in Palestine was a certain Peter, a man from Picardy; high-strung; one to whom a very varied experience brought no satisfaction. His restless disposition had driven him into the profession of arms; he had sought for peace in study; he had tried the companionship of a wife, who had borne him the boon of children; his spirit found no tranquility among cloistered monks; he fled to the greater seclusion of a hermitage. There visions left his soul still unsatisfied, and he went to the Holy Land. The sufferings of Christians at the hands of the Turk filled him with spiritual fury. He returned to Europe, and with inextinguishable zeal, traversed its western half to urge in impassioned eloquence, which made every heart throb and frenzied every mind, the union of all Christendom for the destruction of the Turk and the re-establishment of the True Faith in its first home.

He set Europe ablaze. Fourteen generations of Christians had grieved over the Moslem occupation of the Holy Land. John Zimiskes, the ablest and most popular of Byzantine generals, had carried his arms as far as Lebanon in the year 975, and had recovered what were said to be the shoes of the Saviour and the hair of John the Baptist. But, contrary to the vain-glorious assertions of Byzantine historians, he was unable to penetrate into Palestine. In 1073, Hildebrand, the great Pope-Statesman, was anxious to deliver the Holy Places; but any project that he may have formed came to naught; for the Head of the Holy Roman Empire was bent on subordinating the Church to his Imperial Will; and the Head of the Church was even more resolute in his resolve to make the Papacy independent and supreme. About this time, German prelates headed 7,000 pilgrims, of whom only 2,000 survived to see their home once more. The conquest of Jerusalem remained a dream until Peter the Hermit awoke the sleeper.

But now Urban II responded to his call, and summoned and presided over the famous Council of Clermont in Auvergne. "God wills it," shouted the assembly; "a truce of God" was declared; private war and princely quarrels appeared to be forgotten; and all Western Europe prepared for a Crusade.

The barons were undoubtedly captive to a great idea, and their zeal was sincere. But little of any human action is due to a single motive. Remission of sin was promised to those who should assume the Cross; and love of battle, the charm of novelty, and the desire of acquiring large and lucrative fiefs in the Holy Land also played their part. The imagination of the common people, so lively and virile, often so spiritual and exalted in the Middle Ages, was no less fired than that of the barons. The spirit which directed men to the cloister now summoned them to the camp. A belief that God had decreed the expulsion of the Turk, and would protect and direct them to the capture of the Holy City, filled all men with fanatic fervour. The sound of clarion and trumpet and the clash of arms mingled with the voice of the preacher exhorting seigneur and serf. To men of the eleventh century, the curtains of the Unseen were often withdrawn, and the splendour of God shone forth, or devils appeared, comely to tempt, or distorted to terrify. Guibert tells us that, while at Beauvais, he noticed, at mid-day, a few clouds stretched a little obliquely athwart others, and "All at once, thousands of voices from every quarter cried out that a cross had appeared in the sky."

But, as with the barons, motives other than religious also moved the populace and favoured the Crusade. Private war had been unceasing; famine and pestilence, the attendants on war, had desolated Europe; the serf lay prostrate under the heel of his exacting seigneur.

There would be release from these evils in that land which the Redeemer of Mankind had chosen to be the scene of his birth and Sacrifice.

The wave of enthusiasm struck our own shores, and passed beyond them. William of Malmesbury says in his "Chronicles of the Kings of England" that, "there was no nation so remote, no people so retired, as not to contribute its portion." This ardent love not only inspired the continental provinces, but even all who had heard the name of Christ, whether in the most distant islands, or savage countries. The Welshman left his hunting; the Scot his fellowship with lice; the Dane his drinking party; the Norwegian his raw fish. Lands were deserted of their husbandmen; houses of their inhabitants; even whole cities migrated. There was no regard to relationship; affection to their country was held in little esteem; God alone was placed before their eyes. Whatever was stored in granaries, or hoarded in chambers, to answer the hopes of the avaricious husbandman, or the covetousness of the miser, all, all was deserted; they hungered and thirsted after Jerusalem alone. Joy attended such as proceeded; while grief oppressed those who remained. But why do I say remained? You might see the husband departing with his wife; indeed, with all his family; you would smile to see the whole household laden on a carriage, about to proceed on their journey. The road was too narrow for the passengers, the path too confined for the travellers, so thickly were they thronged with endless multitudes." A French eye-witness tells us that "thieves and evil-doers of all kinds cast themselves at the feet of priests to receive the cross. . . . The rustic shod his oxen like horses; the children on approaching any large town or castle would ask: 'is that Jerusalem?'"

These undisciplined hordes became turbulent; their march was marked by famine, pillage and murder. The few who reached Asia Minor were exterminated.

Macaulay's "schoolboy" knows the story of the disciplined army of the First Crusade; how, after the Caliph of Cairo had wrested Jerusalem from the weakened Turk and offered peace and security to Christians in vain, the slow advance of the invaders, marked by incredible cruelty on both sides, was so far successful that the crusading barons and their followers hurled themselves against the Holy City and took it (A.D. 1099). "Even civilization always bears a brute within its bosom," remarks Sainte-Beuve; and assuredly Mediæval Religion made small attempt to caste out the devils that made the Cross their screen. The loftiest passions are often unstable; the enthusiasm of the crowd readily passes from mood to mood. The fervour of faith became the frenzy of carnage. Raymond of Agiles, an eye-witness, declares that the Mosque of Omar and its portals ran blood up to the knees and even so far as to the reins of the horses. For seven days, Jerusalem was given up to slaughter and pillage.

Yet, in spite of a campaign tarnished with shame and dyed with guilt, the Christian ideal had not wholly disappeared. The growing spirit of Chivalry was not wanting, nor was the Norman genius for statesmanship absent. At the famous "Assizes of Jerusalem," a code of laws was drawn up better than the Middle Ages had yet known. But after Baldwin was crowned at Bethehem (A.D. 1100), the new Kingdom remained unsettled. Neither Christian nor Saracen was likely to forget the atrocities of war; the whole of Palestine was far from being subdued; a few parts were still held by the Infidel; the paths to Jersusalem were still perilous for the pilgrim; but once again the Holy City and other sacred places were under Christian rule. The enthusiasm amd joy of Western Europe ran high. The tide of pilgrimage at once set in, and an obscure Englishman was one of the first pilgrims to reach Jerusalem.

CHAPTER III. SÆWULF'S RECORD.

THERE is preserved in the library of Corpus Christi College, Cambridge, a valuable collection of ancient manuscripts presented by an old pupil of the College, who was no other than Matthew Parker, Archbishop of Canterbury in the reign of Queen Elizabeth. Among these manuscripts is a mere fragment, written in Mediæval Latin, which tells of the pilgrimage to Jerusalem of one Sæwulf, an Englishman, who must have started from his native shores thirty-six years after the landing of William the Conqueror, and less than two years after the coronation of Baldwin.[1] The record of Sæwulf is the broken voice of an obscure, unlettered palmer, which chance has preserved from common sepulture with things more important in the Ancient Silences. It gives us little more than a glimpse of a single year of adventurous pilgrimage in the life of a plain Englishman who, like the Chinaman who undertook a sacred journey nearly five centuries before him, having beheld "a gleam upon the mountain, needs must arise and go thither."

The narrative begins with the statement: "I Sæwulf, an unworthy person and an evil doer, made for Jerusalem that I might pray at the tomb of our Lord." Who Sæwulf was, is open to conjecture. It seems probable that he was the man of that name of whom William, Librarian of Malmesbury Abbey, speaks in his "Book of Bishops"; a merchant who had recurring spasms of penitence, during which he was wont to repair to Wulstan, Bishop of Worcester, a prelate of "pious, simple truth," who commanded the affection of the people and the confidence of the King. This Sæwulf was probably a native of Worcester. Wulstan, we know, was the last of the Saxon

[1] The Latin text is printed with a translation by Brownlow, by the Palestine Pilgrims Text Society. 1892.

Bishops; for the hand of the Norman was heavy on the prostrate land, and it was the policy of the Conqueror, as William of Malmesbury tells us, in another of his works, to replace the native bishops on their death "by diligent men of any nation except English"—a policy which the Church supported; for religion had been in a decaying state in England for some years before the arrival of the Normans. Indeed, "the clergy, contented with a very slight degree of learning, could scarcely stammer out the words of the sacraments; and a person who understood grammar was an object of wonder and astonishment. The monks mocked the rule of their order by fine vestments and the use of every kind of food." Wulstan implored Sæwulf to give up a livelihood which was beset with all manner of temptation, and to take the habit; for his conviction of sin was soon over, and he invariably resumed his former vices. Wulstan told him that the time would come when he would become a monk, "which" says the Chronicler, "I afterwards saw fulfilled; for he was converted in our monastery in his old age, being driven to it by disease." There is nothing in Sæwulf's narrative to indicate that he was in holy orders; more than once he speaks of himself as one oppressed by a sense of sin; and the record of his pilgrimage may very well have been translated into the dry, terse Latin of the monks by another hand, or, conceivably, may have been written by himself in his last years at Malmesbury.

Whoever he was, Sæwulf's early manhood was spent in a disordered land among a dejected people. During the reign of William Rufus, England was visited by tempest and famine and even by severe earthquake; rebellion was rife; the Welsh over-ran the county of Chester and part of Shropshire, leaving them waste; Magnus, King of Norway, swooped down the Irish Sea, occupied Anglesea, and threatened the mainland; the common people were oppressed by their foreign masters and illegally taxed; "the courtiers preyed upon the property of the country people and consumed their substance," says William of Malmesbury, and Eadmer of Canterbury, our best authority on the period, confirms his statement: "As to their cruelty towards their hosts," he writes, "or their unseemly conduct towards their wives and daughters, it is shameful even to remember"; the royal progresses through England were a travelling Sodom and Gomorrah. And we may judge of the tender mercies of the time when we read that traitors to the King, or innocent men deemed to be such, "were deprived of their sight and manhood." These inhumanities also disgraced the far more civilized Byzantine Empire. No wonder that men's hearts yearned for a "City of God," or that their hearts were set on the peace of the convent, or that they disdained the mere perils of pilgrimage!

The existing fragment of Sæwulf's narrative begins with his departure from Southern Italy; but we know, from other sources, what were the conditions and prescribed forms of pilgrimage, and how an English pilgrim would reach Apulia.

First, he had to get the consent of near relatives, in order that the interests of his family or dependents might be protected. To make sure that the would-be pilgrim was moved by devotion or penitence, and not by vain desire to see the world, he was also required to secure the sanction of his bishop, who made investigation into his life and character before granting it. The enquiry was a very searching one in the case of a monk; for his real motive might be to escape from conventual discipline. If satisfied, the Bishop or his delegate solemnly presented him with a pilgrim's staff and wallet, and bestowed his benediction at Mass in the church of the parish in which the pilgrim resided. He was furnished with a document which exhorted all monasteries, priests, and faithful Christians to give him aid and relief on his journey. He was now bound to set off without delay, under penalty of being dealt with as a backslider and perjurer. When the day of departure arrived, a procession of relatives, friends, and pious people accompanied him some little distance, and then, having been blessed by the clergy present, clad in white linen with the cross marked on it, and duly sprinkled with holy water, he went on his way alone.

The long and hazardous sea-voyage to the Mediterranean was shunned. Despite the perturbed state of the Continent, it was safer to make for the heel of Italy by the over-land route. All men who bore arms were under the obligation to defend him; no robber-baron might demand a toll from him—nay the castle welcomed him, and he was seated at table beside the house-priest. The bishop of every town and the abbot or prior of every monastery gave him shelter and hospitality; alms were specially devoted to the relief of the poor pilgrim and the support of monasteries along the pilgrim's path. If he were ill, the doors of whatever hospital might be near were open to him, or he was cordially received into the Infirmary of every convent. A pilgrim's hospice, founded in the first half of the ninth century by Louis the Pious, stood amid the snowy wastes of Mont Cénis to shelter him from its bitter blasts. He would pass through Italy, little affected by the unceasing and bloody conflict of noble with bishop, bishop with city, city with noble, and every one of a thousand petty communes and fiefs with its neighbours; for the charitable monastery would prove a ready asylum. Arrived at a convenient port, a greatly reduced passage-money was required of a pilgrim to the Holy Land; and there were some ports where ships belonging to them were compelled to carry pilgrims free of all charge.

Mediterranean shipping was not notably different in build and badness from that of Northern waters; but was often of larger size. Nearly all that we know about it is derived from the uncouth paintings, coins, and arms of maritime towns of a somewhat later period, which are rather symbols than representations. The sailing-ship was shorter than the galley, which was rowed as well as sailed; it was shaped somewhat like a half-moon and was very broad in the beam. It could sail only before the wind. There was rarely more than a single mast; the sails were square; and the yards could be lowered to the deck like those of a modern barge. These ships were not unlike the clumsy coasters still to be met with off Norway. Passengers were very uncomfortably crowded together, and must have had a terrible time. The outside planks overlapped, and were held together by iron nails; and the seams were stopped up with oakum. Mediæval vessels were crazy craft, and frequently went to pieces when wind and wave ran high: he was a bold traveller who tempted Neptune in those days, and especially bold if, after a first experience, he braved the sea god a second time.

Brindisi was the usual place of embarquation; but for some reason, which Sæwulf does not state, he started from Monopoli, a little port midway between Bari and Brindisi. Now there was a general belief in certain days being unlucky; a belief which persisted in spite of the condemnation of the Church. A Christian Calendar of the early part of the 4th century indicates what days are of ill omen, according to the Astrology of Egypt. Popular belief credited the feast-day of St. Mildred the Virgin (a saint of Kent) with this disqualification; and it was on St. Mildred's day, July 13th, 1102, that Sæwulf set sail in a craft rather crazier than most. A storm came on the very same day the port was left behind, and the ship was wrecked a short distance from the harbour; but, "by Divine Mercy," all aboard got safely to shore. The passengers went on to Brindisi; their ship, having been patched up in some fashion, sailed thither, and the pilgrims got on board again; but alas! it was another of those unlucky Egyptian days! Corfu was reached in two days (July 24th); but a great storm arose after leaving port and drove the ricketty craft before it. However, shelter was gained at another of the Ionian islands—Cephalonia—on August 1st. Here, the company was still further depressed by the death of one of their number. Cephalonia is opposite the Gulf of Lepanto, and, sailing up the gulf, they landed at Patras, which Sæwulf speaks of as a "notable *island*"; not improperly, the word island being often applied to a port in those days. The ship stopped at Patras for a special purpose—that its passengers and mariners should go on shore and pray to St. Andrew the Apostle at the site of his martyrdom. Corinth was reached on Aug. 9th, and Sæwulf and fellow pilgrims left their wretched craft to avoid the long, stormy passage by Cape Matapan. He finds a resemblance between his experiences and those of St. Paul: both had suffered shipwreck, and Paul met with misadventure at Corinth, where "we suffered many hardships." When a pilgrim to the Holy Land speaks of hardship, it was probably of an unusually severe kind. Roman Catholics neither loved nor were loved by members of the Greek Communion; and the behaviour of Crusading hosts in Eastern Europe was too recent to be forgotten.

The pilgrims crossed the isthmus to Livadrostro, and, some riding asses, the rest on foot, reached Thebes. They would find Thebes inhabited chiefly by Jews, who were "the most skilled artificers in silk and purple cloth of all Greece." Sixty-four years later, a Spanish Jew, Benjamin of Tudela on the Ebro, who visited the settlements of his race in many lands and reported on their condition, found 300 Jews at Corinth and no fewer than about 2,000 at Thebes, "many of them being learned scholars, not to be equalled in the land of Greece, save in the city of Constantinople." Leaving Thebes the travellers arrived next day at Negropont (Aug. 23rd). This land-journey had proved untoward; the Greeks were so inhospitable and so suspicious of them that often they had to pass the night in deserted huts and sheds. No wonder that they do not go a little out of their way to visit Athens, in spite of the fact that "in the Church of the Blessed Virgin there is a lamp which is ever burning with miraculously replenished oil," and that Scripture records how St. Paul preached there and "certain men clave unto him and believed." Among these converts was Dionysius, the Areopagite. It may be true that Dionysius "was born and got his learning there": we are indebted to Sæwulf for the information.

At Negropont, the band of pilgrims took passage in a tramp-trader, which first touched at one of the islands of Petali, hard by Marathon; but what Englishman of the year of grace 1102, even if he were an educated monk, knew aught of the "glory which was Greece?" The voyagers now made for Naxos, touching at various islands on their way; their mediæval minds sightless to the classic lustre of the Cyclades. Sæwulf does indeed speak of Naxos as being "near to Crete, that memorable island"; memorable because his own lively experience of what it means to "go down to the sea in ships" recalls the "tempestuous wind" which caught St. Paul off Crete; for certain, he had never heard of that Epimenides of whom the Apostle makes such vigorous use. Patmos is reached, where the Beloved Apostle, banished by Domitian, "entered his tomb alive." Other islands are touched at, among them Cos, and here our author exhibits his learning: it is the birthplace of Galen, "the most famous physician among the Greeks." However, Hippoocrates and Galen were both physicians, and that is near enough. On the trader goes, changing its course, now north, now south; and the pilgrim associates every place visited with some pious legend. Rhodes is reached, and history is again rescued from oblivion: the Colossus was "an idol, 125 feet high; the Persians destroyed it together with almost the whole Roman province on their way to Spain." Sæwulf, or tradition, has confused the first conquering onrush of the Arabs with the Persian advance; but the Colossus was destroyed, not by Persians but by earthquake, nine centuries before Sæwulf's time. Yet there is a basis for his story; its fragments were removed for building purposes about the time of the first Arab conquests. Sæwulf falls into a widespread blunder of his unlettered age when he assumes that the inhabitants of Rhodes drew their name from the Colossus, and that the Epistles to the Colossians were directed to them.

Leaving Rhodes, a great storm drove the ship straight before it; but the sailors got her into the harbour of Patara, "and, by next day, the storm had abated, and we came to Long Island." Here was a ruined city which had been the refuge of exiles, escaped from the Turk. Myra, on the mainland, was now reached; and Sæwulf states that it is "the port of the Adriatic Sea; as Constantinople is of the Ægean": either his geography is not quite accurate, or he would imply that, in his time, Myra received the main Eastern traffic from the Adriatic, and Constantinople from the Ægean. At Myra, he worshipped at the empty tomb of St. Nicholas. Favourable winds bore the ship thence to an island called "Sixty oars," on account of the force of the sea and the effort required to overcome it. A discursion, out of sight of land, brought the pilgrims to Paphos in Cyprus. We do not expect any reference to the Cyprian Venus; but we are a trifle surprised to find that our author now confuses two separate chapters of "Acts" in one jumbled statement.

Leaving Cyprus "we were tossed about by violent storms seven days' space before we could reach our haven; and one night a fierce contrary wind drove us back towards Cyprus; but Divine Mercy, Who is close at hand to those who truly call on Him. vouchsafed no small pity for us afflicted souls, and we resumed our proper course. Yet, during seven nights, we were overwhelmed by such a tempest and were in such peril that almost all hope left us. Nevertheless, at the rising of the sun, behold! the coast of Joppa lay before our eyes; and even as the turbulence of our peril had made our hearts to sink within us, so joy, unexpected and unhoped for, lifted them up an hundredfold more. And so it came to pass that, thirteen weeks after our departure from Monopoli, the sea having been our home, or deserted hovels in the islands (the Greeks not being hospitable), we made the harbour of Joppa, filled with joy and thanksgiving." Sæwulf gives no dates; but many have been fixed by the industry of a French scholar, who compared feast days mentioned in the narrative with the calendar, and its events with ascertained dates. Sæwulf reached the Holy Land, Oct. 12th, 1102.

God had interposed on behalf of "the meanest of His servants and the company of pilgrims"; and Sæwulf renders praise, with the manner of the Psalms of David in his mind. But yet another danger from wind and wave awaits him. He got warning from some weather-wise friends who knew the badness of the harbour. But he shall tell his own tale: "The same day that we anchored, someone, directed by God, as I believe, said to me, 'Master, go ashore this very day, for it may hap that to-night, at dawn, a storm shall come on and stop you from landing.' When I heard this, the desire to land seized me. I got a boat and went ashore with all my party. Even whilst I was landing the sea was vexed; the waves became more troubled, and a tempest came on; yet by Divine Mercy, I landed unharmed. What happened then? We entered the city to find a lodging. Weary and overdone by our long labours, we fed ourselves and went to rest. And then? In the morning, when we came out of church, we heard the roaring of the sea and the populace shouting, and everybody was running in a crowd to the shore, marvelling at such sounds as they had never heard aforetime. And, when we got there, we beheld the waves higher than hills, a countless number of bodies of men and women lying in wretched-wise on the beach; and ships were crashed against each other and broken into small bits. Could anyone hear a sound save that of roaring breakers and splintering ships? For this drowned the outcry of the crowd and the shouting in the ships. Our ship, however, being a big one and strongly built, and some others, laden with corn and other goods and with pilgrims going or returning, held to their anchors still. Yet how were they tossed about? Into what terror were they plunged! How their ladings were cast into the sea! What onlooker so hard and strong as to keep a dry eye! Not long did we gaze when, through the violence of the waves and currents, the anchors parted, the ropes were broken asunder, and the ships abandoned to the fierceness of the billows. All hope of safety was gone. Now they were cast high; now flung down, and hurled by degrees upon beach or rock. There were they dashed against one another in wretched plight, and, little by little, torn to bits by the tempest. Neither would the savage blasts allow of their getting back to the sea whole, nor the steepness of the shore admit of their gaining safety there. But what gain in telling how dismally sailors and pilgrims hung on; every hope gone, some to ships, some to masts, some to spars, some to cross-tenders? What more shall I tell? Some, overwhelmed with fright, are drowned. It may seem unbelievable to many, yet I beheld with my own eyes the heads of some separated from their bodies by the timbers of their own ship. Some, washed from the decks, are borne away again into the deep. Some, who can swim, leap into the sea. So, very many find their end. But just a very few, relying on their strength, gain the land. Thus, of 30 ships of largest size, of which some were Dromonds" (that is to say, having two tiers of double oars), "Gulafri" (a sort of galley) "and Catts" (vessels narrowing to the stern, with overhanging quarters and a deep waist)—"all full of pilgrims and goods—of all these barely seven were still unwrecked when I left the shore. That day more than a thousand folk, of both sexes, perished. Never did eye behold greater horrors in a single day. But the Lord, to whom be honour and glory, world without end, delivered me from all this of His grace. Amen."

The little company had escaped a great peril, but another lay ahead. Two days later they set forth to Jerusalem, and found the way "hilly, very rough, and very perilous. For the Saracens are constantly devising traps for Christians; they lie hidden in the hollows of the hills and in rocky holes, and by day and night remain ever sharply on the look-out for those whom they may pounce upon, by reason of their being few in numbers, or so jaded as to lag behind their band. Suddenly, the Saracens are all round about; the next moment they are gone. Anyone who does that journey. may make trial of this. How many human bodies, torn by wild beasts, lie along the way and beside it! Perchance, some one may marvel how the bodies of Christians should lie unburied. But there is nothing to wonder at; for there is very little earth, and the rocks are not easy to dig, and, even if there were soil, who would be so unwise as to leave his band and dig his companion a grave all by himself? He who should do so would dig his own grave rather than one for his companion. On that wayside, not only the poor and weak, but the rich and strong also, are in peril. If men are cut off by the Saracens, yet more in number die from heat and thirst; many through want of drink; more by drinking inordinately. Nonetheless we and all our company came scatheless to the place we longed for." Sæwulf's account of the dangers which beset the pilgrim is confirmed by that of Daniel, Abbot of Kief, who made his pilgrimage four years later ((1106, A.D.) North of the pilgrim's way lay Acre; south of it Ascalon, strong fortresses, still held by the Saracen.

The track from Jaffa led to the gate of David, and, entering the city, Sæwulf visited its holiest place first—the Martyrium or Holy Sepulchre. The tomb was under cover, because the Church above was so built as to be open to the skies. He tells us that Titus and Vespasian destroyed the whole of Jerusalem to fulfil the prophesy of Christ, and that the city has undergone the same fate seven times since Titus. He has for guides native Syrians, a people whom he confuses with the Assyrians and calls by that name. The guides told him that the Church of the Holy Sepulchre was built in the time of Constantine the Great. Now, the existing Church was only about 80 years old, and there had been two previous buildings, of which the earlier was destroyed by Chosroes II, early in the Seventh Century, and the second by Mohammedans, early in the Eleventh Century.

He was then taken to see the place where Christ was imprisoned, the spot where His Cross and the crosses of the two thieves were found, the column to which Christ was bound (the thong with which He is said to have been bound is still to be seen at Aix-la-Chapelle); all these sacred objects of pilgrimage being near the Holy Sepulchre. He was shown the "navel of the earth," a spot which a contemporary of Sæwulf tells us was in the outside wall of the Martyrium, beyond the altar. Sæwulf assures us that Christ marked it out with His own hand, and declared it to be the centre of the world. This tradition dates from the Sixth Century. Readers of Dante will recall that the poet makes Jerusalem and the Earthly Paradise the Antipodes of our globe; and, indeed, the Holy City was at the middle of the circumscribed world known to the Middle Ages. And had not David sung "God is my King of old, working Salvation *in the midst of the earth?*"

Thence to Calvary; "Which is the very same place where Abraham built an altar to sacrifice Isaac." Traces of the Earthquake which rent the rock, "for that it could not endure the death of its Maker without breaking asunder," were pointed out to him. The guides also took him to Golgotha, the very place where a stream of the Saviour's blood reached the bones of Adam, "and he and the bodies of many saints arose." Again readers of Dante will think of the passsage where the shade of Virgil tells him how, a little before the Roman poet's own death, Christ took from Hades the souls of Adam and Moses and other Scriptural personages of distinction, with many others "*e fecegli beati*," "and made them blessed." Sæwulf has perfect trust in any information conveyed to him by his "Assyrian" guides. Indeed, who so likely to know the truth about this wonderful land as its natives?

Close by the Holy Sepulchre was a little monastery which merchants of Amalfi had founded 54 years before Sæwulf saw it. It was the abode of the Knights Hospitalers, who became so famous; but they had not yet become that military order of which, after so singular a history, England possesses traces in St. John's Gate, Clerkenwell, and a memorial in the beneficent work of which that building is the official centre.

He saw the "Gate Beautiful," through which Heraclius, triumphant bearer of the Cross, entered after his defeat of the Persians; and heard how "the stones fell down and closed the way, until an angel reproved him; and he descended from his horse, and a passage was opened up to him." The guides took the pilgrim to see that stone which was the pillow of Jacob when angels ascended and descended a celestial ladder "and the Lord stood above it" at Bethel. It was now at Jerusalem, and, traditionally, is the very stone which was transported to Scone, whereon the Kings of Scotland sat to be crowned, and is to be seen at the present day, placed below the Coronation Chair at Westminster Abbey.

He was taken to Bethlehem; and complains that there, as at every holy place, the Saracen had destroyed everything. Yet the Convent of the Virgin still stood, and within it he saw the very manger where the infant Jesus lay; the very stone on which His head reposed in the tomb, and which St. Jerome had brought hither from Jerusalem; the marble table at which the Mother of our

Lord sat at meat with the Magi; a well which received their guiding star into its waters; and the burial-place of the Innocents. The story of the Star falling into a well is also told by that fraudulent Fleming who adopted the name of Sir John Mandeville, in his "Voiage and travaile."

As much of Palestine as had been conquered was still the scene of unceasing disorder, brigandage, revolt and warfare; so pilgrims were conducted to the holy places under military escort. Sæwulf went to Hebron, and tells us of the tombs of the Patriarchs, ornamented by the men of old and emitting sweet odours. The tombs were inside a strong protecting fortress. Here, at Hebron, he found, still standing, an ancient Ilex tree, under the shadow of which the Lord had appeared to Abraham and promised that Sara should bear him a son. Apparently, his friends, the "Assyrians," during many centuries of experience, had found what profit accrued to them in tacking on some Biblical association to every available object.

Travelling Northward, he visited Nazareth and Cana of Galilee, whence he beheld Mount Tabor, clad in refreshing green and sprinkled with flowers. Still advancing to the North, he saw the glory of Lebanon above him, and the springs which give birth to the milky waters of Jordan.

More than seven months had passed since our simple-minded, whole-hearted pilgrim landed at Joppa, and now he turns his steps towards home. "Having seen every one of the Holy Places of Jerusalem and its territory, so far as we were able; and our devotions done, we took ship at Joppa on the day of Pentecost" (May 17th, 1903). Each pilgirm would take on board with him a palm-branch as ensign of his success, and a few portable *souvenirs*.

Just as war with the Caliph of Cairo prevented our pilgrim from reaching the Holy Land by way of Egypt (which was the ordinary route from Western Lands), so its continuance compelled him to return by an unusual journey. The ship turned from Joppa to the North. Saracen ships were scouring the sea; and the returning pilgrims found themselves hugging the shore, although they must pass by that one fortified seaport which the Crusaders had not yet overcome. Four days out from Joppa, and when a little to the south of Acre, "behold twenty-six Saracen ships hove into sight. They were the squadron of the Admiral of Tyre and Sidon, sailing for Babylonia with an army to aid the Chaldeans in waging war with the King of Jerusalem" (*! sic*). This statement is an example of how hearsay may germinate in the uninstructed mind. It may not, however, be quite so wild as it seems. Cairo is called Babylon in all Mediæval writings, but, as a matter of fact, Arabs were, about this time, trying to turn Tancred out of his fief at Edessa; and Edessa may, perhaps, be regarded as lying towards the Babylon of Scripture. And a Saracen army was at sea, sent by the Caliph of Cairo, the new "Babylon," to raise the siege of Ascalon, which Baldwin I. was conducting. Probably it was this expedition from Cairo which Sæwulf came across. "Two vessels from Joppa, which were with us, laden with pilgrims, left our ship to itself; for they were lighter craft; and, by hard rowing, fled to Cæsarea. The Saracens sailed all round our ship, and kept an arrow's flight off, rejoicing over so much plunder. However our men were ready to die for Christ; they laid hold of their arms, and used up each moment in fortifying the castle (at the stern) of our ship; for we had in our dromond 200 fighting men. After the space of about an hour, the chief of the expedition, having held a council-of-war, ordered one of his sailors to climb up to the mast-head, so as to find out what it was exactly that we were at. And, when he learned from this man how strong was our defence, he hoisted his high yards and made for the main. Thus did Our Lord, of His Grace, rescue us from the foe that day. Afterwards our folk from Joppa took three of these same ships and made themselves rich men with the spoil thereof."

Sæwulf's dromond hugged the coast for eight days, and then crossed the open sea to St. Andrews', at the eastern extremity of Cyprus; thence it made for Antiochetta on the mainland. "During this voyage pirates often attacked us; but, under the protection of Divine Grace, we suffered naught, whether from hostile attack or from tempestuous tossing." Rhodes was reached on June 23rd; and Sæwulf and some others, who were weary of tacking east and west and of the slow progress made by the heavy vessel, agreed to go a certain distance together, and hired a smaller but swifter craft. Embarked in this, they returned towards the Asian Coast. A contrary wind detained them a few days at a place which Sæwulf calls Stromlo (Astypalæa), "once a fair city, wholly made waste by the Turks." At Scio, "we took leave of our (last) ship and fellow-travellers, and began our journey to Constantinople, in order that we might pray there." While passing Tenedos ,he heard of the ruins of Troy, and "how many miles of ground they covered." He tells us of two fortresses facing one another from opposite sides of the "Arm of St. George" (the Dardanelles), "which are so near as to be only two or three bowshots apart, and which thus make the taking of Constantinople an impossibility." We have another reference to the Trojan war: "The Greeks say that Helen was carried off (from Eregli) by Paris Alexander." And now the fragment ends, leaving our pilgrim landed at Rodosto on the Sea of Marmora, Sept. 10th, 1103. It has taken him more than four months' voyage from Joppa to reach within fifty miles of New Rome. Doubtless he found at St. Sophia, as Benjamin of Tudela did towards the end of the same century, "a quantity of wealth beyond all telling . . . . and the like of these riches is not to be seen in any other Church in the world."

A long, weary journey, full of the excitement of peril,

still lay before him, whatever route he might take. All we know is that, arrived at his native town (Worcester ?), a procession would receive and accompany him to his parish church. There he would render thanks to God for his safe return, and deliver his palm branch into the hands of the priest, who would lay it on the altar.

Some chance has rescued this broken record of an obscure, unlettered palmer from oblivion. He is as the hollow voice of a shade which has burst its sepulture in the silences of oblivion. We catch but a glimpse of some tenuous wraith; once warm and breathing flesh. It tells us of a few months in the brief adventure of Life. Yet we recognize, as in Hiuen-Tsiang, one who, having beheld "a gleam on the mountain," must "arise and go seek it." Sæwulf the Englishman may be but "a poor thing," yet he is our own. There lies the excuse for "a poor humour of mine, sir, to take that that no man else will."

MOHAMMED IBN ABD ALLAH

BETTER KNOWN AS IBN BATUTA, THE GREATEST OF MOSLEM TRAVELLERS, A.D. 1304-77.

CHAPTER I.

THE WHIRLWIND FROM ARABIA AND WHAT FOLLOWED.

MARAUDER as he was, the Arab, like his half-brother the Hebrew, carried an ethical spark in his bosom which could be readily fanned into a consuming blaze. He was accustomed, in the silence of the stony waste and of the stars, to plunge into the depths of his own spiritual being, or to await, in patience, some portent from the unseen. Mohammed, a mystic, like unto the ancient prophets of Israel, hating false gods and illuminated by the "One All Merciful, Lord of Creation and Sultan of Life," in trance, in ecstasy, and in paroxysms of enthusiasm, strove to purge his fellow countrymen of their vain worship of idols and false gods, and to lead them to the feet of the Almighty. At first he preached to closed ears; but persistence and enthusiasm prevailed: the religious intoxication of the Prophet was shared by the unconquered sons of the desert; the Arab took fire from the flaming words which fell from these inspired lips, and was eager to carry the message to the uttermost ends of the earth or to perish in the effort. Within ten years of Mohammed's flight from Mecca (A.D. 622) all Arabia was won to the Monotheist by conviction or by conquest.

The combination of spiritual fervour with a prospect of worldly achievement is formidable. A year after the death of the Prophet, Kalid, riding against the embattled hosts of Persia (A.D. 633), broke into a chant which reveals a baser spring of action in the Arabian mind. "Behold the wealth of the land," he sang; "its paths sweat fatness; food abounds as do stones in Arabia. It were a great thing to fight here for worldly goods; but to battle in a holy war is beyond praise. These fruitful fields and Paradise ! ! !" It was not religious fanaticism alone, although it was religious fanaticism in the main, which put an invincible scimitar into the hands of the tough, tenacious, untamed Arab. He was impelled by religious fervour, without doubt; but religious fervour had the strong support of a lusting after possessions, all the more tempting in contrast with the stinted boons of his desert home. And, should he fall in battle, was he not promised an immediate admission into Paradise with those sensuous enjoyments, which were most in contrast with the penury of the nomad tent, and which were most alluring to the imagination of the average sensual man ?

When material greed supports spiritual fanaticism, there is no need to wonder at success. The Arab advanced against exhausted, loosely organised Empires, sprawling and decayed; he offered righteous government, a pure simple faith, with tolerance of the unbeliever under penalty of a light tribute. The requital of refusal was the sword. Damascus fell three years after Mohammed's death (A.D. 635); Jerusalem, within two year; Egypt, six years later (A.D. 641), and Persia when the Prophet had only lain a decade in his tomb (A.D. 642). Not many years passed before Okba swept across North Africa, rode his steed far into the Atlantic tide, and waved his scimitar over the waste of waters, lamenting that it put a limit to victory. Thrice was the Mediterranean coast of Africa conquered, and thrice was the Arab well-nigh expelled; and then Greek and Roman and all civilized inhabitants of the coast, preferring the rule of the Moslem to that of the barbarous Berbers who had replaced him, welcomed the fourth invasion, and settled down under Arab rule. By the close of the century which in its youth saw the hurried night-flight of Mohammed from Mecca, the Moslem held sway from the Oxus to the Western ports of Barbary. At the beginning of the next century the great Iberian peninsula was added to the dominion of the Caliph; and, although Ironic Destiny turned back the triumph of the Prophet in the decisive battle of Tours (A.D. 732), a hundred years after his death, the great Iberian Peninsula was held by the Arab from sea to sea and as far north as the Cantabrian Mountains and the southern spurs of the Pyrenees; while the Koran was preached, although it did not everywhere prevail, east and west, over a broad belt more than seven thousand miles in length. The muezzin called the Faithful to prayers from the Atlantic to the Yellow Sea.

When a race, endowed with natural gifts, subdues an enlightened people, it becomes inseminated by the higher culture it encounters, and is stimulated to evolve an art, a literature, and a polished civilization of its own. So was it when Rome conquered Hellas; so was it when the Northmen established themselves in France and Sicily; so was it when the thundering steeds of the desert bore their wild riders north and east and west, and the ancient Parthian monarchy and the fairest, the wealthiest, and the most cultured of the Roman provinces fell before the triumphant Arab. Like the Norman, like the Roman, he had the natural gift of governing as well as a passionate wisdom. He steeped himself in the lore of Hellas; it was through him that the philosophy of Aristotle was transmitted to the Schoolmen; it was through him that St. Thomas Aquinas was able to construct that venerable philosophical system, based on the Peripatetic, which has received the sanction and endorsement of the Church of Rome; it was through him, therefore, that Dante beheld that "glorious philosopher," that "guide of human reason," that *Maestro di color che sanno*," "Master of those who know," seated amid a philosophic family. The great names of Averrhoes, Avicenna, Avempace,

Algazel, and Avicebron attest the freedom of Arab speculation in the tenth, eleventh and twelfth centuries. Mohammedans were the begetters of chemical science ; they eagerly pursued the study of botany ; they contributed much to geography ; they carried medicine far beyond the ancient limits of Galen and Celsus ; they became bold, brilliant and successful operators, and introduced new methods into surgery ; they cultivated letters and left a noble literature behind them ; they were poets almost to a man : Princes wrote verses to the stars in some interval between private plot and public slaughter ; water-carriers and camel-drivers vied with professional poets in singing the praises of love in those delicious hours when the refreshing breezes of the night might carry songs beyond the lattice of the harem to be received with the light laughter of girls ; even the forbidden wine-flask became a theme for song. Much of Arabic love poetry is immortal, and few are the literatures in which it is surpassed. In Architecture and the Decorative Arts, the Arabs achieved inimitable elegance and grace ; as workers in metal they were supreme. After a prolonged struggle, they subdued and civilized the wild Berber. They regarded the Jew as a brother, less well informed in sacred things than themselves ; and they treated even the "tritheistic" Christian with forbearance. Indeed they were not too anxious to proselytize ; for the unconverted were taxable, and they did not wish the sources of public income to dry up. But taxation was light, and, in the main, the Arab yoke was far from heavy. Slaves were treated with humanity, and might earn their freedom at any moment by a simple profession of faith : the Negro, the Spaniard, the Berber, the Turk, could acquire the full right of a man by the repetition of a short formula. During the declining years of the Byzantine Empire, and until Liberty and Literature arose in the Italian Communes, the Mohammedan bore the torch of learning and kept human justice enthroned.

But Islam was another illustration of the profound truth already recorded in this volume as one of the melancholy tenets of Buddhism: Every human institution bears within it the seeds of its decay. Though a sense of righteous dealing dwelt from of old in the bosom of the Arab, in his native desert the sword which executed it was held by his own right hand. The predatory tentsmen were divided into clans; and between the clans there were blood-feuds. They were a democratic people; but they had a deep reverence for men of noble blood; and their feuds were taken up by the chief men of the cities of Arabia, and by those leaders who, later, became the governors of new provinces. And the conquered Berbers had precisely the same characteristics: they also were predatory, democratic, and revered their noble families. Moreover, both races were readily moved to the more violent of the emotions of religion. Before long Moslem fought against Moslem, and a thousand forms of religious dissent weakened, although they did not destroy, the essential unity of Faith. Again, the extensive and rapidly acquired Empire was too vast and too ill-organized to be ruled by one, all-powerful Caliph. The centre of government was transferred, during the revolutions of Islam at variance with itself, from Damascus to Bagdad and from Bagdad to Cairo; but the Caliph of Cairo was defended by, and therefore in the hands of Mamelukes—slaves, bought in childhood and trained to arms. The Mameluke became the ruler; and, by the middle of the Thirteenth Century, the Caliph was a mere nominal Spiritual Head, far feebler than the Pope in Rome. For, distant provinces were continually falling away from central authority; and it was never long before the ally who came forward to support the Caliph found it to his advantage to turn against him. The Mohammedan world was divided, not merely between the Shiite and Sunnite sects, but between many ambitious and rival States. Long before the Fourteenth Century, Islam was past its prime. There was decay in matters political, in literature, and in art. Yet the amity in Islam was greater than its discord. The need of mutual protection against the Christian, and the duty of every Mohammedan to make a pilgrimage to Mecca at least once in his lifetime, helped to preserve true brotherly feeling among all followers of the Prophet, whatever their rank, their wealth, or the colour of their skin. The study of the Koran implied a study of Arabic: there was therefore a common language to serve the needs of intercommunication. The Koran was carried into mysterious lands, known before its arrival only in the distortion of legend and in fables of romance. Passionate devotion to a Faith which antagonistic or far-separated races came to hold in common swept away these obstacles to commutual intimacy. Huge hosts of Pilgrims from many lands met at Mecca, and different caravans and different sects united in prayer and praise. Some had encountered peril by sea; all had baffled the craft or repelled the attack of robber-bands; all had endured trials of the desert; all had triumphed over those countless dangers which lurked along difficult ways. Thus, disciplined in endurance and accustomed to adventure, latent powers of mind and character were aroused. Strange sights awakened the curiosity of the trader; novel wares excited his cupidity and converted him into an explorer of the world. In spite of the intertwining of religious zeal with commercial instinct, Pagan princes saw their opportunity of enrichment, and welcomed the Arab, Moorish, or Persian merchant. And, in days of peace, the whole Mohammedan world was open to every Mohammedan traveller; rulers received him with elaborate courtesy and sped him on his way, rejoicing in gifts. It mattered not whether he entered the gateway of some princely residence, or stood on the threshold of some peasant's hut; he was sure at least of welcome and refreshment. The trader might settle anywhere and find amity awaiting him; an honest man was an honoured guest in whatever land he might pursue his calling. A Christian, Missionary to the East, who died in Ibn Batûta's time, bears witness to the brotherly love which obtained among Moslems of different races. So we shall not marvel overmuch at Ibn Batûta accomplishing what even to-day would be considered world-wide travel, or at his discovering children of the same father, who in their childhood watched the sun setting over Atlantic waters, prosperously dwelling in their maturity, one, where the dawn breaks from the Yellow Sea; one, where the oasis lies an incongruous and solitary blossom amid the sands of Sahara.

CHAPTER II. A RESOLUTE PILGRIM

AMONG Mohammedan pilgrims and travellers Ibn Batûta stands without a peer. He was born in a city which was once an extreme outpost of Roman rule in Africa, the Ancient Tingis, the modern Tangiers, in the Sultanate of Fez, 24th February, 1304. He devoted his youth to the study of the Koran and its exegesis; becoming thereby an expert in theology and jurisprudence. For, throughout the Mohammedan world the Koran is the living fountain of all law and of all piety: hence Moslem theology and law are inextricably intertwined.

"Life is a pure flame, and we live by an invisible sun within us," is one of the quaint metaphors of Sir Thomas Browne. The old Norwich physician is writing of the body; but his remark is profoundly true of the soul of men. By the time that Batûta had reached the age of 21, he tells us that he was all aflame with "inner desire and determination to visit the Holy Places; tearing himself away from those who were dear to him, both male and female, and taking wing from home as a bird doth from its nest." He started from his native city when not quite twenty-one years and four months old (14th June, 1325), making, first, for Tlemçen, the capital of a Moslem State 300 miles distant from Tangier. Tlemçen remains in the present writer's memory as a gem set among the Algerian Mountains, remarkable for the ruins of Mansûra, which almost run up to its walls—a rival city built by a rival prince during a siege which dragged on longer than the ten years' assault on Troy—remarkable also for a master-piece of decoration in that Thirteenth Century which was the great period of Moslem Architecture no less than of our own. In this beautiful city rested a Tunisian Embassy which had completed its mission and and was about to return; and this he joined. When he arrived at Bougie, he became a prey to fever; but the patient was a man of mettle and he pushed on. Fever was not the only foe. All North Africa was more or less unsafe, by reason of Nomadic Berbers and brigands; and hostilities were frequent between the States into which the great Empire of the Undivided Caliphate had broken up. The returning Embassy was exposed to danger on its journey "from the perfidy of Arabs."

Arrived at Constantine, he received the first of those welcome donatives which it was incumbent on the Rulers of Islam to bestow. It was a scarf for head-gear; and tucked in its folds, with considerate delicacy, were two gold coins.

At Bona, the ancient Hippo, whereof once Augustine was bishop, fever again preyed on him, and he became so ill that he could only keep his saddle by taking his turban off and tying himself on with it; nor could he stand at all during the whole long journey to Tunis. When the Embassy arrived at its destination, the inhabitants came outside the walls to welcome the cavalcade. Weak, weary, and worn down by illness, unfriended and solitary, among strangers who were joyfully greeted by relatives and friends and fellow-countrymen; remote from all that was hallowed by family affection or endeared by early association, a terrible tempest of longing swept the bosom of our pilgrim. He saw all the others saluted: "there was no salutation for me" he says, "I knew no soul there. I burst into a flood of tears. A pilgrim saw this; he came forward and did me courtesy; nor did he cease to take me off my thoughts by his conversation until I was housed in the city." This is the sole occasion on which we hear a word of home-sickness during a journey which lasted more than a score of years. The born traveller, like the born sailor, may feel the pang and have it renewed, but he brushes it aside. Moreover, we shall shortly find Ibn Batûta setting up a travelling-home of his own.

The Caravan for Mecca was about to start from Tunis; and we find our jurisconsult become its Cadi, or justiciary. A hundred bowmen accompanied it through a district always perilous by reason of marauding nomads, who lurk among its hills. It was the rainy season; the weather turned so wet and cold that the caravan halted at Sfax, and remained there some time, hoping for improvement. Ibn Batûta seized the opportunity to marry the first wife of whom we are told. She was a daughter of a syndic of Tunis; and probably this was his first, but far from being his last, entrance into matrimony. For he was a man of taste, and we shall find him, in the course of time, become an experienced Benedict, and by no means indifferent to the charms of his pretty slave-concubines. All delay was intolerable to Baṭûta; so, accompanied by his bride, he set off at the head of an armed band, bearing its standard. He soon entered a district notorious for brigandage even to-day, when conquering France and Italy hold the land and bestow sanguinary lessons on wild tribesmen and robbers-in-blood. Fierce nomads hovered around the little company, awaiting an opportunity to attack; but happily the caravan caught it up at one of those tombs of saint or warrior which the Moslem holds in such veneration. Probably Batûta's father-in-law was in the caravan; for we are now told of dissensions between the two men, although there is silence as to the subject of dispute. If the Prophet granted the doubtful privilege of a plurality of wives, he mitigated the inconveniences of polygamy by extreme facility in divorce. Batûta availed himself of this, and sent his bride back to her father. The ill-luck, which so soon attended this first matrimonial venture, did not deter him from a second experiment: he lost no time in marrying a fellow-countrywoman, presumably also a fellow-pilgrim; she was the daughter of a dignitary of Fez. The pilgrims halted a whole day to indulge in wedding festivity. On the 3rd April, 1326, nearly ten months after Batûta's departure from Tangier, the caravan drew up at Alexandria, and his long and not too safe journey along the southern coast of the "mid sea, moaning with memories," was at an end.

Alexandria was, at that time, one of the great commercial centres of the world. Shipping from all Christendom and North Africa were to be found in its haven. Batûta tells us that it surpassed all ports he ever saw, excepting Colon and Calicut in India, the Italian settlement in the Crimea, and Zaitun (Thsiuan-Cheu) at that time the great port of China. Alexandria was almost as remarkable for Moslem piety as for trade. Batûta made a point of visiting a learned and pious person there, who, like all Mohammedan saints, was reputed to possess miraculous powers. The saint's acuteness penetrated into the character of his visitor: he perceived a born-wayfarer in the prescriptive pilgrim, and told him that he had a taste for travel. "'Yes,' was my reply," says Batûta, "although at that time, I had formed no project of distant travel. . . . 'You will see my brother in Sind, another brother who is in India, and yet a third who is in China, and will bear my salutations to them.' I was astounded at what he said, and made up my mind to visit these countries; nor did I give up my resolve until I had beheld all three men." "Only strongly impassioned men may achieve great results," says Mirabeau. We shall see what Batûta's passion was and what he accomplished.

His keen eye noted the glories of Alexandria; the great lighthouse of Ptolemy, in the last stage of decay, and that great column of Diocletian, mis-called Pompey's Pillar. Stung more than ever by a divine gadfly, he must run all over Lower Egypt, visiting every living saint of renown and every relic of the past, especially such relics as were the tombs or dwellings of departed saints. The attention which holy men paid to their dreams and the confidence with which they interpreted them recall the Hebrew Scriptures. Batûta tells us that he visited an unusually gifted and eminently holy seer; and from that time "good fortune attended me throughout my travels." But our traveller was no mere inattentive dreamer: the minuteness and accuracy of his observations are remarkable; and his statements are fully confirmed in the literature of contemporary and later travel, and other records of the age in which he lived.

Among the places he visited, we find him at Damietta, where was preserved the cell of the Chief of the Calenders. The very name Calender recalls one's youth and those fantastic fables of the "Arabian Nights" which delighted it. A Calender was a Moslem under vow to deliver himself from the allurements of earth and to consecrate his life to things spiritual. It was the usage of all Calenders to shave off beard and eyebrow; and Batûta supplies us with a story to account for their disfigurement. The founder of the sect was a personable man, and a certain lady fell in love with him and pursued him in every conceivable way. But all her lures and devices coming to nought, she contrived a still more ingenious stratagem. She got an old woman, who, of course, could not read, to stop the beloved one, who was as good-natured as he was devout, when on his way to the mosque, and ask him to read a letter which she said she had received from her son. He complied, and then quoth the old woman: "My son has a wife who dwells in yonder house. Will you be so good as to read it in the passage so that she may hear what her husband says?" He agreed to this also; but no sooner had he crossed the threshold than the old woman clapped the door to, and the love-sick lady appeared, attended by her slaves, who forced him into an inner room. She cast herself at him, and began to take liberties with him. So he made the excuse that it was necessary for him to retire privately. No sooner was he alone, than he whipped out a razor which he had with him, and divested himself of beard and eyebrow. Then he presented himself before the enamoured woman, who was so disgusted at the disfigurement that she had him chased from the house. "Thus," says Batûta, "by Divine Providence, his chastity was preserved, and his sect shaved eyebrow and beard from that time forward."

This is one of the many anecdotes which Batûta thrusts into his narrative. It is much more amusing than most of them. All Orientals (and Moors are essentially Orientals) dote on pointless fable and wild romance. They are insatiate for marvel, and gulp down any stretch of fancy coloured by religion. Batûta's farrago of stories is, for the most part, silly. Happily, these legends are short. He wrought diligently in hagiology; he was a-gape for yarns, remembered them all and carefully recorded them; for they suited his own taste and that of his nation and time. They are the gatherings of a man profoundly learned in the Koran and Mohammedan lore; one concerned, like the Pharisees of old, with minor questions of the Law and minutiæ of ceremonial observance; vexed, as it were, about tithes of small herbs. His main interest was his religion, and in his religion he was a meticulous pedant. He had a natural love of the miraculous, and religious credulity case-hardened it. Every mosque was a magnet to draw him from afar; he made a pilgrimage to every Mohammedan shrine he heard of; he cannot away without its legend. He reports wonders as dull as they are extravagant. They possess neither genius nor charm nor authority. Sometimes Oriental taste for the tawdry is to blame: sometimes he is flatly gulled. But, in mundane matters, restless impulses converted the credulous pundit into a man of the world. He records accurately what he actually saw and heard, or what he believed he saw and heard. He was interested in all that life had to offer; but supremely so in all that had to do with Islam.

From the mouths of the Nile, Ibn Batûta approached that ancient land where mournful memorials stand out, clear and awful, in the flood of light; where every winding of the mysterious valley repeats the enigma of the tomb. He came to Cairo, and saw the Pyramids,

> " Memphis, and Thebes, and whatso'er of strange
> Dark Ethiopia on her desert hills conceals."

He tells us of all in architecture that struck him as worthy of mention, of the products of the soil, of the habits of the people, and of their government. He praises the emulation of the provincial Emirs of Egypt in good works and the building of mosques. He watches the gathering of great personages at the procession of the Mahmil, or drapery woven to cover that sanctuary at Mecca wherein lay the object of Arabian worship ages before Mohammed was born. For the Sacred Stone fell from Paradise with Adam ; and the Archangel Gabriel carried it to him for the house which he built to God.

Magistrates and juris consults, the great officials of the Sultan and the Syndics of Corporations, some on horse-back, some on foot, assemble at Cairo and await the Holy Drapery. The Emir who, this year, is to head the annual pilgrimage, arrives with attendant troops and camels and water-carriers. A conical box encloses the sacred cloth. All the nondescript population of the city follow it. By some trick of the camel-drivers, their beasts are urged to strange screeching ; and the motley throng makes its slow progress round the city, a winding river of vivid colour and odd effect ; a procession not without dignity, but which an ancient Athenian had perhaps found a tawdry show compared with the simple grace of the procession of the *peplops* in his City of the Violet Crown.

From Çairo, our pilgrim makes his way to Panopolis, then " a great town, fine and well-built," and so to Syene, partly following the river where each new morning mocks the ruined temples, and partly taking short cuts across the desert.

A holy man told him that he would find it impossible to fulfil his pilgrimage just then ; but he pushed across the unpeopled sands which lie between the Nile and the Red Sea, and, after a trying journey of fifteen days, found himself among a "black" race, called Bodjas, who were settled at Aidhab, at that time a port of considerable trade. These people wore yellow garments and affected the smallest of head-gear. They would seem to have preserved their independence by martial spirit; and, as is so often the case among a warrior-people, daughters were not allowed to succeed to property. At this moment, they were at war with the Mamaluke soldiery of Egypt; and it was impossible for pilgrims to get transport across the Red Sea.

CHAPTER III

A ROUNDABOUT PILGRIMAGE

Now, besides the shrewd reading of Batûta's character by the holy man of Alexandria, who saw in him the born traveller, another Sheik had also read his man aright and foretold that he should meet the seer's brothers in widely separated parts of the world. Oracles are often suggestive and start the way to their own fulfilment. These predictions actually came about. Batûta assures us that he had at the time no intention of running over nearly all of the known earth; but by now an inborn tendency to keep moving had developed into a veritable *wanderlust*. "A brief space," sings Pindar, "a brief space hath opportunity for men; but of him it is known surely when it cometh, and he waiteth thereon." Batûta's opportunity had come to him. Stopped from reaching Mecca during the present pilgrimage, he resolved to retrace his steps to Cairo, push on to Palestine, visit its sacred spots and the renowned cities of Syria, join the Syrian Caravan, and take the long, fearsome journey from Damascus over the Arabian waste. Here was occasion to visit holy places only less interesting to the Moslem than to the Christian, to wander at leisure in notable lands, and to compare the amazing ways of the tribes of men. He sold all that might encumber him, and returned to High Egypt. The Nile was in flood; he sailed down it, spent a night at Cairo, and pushed on, (A.D. 1326). There was a caravan-route to Palestine, north of Sinai, with stations in the desert. Each station had its *Khan*, or inn, an institution which afforded bed and stabling, but not food or fodder. But there was a shop at each station, where all that might be wanted was sold; and there was a water-cistern, free to all comers at the door of each inn. At the frontier of Palestine, there was a custom-house, and a passport must be produced before one was allowed to cross the boundary in either direction. At Khalil, a town of Hebron, remarkable for its beauty, and also for the unusual distinction of being well lit at night, Batûta admired a mosque said to have been reared by those genii whom the wisdom of Solomon had made his servants, and whom he evoked by his mystic talisman. Passing through Palestine, our pilgrim visited those very few places the sanctity of which could be established by indisputable record and those very many places which owed their fame to rank imagination or crafty legend begotten of sordid avarice. He went to the birthplace of Jesus, because the Moslem regards Jesus as a fore-runner of Mohammed: and from Bethlehem he came to Jerusalem. He thought the Mosque there as fine a building as any on earth. It occupied one side of a vast courtyard, and its fretted walls and roof shone with gilding and vivid colours. In the middle of the Mosque was a rock, so brilliant in hue that no idea of its glory could be given. And this was the rock whence (so says tradition) Mohammed rode up to heaven on the sacred winged ass.

Tyre, "mother of cities fraught with pride," Acre and Askalon were in ruins—the result of the Crusades. Tiberias rejoiced in a bathing-establishment. Having plenty of time to fill up before the Syrian caravan should leave Damascus, the pilgrim wandered hither and thither, backwards and forwards, and saw many famous cities, such as Beyrout, Tripoli, Aleppo, Baalbec, Emessa and Antioch. He found all the people who inhabited the district of Gabala sadly misguided; for they believed Ali, son-in-law of the Prophet to be a god. They neither purified themselves, nor prayed, nor fasted. They had turned mosques into cattle-sheds; and, should any pious wanderer wish to pray in one of the desecrated buildings, these heretics were wont to gibe at him and shout: "Don't pray, ass that thou art; fodder shall be given thee."

Nomads from Central Asia had penetrated Asia Minor and reached the Mediterranean shore. Here and there they had settled; just as Scythian and Hun, Goth and Vandal once forced their way into the Roman Empire and effected lodgement within it before they rose and overthrew it. But the Emirs, whatever their nationality, would seem to have maintained decent government. Sometimes the despotisms of Islam surprise us by such unexpected qualities as sagacity, prudence, and self-restraint. At Latakia, Batûta found that, when anyone was condemned to die, the official appointed to superintend the execution was expected to go up to wherever the condemned man might be, return without apprehending him, and ask the Emir to repeat the sentence. Not until three such journeys had been made and the sentence thrice delivered was it carried out. On the other hand, secret murder was a favourite political engine. Our pilgrim beheld, on the heights of Lebanon, strongholds of that military sect, the Hashashin, to which we owe the word assassin. "They will admit no stranger among them, unless he be of their own body. The Sultan, El Malik El Nasir, uses them as his arrows; and, through them, he strikes down those of his foes that dwell afar from him; such, for instance, as may dwell in Persia or anywhere else. Various duties are allotted to different men among them; and when the Sultan wishes one of them to waylay some foe, he bargains as to the price of blood. Should the murderer accomplish his work, and return to safety, his reward is paid to him; and should he fail, his heirs receive it. These folk carry poisioned knives wherewithal to strike their prey."

Laodicea would seem to have been held by a ruler who, like the robber-barons of Germany or the pirates of Dalmatia, was a terror to the trader: "he is said to take by violence all the ships he can." Like all travellers, Batûta is enthusiastic about the glories of Lebanon. He found it "the most fertile mountain on Earth, where are copious springs of water and shady groves; and it is laden with many kinds of fruit. And I beheld there very many of that host of hermits who have left the world that they may devote themselves to God."

Two thousand feet above the sea-level lay Damascus, most ancient of cities, with a delightful climate and a productive soil. "The chief Mosque is the most splendid in the world, most tastefully built, excelling in beauty and grace." His interest in mosques and public worship is inextinguishable; and he recounts the dramatic methods of a certain preacher. "There dwelt at Damascus an imam whose orthodoxy was not above suspicion; indeed he had already suffered imprisonment on that score. It so fell out that, one Friday, I was at his preaching. He came down the stairway of the pulpit calling out: 'God came down to the Earthly Paradise in the very same way as I am coming down.' A theologian who was there denied this; and the congregation, set on the preacher and beat him." A complaint was made against this too literal expositor; he was cast into prison, and there he died.

Islam has always been remarkable for charity. Damascus boasted many benevolent institutions. "As I was passing along a street one day," says Batûta, "I saw a slave-child who had dropped a porcelain dish, made in China, which lay in pieces on the ground. A crowd gathered round the little Mameluke, and one of them said, 'Pick up the pieces and carry them to the overseer of the Utensils Charity.' This man took the little slave with him to the overseer, who at once gave him what money was necessary to buy such another dish. This is one of the best of these endowments; for the owner of the slave would doubtless have beaten him or scolded him severely. Moreover he would have been heart-broken. So the endowment really relieves sorrowful bosoms." Batûta gives more than one little indication that children (and even his own wives occasionally) could touch his heart.

The Moslem can be very pitiful; he usually treats his slaves kindly; and one does not wonder that our pilgrim speaks warmly about the piety and high civilization of Damascus in his time. He was licensed to teach in that beautiful city; but found time to visit the cavern which is one of the places where Abraham is said to have been born, and the grotto where Abel's blood was still to be seen; "for his brother dragged him thither."

Batûta started with the Pilgrim's Caravan to the Holy Cities on September 1st, 1326. Many hundreds of perilous miles lay before him. The mere solitude of the desert always inspires insupportable dread, and to secure a sufficient supply of water is a problem not always to be solved. Batûta was told how, during one pilgrimage, water gave out, and "a skin of it rose to a thousand *dinars*; yet both seller and buyer perished." Ancient travellers always speak with awe of the weird noises which suddenly break the silence of the desert and inspire a new dread. Shifting sands cause these sounds. Batûta tells us of one huge sandhill called The Mount of Drums, because the Bedouins "say that a sound as of drums is heard there every Thursday night." But this particular pilgrimage, although made along a difficult and dangerous route, was comparatively uneventful, as were all the journeys Batûta made to Mecca. He gives small space to it, and we shall find the record of a much livelier and more interesting pilgrimage from Damascus in the pages of Varthema. The journey was often one of perils, grave and manifold.

CHAPTER IV

GLIMPSES OF ARABIA, PERSIA AND EAST AFRICA IN THE FOURTEENTH CENTURY

AFTER duly visiting the tomb of the Prophet at Medina and performing the prescribed rites at Mecca, Batûta, still insatiate of travel, joined the Persian caravan on its homeward journey, and soon came to the place where, to this day, the devil is lapidated. "It is a great collection of stones. Everyone who comes to it hurls one. They say there was once a heretic who was stoned to death there." From Medina, Central Arabia was crossed, and a journey of 600 miles brought the caravan to a town in the Nedjd which was one of the claimants to the possession of the bones of Ali, the son-in-law of the Prophet. Where Ali really was buried is unknown. But the excited mind worked a great effect on the body here, for, on a certain night of the year devoted to religious revival, "cripples were brought to the tomb, even from far-away lands, and were laid on it soon after sunset. Then there was praying and reciting of the Koran and prostrations; and, about midnight the halt rose up, sound and hale."

At Bussora, the port so opulent and its trades so flourishing in the days of Haroun-al-Raschid, one dared not venture to travel abroad without the protection of a Bedouin escort: "There is no journeying possible in these parts except with them." Yet traces remained of the former wealth of the city. "Bussora is richer in palm-trees than any place in the world. Its people are generous and friendly to strangers. One of the finest mosques is paved with red pebbles. And therein is kept that beautiful copy of the Koran which Othman was reading when he was murdered; and the stain of his blood is on it yet."

In this district he came across vestiges of the worship of Baal. Certain of the fanatical sect called Haïderia lit a fire of wood, ate of the burning embers, rolled in them, and then trampled them with bare feet until all flame was put out. Later on, he saw the same strange feat done by the same strange sect in India, when there came to a place near Delhi, where he was encamped, men led by a very black man and wearing collars and bracelets of iron. "They stayed all night with us. Their chief asked me for wood to light a fire for them to dance by, and I requested the deputy-ruler of that part to let them have it. After the second evening prayer, the pile was lit, and, when the wood had become burning charcoal, they struck up music and began to dance into the fire; and they rolled themselves in it. Then their head-man asked me for a tunic, and I gave him one of very fine make. He put it on, rolled in the fire, and beat the embers so that the fire ceased to flare, and it went out. He then brought the tunic to me, and I found it to be undamaged. And thereat I marvelled greatly." And between these two experiences he came across Haïderia in Eastern Persia at Turbet-Haïdarj: "They wore an iron collar, and, what is stranger still, their *virilia* are incarcerated to ensure their chastity."

He now sailed down the united Tigris and Euphrates and along the coast of Persia in a small boat, and, landing at a port, travelled across the plains of Southern Persia, with high mountains right and left. He found the ways in mountainous Lâristân cut through the rocks. These parts were governed by a tributary ruler. "In every one of the stations in this country are cells made ready for those bent on religious undertakings and for travellers. Every newcomer is provided with bread, flesh, and sweetmeats." After two months of travel, Batûta came to Ispahan, in the heart of Persia. The Sultan had already provided him with money to cover the cost of his wanderings in Persia. Eastern rulers regarded munificence as a duty: Eastern travellers claimed it as a right. From

Ispahan he went southward to Shiraz, which he found a large and well-built city, but inferior to Damascus. "The inhabitants are honest, religious, and virtuous, especially the women. I went thither in order to visit that paragon of saints and of those that have the power to work miracles, Majd Oddîn. I put up therefore at the College which he founded. He was judge of the City: but, being advanced in years, his brother's sons took on his duties for him. . . . He is much venerated by the Emirs of that land, so that, when they are before him, they lay hold of both their ears; which is the mark of devotion due to the Sultan."

At El Hilla, on the banks of the Euphrates, he found a curious belief that the last of the Imams was still alive and dwelt there; but that he was invisible to mortal eye. "Every day, a hundred armed men come to the portal of the mosque. They lead with them a beast saddled and bridled; and a gathering of folk beat drums and blow trumpets. They cry aloud: 'Come forth, Lord of the Times; for the earth is filled with evil doing and deeds of shame. Now is the hour for thee to appear, so that, through thee, Allah may divide the truth from the lie.' They wait on until night, when needs must that they go home."

"It is an uncontrolled truth," says Swift, "that no man ever made an ill figure who understood his own talents." Ibn Batûta, theologian, jurist, and, by this time, experienced man of the world, knew his powers; and one of his powers was knowing how to employ the rest. We now find him accompanying the Tartar Ruler of Persia, the "Sultan of the Two Iraks and Khorasan, to Tabriz, whither the monarch marched with his army." Tabriz is not more than a hundred miles from Armenia and the Caspian Sea. Batûta tells us how his eyes were dazzled by the lustre of precious jewels which well-dressed slaves purchased to decorate their Tartar mistresses. The Sultan gave him a fine dress and other handsome presents; and he resolved to make a second pilgrimage to Mecca; whereupon the Sultan ordered that he should be provided with all that was necessary to further such a worthy end. But, before starting he had time to travel along the banks of the Tigris as far north as Diarbekir; for he wished to visit a saint and worker of miracles, reputed "not to break his fast during forty days at a stretch, save with a crust of barley bread." On getting back to Bagdad he found the caravan ready to start, and took his departure with it.

Persia, exhausted by the long struggle with the Roman Empire, fell an easy prey to the Arabs; and, although it enjoyed a second era of power and prosperity under the Caliphs of Bagdad, first Seljuk Turks conquered it, and then Mongolians, under Chingiz Khân, which, being interpreted, is the Great Khân, no other than the "Tartre Cambyuskan" of Chaucer's Squire's Tale, the "Cambuscan bold of Milton's Il Penseroso. Mongolians had now possessed the land for little less than a century, and they and the Sultans of Egypt held each other in dread. Religious differences have always been convenient as a war-cry; and, from of old, religious unity has been wont to fulfil some of the functions of our modern patriotism. The Caliph at Cairo was the head of the Orthodox Sunnites, Moslems who hold the Sunna, or body of tradition which professes to preserve such teaching and laws as the Prophet gave by word of mouth as of equal authority with the Koran; but the Tartar Sultan of Persia was a Shiite, or one of those who reject the Sunna, and hold that Ali, son-in-law of the Prophet, was Mohammed's legitimate successor. Hence Batûta found the Shiite Sultan putting pressure on the Sunnites of the great cities of Bagdad Shiraz, and Ispahan to make them renounce the form of faith sacred to them because it was that of their fathers and further endeared because the Caliphate at Bagdad had brought such lustre to the Persian name.

Our pilgirm arrived at Mecca, for the second time, without meeting with any remarkable adventure in crossing

Central Arabia. One is surprised to find so restless a spirit content to remain three years in Mecca. But Batûta was a theologian and jurist; one, moreover, who held the outward observances of Islam in high respect; and he dwelt during the whole of that time at a Mohammedan theological school. And now the old passion for travel returns, and he is completely in its grip. He is away to Jidda on the Red Sea, embarks on one of those Eastern ships which were even more wretchedly built and worse navigated than those of the Western nations, and is forced by tempest into a port between Aidhab and Suakin. Nothing daunted, he puts to sea again and arrives in Arabia the Happy. A Cadi welcomes the distinguished sage and traveller, entertains him for three days, and, on the fourth, takes him to the court of the Sultan at Zebid, one of the chief towns of Yemen. Batûta a true Oriental delights in pomp and ceremony, and describes the audience in full.

"The Sultan is to be saluted by touching the ground with forefinger, raising it to the head, and saying 'May Allah give thee enduring rule.' This I did, copying the Cadi; who seated himself at the right hand of the Sultan, and told me to be seated facing him. The monarch sat on a daïs, which was covered with ornamental silk stuff; and right and left of him stood his warriors. Around him are sword and buckler-bearers; nearer are bowmen; and in front of these, on either side, the chamberlain, the first men of the State, and the private scribe. Djandar, the Emir, is also present before him and the officers of the guard; but the latter keep their distance. When the Sultan takes his seat, all cry aloud, 'In the name of Allah!' and they repeat this when he rises; so that all who are in the Hall of Audience know precisely when he sits down and when he rises. Directly the Monarch is seated, all those who are wont to visit the Court and do him obeisance, come in and salute him. This done, each takes his allotted place to right or left, nor does he leave it or sit down unless commanded to do so. In the latter case, the Sultan says to the Emir Djandar, who is Chief Constable of the Palace, 'Tell such an one to be seated.' And the man so commanded comes forward a little way and sits down on a carpet in front of and between those who are grouped to right and left. Meats are then brought forth; and these are of two kinds, one kind being for the many, the other kind for people of importance, that is to say, the Sultan, the Chief Justice, the principal Sheriffs, jurisconsults and guests. The other sort of viands serves for the rest of the Sheriffs, jurisconsults, judges, sheiks, emirs, and officers of the army. Everyone takes the place allotted to him at the feast and everybody has room enough. I found the same form observed at the Court of the Sultan of India; and I know not which monarch hath copied it from the other."

After visiting several cities of Yemen, which were flourishing centres of trade at that time, Batûta reached Aden, "a large city, but without water, and nothing can grow there. Rain is caught and stored up in tanks, and that is the only water to drink. But rich traders make their abode in Aden, and hither vessels come from India."

Now the Arabs had sought for wealth in the products of Ethiopa; they had advanced along the Eastern Coast of Africa, and had established ports considerably south of Zanzibar. Batûta had a fancy to see these tropical parts; so he sailed from Aden as far as Kiloa or Kilwa, which is nine degrees south of the equator. The ship touched at various ports where there were Arab settlements; some of them by no means salubrious or agreeable. At Zeila, he experienced "an unbearable stench from decaying fish and the blood of camels, which are slaughtered in the streets:" At another station, Mogdishu, he was received with much civility. "When a ship draws up, the young men of the place come forth, and each accosts a trader, and becomes his host. Should there be a theologian or a man of station on board, he is taken to dwell with the Cadi. When it was known that I was there, the Cadi came to the beach, and his students with him, and I took up my abode with him. He led me to the Sultan who is styled the Sheik. . . A servant brought vegetables and fawfel-nut . . . and rose-water to us . . . and this is the highest honour that can be done to a stranger . . . The people are far too fat, because they gorge. One of them will eat as much as a whole congregation of worshippers ought to do." From Mogdishu, the ship went on to Mombasa and Kiloa for a cargo of ivory. Batûta tells us of the productions of tropical East Africa, and how " the greatest gift to the peoples here is ivory, which is the tooth of the elephant."

From Kiloa, he coasted back to the straits of Bab-el-Mandel, ran along the Gulf of Aden, and landed at Zafar, in Oman. He tells us, as does Marco Polo, how the natives feed their cattle on fish. Zafar " is a filthy place, plagued with flies by reason of the markets for fish and dates. Copper and tin pieces of money are used. The heat is so great that those who dwell there must bathe several times a day; and they suffer greatly from elephant's leg (elephantiasis) and from ruptures. It is indeed beyond a marvel that they will hurt no one unless it be to return some hurt done to them. Many Sultans have tried to subdue them, yet naught but bale have they gotten thereby."

Batûta travelled past the shores of Oman in a small coaster which touched at many ports. He found the banana, the betel-tree, and the cocoa-nut flourishing in this corner of Arabia, and describes them and their uses. Wishing to see what the hinterland was like, he took a seven-days' journey from the coast, but found that it took six days to cross a desert. The inland people would seem hardly to have emerged from primitive promiscuity; for he tells us that " there wives are most base and husbands shew no sign of jealousy." Jealousy as to the harem is an excellent masculine virtue to our good Moslem.

Crossing the Persian Gulf, the island of Hormuz was reached, whither traders had recently migrated from old Hormuz on the Persian mainland. Vases and lamp-stands of rock-salt were among the manufactures of this important mart and port of call; and hard by were the renowned fisheries for "orient pearl." He was told, and believed, that the divers remained two hours under water, and was astounded to see people amusing themselves by crawling from orbit to orbit of the battered skull of a spermaceti whale which had been washed ashore.

Crossing the narrow strait to Persia, he hired an escort of Turkoman settlers, "a hardy and brave race, who occupy these parts and know the roads. Without them, there is no travelling." His object in returning to Persia was to visit a man of saintly repute who dwelt far away in Lâristân. It took four days to cross a waterless desert where the Simoon blows in summer, "and kills everyone in its path; and their limbs drop away from the trunk." At Lar, the capital, he found the saint in his cell, seated on the ground. He was clad in an ancient garment made of wool. Yet he was in the habit of giving costly presents, and had food and fresh clothing ready for all who visited him.

CHAPTER V

TO INDIA BY WAY OF CONSTANTINOPLE AND THE STEPPES

BATUTA joined the Persian Caravan to Mecca, and once again journeyed across the territory of the Wahabi in Central Arabia. This, his third pilgrimage, over, he resolved to see India. But the wretched ship in which he put forth was storm-tossed, and finally driven into a little port on the Egyptian coast. So he made across the desert, seeing, now and again, the tents of a few wandering Arabs or an ostrich or gazelle. After much hardship, he reached Syene and travelled once more along the banks of the Nile to Cairo. And now the fancy seized him to revisit Asia Minor, see Southern Russia and Turkestan, and get to India over the Hindu Kush. He retraced his old route through Palestine and Syria as far as Latakia. There he embarked on a Genoese vessel for Alâia, on the south coast of Asia Minor, which he calls " Rûm, because it belonged of yore to the Romans ; and, to to this day many of them dwell here under the protection of the Moslems." He was now farther north than he had been before. One of the petty Sultans gave him and those who were with him the usual gracious greeting of the East, and furnished them with provisions. On reaching Anatolia, he found the country broken up into a multitude of contending States, many of these being held by Turkomans. The secular efforts of the keepers of wandering herds on the Steppes of Asia to settle in the rich, civilized countries of Europe and Asia had established the nomad in Persia and Asia Minor. Successive waves of conquest had swept over the fair lands south of the Oxus and Caspian, and, one by one, the victorious tribes settled down and received a higher civilization than their own from the subjugated tillers of the soil. But now the Empire of the Seljuk Turks was broken into fragments. Among the new rulers the Ottoman Turks, a small class of the tribe of Oghuz, were gradually and with difficulty gaining territory and power in Asia Minor. But there was as yet no hint that they were destined to inherit the Roman Empire of the East and to rule from the Danube to the Euphrates. Some of these little States were ancient provinces, with splendid and busy cities that rivalled Cairo in wealth and beauty. Some were carved out of the mouldering Byzantine Empire; some had been torn from Persia. There were also solitary fortresses and towns held by Turkomans who lived by rapine and piracy; and some States only preserved their precarious existence by the aid of a force of slaves who had been purchased or torn from their Christian parents in childhood and rigidly trained to military life. These Mamelukes were sent by their overlord, the Sultan of Egypt.

Yet the tradition of good government was far from being lost. The new rulers were vigorous and prudent. It would seem that one of the secrets of Ottoman success lay in that close supervision of subordinates which recent conquest requires. Consequently, on the whole, the country was prosperous. Batûta found that the ruler of one province never remained more than a month in one place. He moved about to inspect fortresses and see the condition of various districts. This man had besieged a city for twelve years. It is not without precedent in Moslem history for a siege to last longer than that of Troy; a fact which shows how little the husbandman was interfered with in these local wars. Even in France at the close of the Dark Ages, the tiller of the soil was safe from the invader of his field if he laid his hand on the plough. Batûta wandered at large, and was received in all places with warm hospitality. On landing, he took up his abode in the college of a sheik;

and, on the second day, a poorly-clad man came to invite him and those who were with him to a feast. He wondered "how so poor a man could bear the charges of feasting us, who were many." The sheik explained that the man was one of a society of silk-merchants who had a "cell" of their own. The guests were received with much courtesy and hospitality, and were liberally supplied with money to cover their travelling expenses. Batûta learned that, in every town of the Turkomans, there was constituted a brotherhood of young men to supply strangers with food and other necessaries. A president, styled The Brother, was elected by those of the same trade, and even a foreigner might occupy the post. Each guild built a "cell" for itself in which food, a saddled steed, and all that might be wanted by travellers was stored. One of the duties of a President was to call daily on the members of his guild or brotherhood, and assist them in their diverse needs. Every evening the brotherhood returned his call; and whatsoever had not been needed was sold to support the "cell." Should any traveller have arrived during the day, he was entertained. Otherwise "the brotherhood of youths" spent the evening in song, dance, and feast. On one occasion, directly Batûta's party arrived at the gate of a city, two knots of men rushed to seize the bridles of their horses, and there was a struggle between them. This proceeding greatly alarmed the travellers, the more so that none of them was able to speak the language. But a man who knew Arabic came forward to assure them that there was no cause for fear. The rival parties were two brotherhoods disputing as to which should entertain the travellers. The antagonists cast lots, and the travellers went to the cell of one guild on the first day and to that of the other guild the next day. At another time, Batûta put up at the "cell" of one who was a member of a society of youths and who had a great number of disciples distinguished by their coarse ragged mantles and closely fitting hose. The petty Sultans, too, would provide horses or provisions.

The ruler of Bigni, a man proud of the possession of "a stone which had fallen from heaven," gave Batûta gold, clothes, two horses and a slave. Although a severe Sunnite, our traveller shows no great religious hatred to Shiites, Jews, or Christians; but he liked to keep heretics and infidels in their place. He tells a story which is instructive as to the medical attainments of the Jew and the relations between Jew and Moslem. At Bigni an old man came and saluted the Sultan. All rose to do him honour. "He sat himself on the daïs, opposite the Sultan, and the readers of the Koran were below him. I asked the sage, 'who is this sheik?' He smiled and kept silent; but when I asked again, he replied: 'he is a Jewish physician of whom we all have need. That is why we rose when he came in.' Whereat I fumed, and said to him: 'thou dog, son of a dog, how darest thou, a mere Jew, to seat thyself above the readers of the Koran?' I had raised my voice, and this astonished the Sultan, who asked why I had done so. The sage told him, and the Jew was humbled, and went away very much cast down. When we returned, the sage said to me: 'well have you done! Allah bestow his blessing on thee! None other but thou had dared to speak thus to the Jew. Thou hast taught him to know his place.'"

Language-difficulty caused some embarassment during this long journey through Asia Minor; so an interpreter, who had done the pilgrimage to Mecca and who spoke Arabic, was engaged by Batûta's party. But the Hadji cheated them abominably; so one day they asked him what he had stolen from them that day. The thief, quite unabashed told them the precise amount; "whereat we could but laugh and put up with it."

Batûta embarked from Sinope, on the southern shore of the Euxine, for Sodaia, in the Crimea. Sodaia was one of the great ports of the world. Venice had established a factory there a century back, but had been ejected. The Crimea was chiefly in the hands of the Genoese, who were established at Caffa; but the Italian cities were in pressing danger of ejection and of losing their Levantine and Euxine trade. After suffering much distress on the voyage and "only just escaping from being drowned," we find Batûta at Caffa; and for the first time suffering from the annoyance of those Christian bells which have been a nuisance, not merely to Moslems, but to the more sensitive among European ears from the days when they were perhaps necessary, yet when Rabelais objurgated them in his chapter on the "Island of bells," to these modern times of clocks and watches. In all these cosmopolitan towns, each nation occupied a separate fortified quarter. The trade of Southern Russia was great; and one is surprised to find that horses were exported to India.

Batûta made across a land where the quiet air was no longer annoyed by the insistent clang which was an insult at once to his faith and his ears. He found Southern Russia a plain without hill or tree. Waggons might travel for six months through a green desert the silence broken only by lowing of cattle, hoarse voice of an occasional herdsman, or languid stir of some collection of huts which passed for a town. Cattle were protected by severe laws severely enforced. "Should a beast be stolen, the thief must return it with nine more. If unable to furnish these, his children are taken into slavery; and, if he have no children, he is slaughtered like a sheep . . . The only fuel is dung."

Batûta was bent on visiting Uzbek Khan, the powerful Tartar who now represented the dynasty founded by Chinghiz Khân, the blacksmith. Uzbek "was one of the seven mightiest monarchs of the world, the others being the Sultan of the West; the Sultan of Egypt and Syria, the Sultan of the two Iraks (Persia and Mesopotamia), the Khân of Turkestan, the Sultan of India, and the Emperor of China. Our traveller hired a waggon, and, after many monotonous days, arrived at the camp of the Khân. He was amazed to behold "a city in motion; complete in its streets, mosques, and cooking houses." Nor was he less bewildered at the consideration given to women by all men, from the Khân downwards, and at seeing them going about unveiled, yet "religious, charitable, and given to good works." The wife of an Emir would ride, magnificently attired, in a coach. "Often she is accompanied by her husband; but one would take him for a mere attendant." Uzbek Khan was "wont to give audience on Friday, his four wives, unveiled, sitting enthroned to right and left of him, a son on either side, and a daughter in front. Princes and Emirs are gathered around. People enter into the presence in order of rank. When a wife comes in, he takes her by the hand and leads her to her throne. Each wife has a separate abode; and not to visit these ladies is looked upon as a breach of good manners." It is evident that the ancestral habits of a nomadic people were carefully preserved under conditions which were rapidly changing. The Sultan sent his visitor a horse, a sheep, and koumiss in a leathern bottle.

Batûta wished to see for himself the great change in the length of day and night which takes place as one travels northward. So Uzbek sent him to far-distant Bulgar, on the Volga, a place in the latitude of Newcastle. Here he was told of a "Land of Darkness," which lay forty days' journey to the North. "Traders alone go there; and only in big companies. Dogs draw them over the ice in sledges; and the travellers must take all food and wood for fuel with them. The dogs are fed before anyone, and experienced dogs, who have done the journey several times, are chosen to lead the pack. On arriving at the proper place, each trader puts down his goods and retires. Next day, he finds furs put down as barter. Should he be content with these, he carries them off; but should he not be satisfied, he leaves them where they are, and more are added. But sometimes the natives will take back their own goods, and leave those of the traders. The traders never see anyone, and know not whether they deal with human beings or with demons." Strange as this practice seems, there is other evidence that exchange of goods was made in this way in very high latitudes. Sledge-dogs were used very much farther south than they are to-day. Batûta speaks of the Russians as being "Christians with red hair, blue eyes, ugly, faithless, and rich in silver shrines."

When Batûta returned to Uzbek, he went on to Astrakhan with him. "Here the Sultan dwells in very cold weather . . . The city is on one of the great rivers of the world (the Volga), which is crossed by laying thousands of bundles of hay on the ice."

Now, the third of Uzbek's four wives was a daughter of the Christian Emperor of Constantinople. History makes no mention of this lady; but there is no reason to doubt the fact, however surprising; for, since 1265 A.D. the Byzantine Emperor had more than once given a natural daughter or legitimate sister in marriage to powerful Mongolian Sovereigns, in order to get their support against the encroaching Turks of Asia Minor.

This particular lady was expecting her confinement and desired to return home for the event. She had requested the Khan to allow her to do so, and he had sanctioned the journey. Batûta saw an opportunity of seeing the famous Christian metropolis, if the Khan would allow him to join the escort. Such a petition from a foreign stranger naturally aroused suspicion as to his motives; but Batûta was skilful in allaying this; and we find him setting forth with a parting gift from the Khân of a fine dress, several horses, and cash. Even the Khân's ladies and his sons and daughters gave him presents. The princess was escorted by 500 horse and 4,500 foot. The Khan, accompanied by his head-wife and heir-apparent rode with her the first stage; the heir-apparent and his suite went on the next stage of a journey that took two months. For some reason or other a very round-about route was chosen; first a waterless, uninhabited waste was crossed; then the Caucasus approached to within a day's march. When a border-fortress was reached, the escort returned; and now the real motive of the lady becomes discernable. The unhappy woman had been the victim of state-craft, a puppet danced off to a semi-barbarian husband in the interests of Constantinople. In spite of the respect paid to women in her new abode, she was heartily sick of Tartar discomfort and Moslem ways. Accustomed to the luxurious ease and refinements of the Byzantine Court, she loathed the uncouth manners of a half-tamed people and their rough life. She sighed for the amenities of her father's palace and the high civilization of his city. She left her travelling mosque at the fortress, drank wine, and is said to have eaten swine's flesh. From Batûta's point of view, she relapsed into infidelity; yet he has no bitter word to cast at her. When a day's journey from her native city, a younger brother came to meet her with 5,000 cavalry, all in shining armour. Next day the heir-apparent arrived with 10,000 cavalry, and when quite near to Constantinople, the greater part of the population turned out, decked in their best, and shouting so that it was difficult to decide whether they or the drums made most noise. The parents came forth from the gate in full royal state, and the poor released princess threw herself on the ground before them, kissed it, and even kissed the hooves of their horses. All the bells of Constantinople were a-ringing, and the royal party entered the city with glittering pomp.

Batûta was unwilling to enter "Istambûl" without the Emperor's special sanction; it was not too safe a place for a Moslem. Andronicus Palæologus the Younger gave him a safe-conduct; but he was searched for concealed arms at the fifth gate—a practice which, afterwards, he found to obtain in India. As he passed through the gateways the guards muttered: "Saracens! Saracens!" And Saracens they had indeed occasion to hold in mortal horror and dread.

Our pilgrim-traveller gets sadly muddled about names and dates just here. Evidently, he derived the information he gives us from a Jew, who acted as interpreter, and who either spoke Arabic imperfectly or heartily enjoyed "pulling his leg." And as to dates, just here, Batûta's memory fails him a little. He was told that the Pope of Rome paid an annual visit to Santa Sophia, and was received with the greatest veneration and ceremonial. And he calls the Emperor Andronicus, "George." Andronicus plied him with eager questions as to Jerusalem and the Holy Places of Palestine. He only saw the outside of Santa Sophia.

Now, the Princess made open objection to return to her husband, and had her will. She gave Batûta a money-present for his services; but the Byzantine Empire was in decay, and, to his loss in exchange, the coins debased. He returned Eastward with a small escort, and met Uzbek Khân at Sara. We read in Dan Chaucer how

> "At Sarray, in the land of Tartarye
> Ther dwelt a king that werreyed Russye."

Nothing will content him but to see those famous cities beyond the Oxus, and Balk, with its great mosque of the precious pillars, before he proceeds to India. He travels 40 days through a desert. The whole district is one vast desolation; and he tells us how Chinghiz Khân, the blood-stained blacksmith, a conquering hero, a strict Moslem, and therefore "a man of liberal mind," subdued district after district until he was lord of China and the Middle East; how he carried off the youth of Bokhara and Samarkand, Khôrasân and Irak, and slaughtered and pillaged so that he left nothing but ruin behind him. Batûta visited the Great Khân of Turkestan and more than one camp of petty rulers.

"The purple robe makes Emperors, not priests," said Ambrose the Bishop of Milan to the Emperor Theodosius; and the Emperor remarked how hard it was for a ruler to meet with an outspoken and unfearing man. Batûta tells us of an amusing incident which indicates, not merely how an imam could be outspoken to a king, but also that, if Mohammedanism had admitted of a sacerdotal hierarchy, the same exercise of priestly authority which cast Theodosius prostrate and weeping before the Altar at Milan and kept Heinrich shivering in the snows of Canossa, while awaiting the condescension of Hildebrand, would have obtained in the Moslem as in the Christian world. When Tirim Siri Khân wished prayers to be delayed until he should come to the mosque, the imam bade the messenger return to the Khân and ask him whether prayers were ordered of God or of him, and commanded the muezzin to summon the faithful as usual. After the second prostration the Khân arrived, meekly remained at the doorway, and joined in the prayers. When worship was over, he grasped the hand of the imam, who laughed heartily, and the twain sat together afterwards, Batûta being with them. The Khân told the traveller to declare to his countrymen how the Ruler of the Turkomans had sat with a poor man of the poorest Persians. This worthy imam lived by the labour of his hands, and refused all the gifts his sovereign offered him. No wonder that warm friendship sprang up between these two men, and that both were respected and obeyed. But greater regard was paid to the statutes than to this monarch even; for, after Batûta left, Tirim Siri broke a law laid down by his grandfather and therefore was deposed.

In one province he found "a laudable practice. A whip is hung up in every mosque, and whoever stays away from worship is beaten by the imam before all the congregation, and fined to boot, the fine going towards the upkeep of the mosque." The time came when Batûta, clothed with authority, itched to exercise it in the same praiseworthy way.

Batûta now visits Herat, turns north-westward to Meshed, the capital of Khôrasân and holy city of the Shiites, thence travels to Jam, the birthplace of Jami, the Persian poet, and at Tus finds the tomb of the Caliph Haroun-al-Raschid, who died there when on a military expedition. Now, Haroun-al-Raschid was a Sunnite; so the orthodox "place lighted candles on his grave, but the followers of Ali (Shiites) are wont to give it a kick." One recalls the story of how, when the Indian Emperor had his attention drawn to a dog defiling the grave of a heretic, he remarked that "the beast resembles orthodoxy." Heterodox or orthodox, according to point of view, here were flourishing colleges filled with students, and saintly men dwelling in secluded cells. To work miracles has always been a distinction of the saint; but the Eastern saint was also permitted to live on to an age incredibly ripe. Batûta is always running across some man of the age attained by old Parr, and upwards. A century and a half is a moderate number of years for these holy beings, and Batûta accepts it as veridical; especially when corroborative evidence is given. But three and a half centuries claimed by a man who is no Struldbrug, but looks not more than fifty, staggers even him. The impostor assures his visitor that every century he grows a fresh crop of hair and cuts a new set of teeth, and that he had been a Râja who was buried at Multân in the Punjâb. "I very much doubted as to what he might really be; and I do so to this day."

CHAPTER VI

AN EASTERN DESPOT

He waited forty days for the snows to melt on the "Hindu Kush—the Slayer of the Hindus, so called because most of the slaves brought from India die here of the bitter cold thereof." The Afghans were at that time subjects of the Khân of Turkestan (Transoxiana); a turbulent, violent race, impatient of the slightest curb. Bandits attacked the party he joined in the Kabul pass; but bow and arrow kept them at a distance. Fierce invaders had poured down the mountain passes from Afghanistan from the end of the twelfth century and established a Mohammedan Empire at Delhi.

Batûta passed into Sind. At the Indian border the usual written description of his personal appearance and the object of his visit was sent to the Sultan. There was a system of stations at a short distance from each other, and couriers of the Sultan went to and fro, some on horseback, some on foot. To secure rapid transit, each courier was provided with bells attached to a whip, so as to announce his approach to a station and to warn the courier there to be ready to go on with the royal despatch.

Now, the Mohammedan Sultan of Northern India was a striking illustration of the fact that humanity is not necessarily coupled with generosity. Mohammed Tughlak was renowned throughout the Moslem world for his lavish munificence; but the cold-blooded cruelty of the despot was not less great than his bounty. Batûta not merely wished to see India; he hoped to achieve lucrative establishment at the Moslem Court. At Multân he found a body of adventurers, who sought to place their talents at the service of the Sultan, and awaited his invitation to court. Any shipwrecked sailor, even, had only to make his way to Mohammed Tughlak to be relieved. Batûta has tales of him which we may believe at our pleasure.

The Sultan told one of his courtiers to go to the treasury and take away as much gold as he could carry. He took so much that he fell under its weight. The Sultan ordered the coins to be gathered together, weighed, and sent to him. Once he had one of his Emirs put into a balance, and gave him his weight in gold, kissing him, and telling him to bestow alms for his soul's welfare. He kissed the feet of a "theologian and gatherer of traditions," and presented him with a golden vase filled with gold coins.

On the way, Batûta saw one of the three brothers whom the Sheik at Alexandria had prophesied he should meet, and found him "a man very much broken by temptations of the devil. He would not allow any one to touch his hand or even to draw near him; and, should anyone's garb chance to touch his, he washed it immediately." On the road from Multân to Delhi, Batûta was most hospitably received by the Emirs. But Northern India was no more reduced to order by the Mohammedan Sultan than by the Emperor Sîlâditya in Hiuen-Tsiang's time. Between Multan and Delhi, while travelling with a party of twenty-two, Batûta found two horse and twenty foot opposing their progress. Our pilgrim was a many-sided man, quite capable of taking his share in a fight. The robbers lost one of their horsemen and twelve of their foot, and then fled from the field.

When Ibn Batûta arrived at the Moslem capital, which was ten miles to the south of the Delhi of our day, he found that the Sultan was not there. But great honour was done to the man whose fame as theologian, jurist, traveller and threefold hadji had preceeded him. He was received and entertained by the Sultan's Mother and the Vizier, and received a welcome present of money in return for the presents he had brought with him.

A month and a half after his arrival a child of one of his numerous marriages died. She was a little less than a year old. "The vizier gave her funeral honours as if she had been a child of high rank in that country, with incense, rose-water, readers of the Koran, and panegyrists. And the vizier paid all the costs thereof, giving money to the leaders and food to the poor. This was done by the Sultan's orders. And the Dowager Sultana sent for the mother of the child, and gave her valuable dresses and ornaments; which was much to her solace."

News now came that the Sultan was drawing near; so the vizier and others set forth to meet him. Everybody, the adventurers in search of employment included, bore presents to the palace, of which the sentries at the palace-gateway took note. When the Sultan arrived, these gifts were spread out before him, and the travellers were presented to him in order of rank. Batûta was received with special marks of approval. The Sultan graciously condescended to take his hand, promised to see to his interests, and gave him cloth of gold which had adorned his own person. Each visitor had a horse and silver-saddle sent him, and was appointed either judge or writer. Batûta was made Judge of Delhi, with a stipend and the rents of three villages attached to his office. When the messengers brought news of these appointments, the new functionaries were expected to kiss the hooves of their horses, go to the palace, and invest themselves with their robes of office.

Batûta gives an account of the Sultan which is confirmed by Ferishta, the Moslem historian. Mohammed was a typical Oriental sovereign of the first order, that is to say, a man of letters and learning, "approachable, one of the most bountiful of men, splendid in his gifts (where he took a fancy)." But despotism breeds tyranny, and tyranny, brutality. "Notwithstanding his humility, justice, kindness to the poor, and marvellous open-handedness, he was swift to shed blood. Hardly a day went by without someone being slaughtered before the gates of his palace. Often have I seen people suffer there, and their bodies left where they fell. Once, as I rode up, my horse plunged and quivered with fear. I looked ahead, and saw something white lying on the ground. I asked what it might be. One who was with me replied: 'it is the trunk of a man who has been dismembered.' It made no difference whether the offence were great or small; the punishment ordered by the Sultan was the same. He spared none on account of his learning, his upright character, or his position. Daily, hundreds of prisoners were brought to the audience-chamber, arms chained to neck, and feet pinioned. Some were killed, some tortured, some severely beaten. He sat in his Audience Hall every day, Fridays excepted, and had everybody in prison brought before him. But Friday was a day of respite for them; then they kept calm and purified themselves.

"The Sultan had a brother. Never have I seen a finer man. The monarch suspected that he had plotted against him. He questioned him concerning this; and, for fear of being put to the torture, the brother made avowal. But, in fact, whoever should deny any charge of this kind which the Sultan might choose to make would most assuredly be put to the torture; and death is usually chosen. The Sultan had his brother's head cut off in the middle of the court-yard, and, as is the custom, there it remained three days. This man's mother had been stoned to death in the same place two years before; for she had confessed to adultery or some debauchery. . . . . On one occasion, when I was present, some men were brought forward and charged with having conspired to kill the vizier. They were sentenced to be thrown to the elephants. These beasts are trained to put an end to culprits, their feet being shod with steel with a sharp edge to it. They are guided by riders, take up their victim with their trunks, hurl him up into the air, thrust him between their fore-feet, and do to him just what the riders bid them, and that is whatever the Sultan has ordered. If the command be to cut the victims to pieces, the elephant shall do this with his tools, and then shall cast the pieces to the crowd gathered around; but if it be to leave him, he is flayed before the monarch, his skin stuffed with hay, and his flesh given to dogs."

This genial sovereign had craftily contrived to bring about the death of his father and a brother by the collapse of a pavilion. But the reign of every Sultan was polluted by parricide or fratricide in the frantic struggle for the throne. And, even more than has been the case throughout history, all the ostentation, luxury, and culture of the Court, the powerful, and the wealthy, was as fine meal ground from the ear which the humble had sown and reaped. The people were crushed, enslaved, outraged and despoiled.

A case was brought before our judge which reveals that the trial by ordeal, of which Hiuen-Tsiang told us, was still employed. A woman reputed to be a *Goftar*, that is to say, a witch who could kill anyone by a glance, was brought before Batûta on the charge of having murdered a child. Not knowing what to do, he sent her on to the vizier, who ordered four large water-vessels to be tied to her, and the whole bundle to be thrown into the Jumna. Had she sunk, she would have been deemed innocent and pulled out. Alas ! she floated ; so she was taken away to be burned.

One day, two Yogis, master and disciple, arrived at the Sultan's court. Their heads and arm-pits were bare, the hair having been removed by means of some kind of powder. They were received with much respect ; and Batûta was treated to an exhibiton of that Eastern skill in jugglery which astonished all ancient travellers. The disciple assumed the shape of a cube, rose in the air, and floated over the heads of the spectators. Our judge was so frightened at this uncanny trick that he fainted. When he came to, the disciple was still up above his head. The head-conjurer then cast a sandal to the ground. It rebounded, hit the cube, which descended, and lo ! there was the disciple again. Batûta's heart beat at such a rate that the Sultan ordered a powerful drug to be given him, and told him that he should have been shewn more astounding things, but that he feared for his wits. Probably, however the illusion was produced, our traveller saw something very much like what he describes. Marco Polo and other old travellers tell of the astounding feats they saw, and Jehangir, fourth in succession of the Great Moguls, devotes several pages of his diary to a careful record of many similar marvels which he would seem to have observed closely.[1] We shall hear of something stranger yet, which befel Batûta in China.

Our new-made judge was not only a restless being, but one possessed by an immoderate desire to do things on a big scale. His qualities were exaggerate, and a virtue tended to swell into an iniquity. One pious pilgrimage to the Holy Places did not suffice him : he must visit them again and again. We shall see how fully he availed himself of the liberty in marriage, divorce, and concubinage accorded by his creed. Egoism was a strong element in his character. He could not set bounds to his expenditure. In a word, he borders on megalomania. In a short time, his debts are four and a half times his total income. His excuse is that he was ordered to attend the Sultan in an expedition to put down an insurrection. Many servants are required in India ; but his retinue was immense. He was ingenious enough to escape from his difficulties. Mohammed Tughlak plumed himself on his real or supposed proficiency in Persian and Arabic and on his patronage of letters. Batûta went to him with a panegyric in Arabic so adroitly expressed that he charmed His Majesty. Then Batûta laid bare his distress. The Sultan paid his debts and dismissed him with the same warning which Mr. Micawber gave David Copperfield. The judge was excused from accompanying his Master, and was given charge of a tomb and the theological college attached to it.

[1] *Memoirs of the Emperor Johangueir*, by himself. Tr. from Persian by D. Price. Oriental Translation Fund. 1829. pp 96–104.

Encouraged by the Sultan's liberalty, perhaps incited by his example in prodigality, and untaught by his recent dilemma, he arranges everything on a stupendous scale. "I set up 150 readers of the Koran, 80 students, 8 repeaters, a lecturer, 80 conventuals, an imam, muezzins, reciters selected for their fine rendering, eulogists, scribes to note down absentees, and ushers. All of these were men of breeding. And I set up an establishment of menials; such as footmen, cooks, messengers, water carriers, betel-servers, swordsmen, javelin-men, umbrella-carriers, hand-washers, criers, and other officials—460 of them, all told. The Sultan commanded me to supply 12 measures of meal and an equal quantity of meat daily at the tomb. This seemed to me a pitifully small amount. . . . I made it 35 measures of meal, and 35 of meat, and sugar, sugar-candy, butter, and fawfel-nut in due proportion. Thereby I fed all comers."

There was some excuse for the expenditure on food. Famine is the recurrent curse of countries with imperfect means of transport, and "the land suffered from famine at this time. Thus suffering was relieved; and fame of it borne afar." But Batûta does not conceal his having used money which his friends lent him during his stay at Delhi. Indeed he vilifies them for expecting him to return any part of it. He tells his tale in the tone of a man who believes himslf to have been treated ungenerously and unjustly.

Later on in his narrative, he has occasion to refer to the fact that at some time during the few years of his residence at Delhi he added to the number of his wives by marrying the daughter of the Emir of Mobar, in Southern India. "She was a religious woman, who would spend the whole night in meditation and prayer. She could read, but not write. She bore me a female child; but what is become of either of them is beyond my ken." The indelicacy of the dress of women in Delhi shocked him: "they merely cover the face, and the body from the navel downwards only." He tried to get them to robe themselves completely, and failed.

"How wretched
Is that poor man who hangs on princes' favours!"

It seems that the capricious Sultan had placed much confidence in a certain holy man; but suspicion of the sheik's fidelity was aroused, and spies were set to take note of his visitors. Among his friends and visitors was Batûta. Everybody on the list was ordered to appear at the fatal portal. Batûta thought his last hour had come and betook himself to his prayers; he repeated "God is our succour and exceeding help" no less than 33,000 times in a single day; he fasted for four days, taking nothing but water and expecting the executioners every moment. He alone escaped the fatal scimitar.

He had seen enough of Imperial caprice to know that respite was not security, or innocence a lasting defence. He resigned his office and went to a worker of miracles, "the saint and phœnix of his time," who was one of his friends. He gave all that he possessed to holy men; put on the robe of an ascetic, and ate nothing but rice. But the blindfold goddess had him on her wheel, and was to give it many a turn yet. Five months passed, and then the Sultan sent for him and gave him a gracious reception. But he deemed it wise to return to his rigorous life, and was more severe in it than before. Yet forty more days passed, and then the Sultan again commanded his presence.

There was now a much greater trade with China than in the time of Hiuen-Tsiang. An Embassy, headed by a high mandarin, had come from China (A.D. 1342) with presents of 100 male slaves, 50 slave-girls, rich dresses, quivers of gold, and jewelled swords. In a certain lower reach of the Himalaya was a plain which had been overrun by the Moslem conquerors. Once a Buddhist temple stood there; and Chinese pilgrims were wont to journey across Thibet to pray at the sacred spot. Moreover the inhabitants of the district were cut off from their wonted toil in Thibetan fields beyond the border. The place was secured by Nature from any attack from the North ; and the Great Khân of China begged that restrictions should be removed and permission given for the temple to be rebuilt. The Sultan was willing to grant the request on certain pecuniary conditions, but he cast about for some one to accompany the returning embassy and represent him at the Chinese Court. Who so suitable as Batûta, a man of the world, experienced in travel, highly educated, and sharp-witted ? His innocence was established. Such a degree of asceticism, so long endured, was proof of piety. The Sultan ordered him to go. The garb of the ascetic was thrown off. He would feel more secure in China than at Delhi.

CHAPTER VII

PERILS BY LAND AND SEA

Our ambassador sets off with the returning mission attended by two favourites of the Sultan, and a guard of 1,000 horse. He has charge of gifts which far surpass the Chinese presents—100 horses of the best breed, richly caparisoned, 100 Hindu singing and dancing girls, robes of rich brocade, jewelled arms, instruments of gold and silver, silks and stuffs, and 1,700 rich dresses.

He has not travelled 100 miles from Delhi when he finds a district in revolt against the Mohammedan conquerors. The Hindus are besieging a city; the cavalry attending the embassy rushes at the investing forces, loses many men, but leaves not an enemy alive. The news is sent to the Sultan, and a halt is made for his instructions to arrive. Batûta is sitting in the grateful shade of a garden when word comes that a fresh body of Hindus is attacking a village hard by. He rides off with an escort to see how he may help. The insurgents are already fleeing from a hot pursuit, and he finds himself left with only five others and a few mounted men. His horse gets its forefeet wedged between some stones, and he has to dismount; his companions ride off, and he finds himself alone. Suddenly, two score of the enemy's horse appear and ride at him. He is stripped to the skin, bound, and threatened with death. He is unable to talk the language of his captors, is kept a captive during two days, and then they ride away. He shuffles off to a neighbouring jungle, and hides there. He cautiously tries every foot-track to find that not one of them but leads to some enemy village or to some village in ruins. He keeps himself alive by sucking wild fruit and chewing leaves. Seven days have passed, and he is quite exhausted, when he sees "a black man, carrying a small water-vessel and walking by aid of an iron-tipped staff." The man is a Mohammedan, and gives him water and pulse, which he has with him. Batûta tries to walk with him ; but he is too weak and faint ; his feet totter, and he falls to the ground. The "black man" throws him across his shoulders ; all consciousness is lost, and he comes to himself at the Imperial gateway one daybreak, the East aglow with the rising sun. That good Samaritan, the "' black man," stands out in bright relief from a background of crime and cruelty and shadows of feet swift to shed blood.

Mohammed Tughlak received Batûta more kindly than ever, gave him handsome compensation, and commanded him to return to the Embassy. On his way to Cambay, we hear more of Yogi magicians and how they will remain long time without food. "I have seen, in the city of Mangalore, a Moslem who had learned of these folk. A sort of platform was set up for him ; and thereon he had stayed 25 days, neither eating nor drinking. Thus did I leave him ; and I know not how long he kept there afterwards. It is said that they make up pills, and, after swallowing one of them, can do without food or drink. They foretell hidden things. The Sultan honours them and admits them to his society. Some among them eat vegetable food only ; and these are the greater number. There are among them those who can slay a man by a glance at him. The common people hold that, if the chest of the dead man be opened, no heart is to be found within ; for it has been consumed. Women do this in the main, and such an one is called a hyæna."

Batûta's chief interest was in Islam ; but he noted natural products carefully and was alive to the odd. North of the Hindu Kush he had seen a woefully obese man ; and now, on this 1,500 mile journey to Calicut, he came across the ruler of a small State, "a black giant," who thought little of devouring a whole sheep at a sitting.

He took ship near Goa, and the craft ran along the

Malabar coast, "the land of black pepper." Twelve kinglets ruled as many states in Malabar at that time, and each king had an army of from 5,000 to 50,000 men at his command. Many ancient polyandric practices were retained; which explains why each Râja was succeeded by a sisters' son. No landing was made until a king's son had been handed over as a pledge of safety. Many Arab traders had settled in the ports, and become wealthy. Punishment, swift and severe, followed on the smallest infringement of *meum* and *tuum*. We are told how a Hindu noble, out riding with his father-in-law, who was no less a personage than the Râja, picked up a mango which had dropped from an overhanging tree. The Râja ordered that both he and the mango should be cut into two halves, and half of the mango and half of the culprit laid on either side of the public way precisely where the enormity had been done. One may suspect that the son-in-law was not wholly *persona grata* to the despot.

The Embassy had to tide over three months at Calicut awaiting the season for the sailing of the fleet of junks from China. There were thirteen of them at Calicut, and they also traded to Hili and Quilon. He tells us that the biggest junks were as floating cities. They would carry a crew of 1,000 men, whereof 400 were soldiers. The junk was worked by oars and sails of bamboo-matting, slung from masts varying in number from three to twelve, according to the size of the junk. Ten to thirty men stood to pull at each oar. Garden-herbs and ginger were grown on deck, and on it, too, were houses built for the chief officers and their wives. The quarters of the junk were three-fold, fastened together by spikes. Each junk of the biggest size was accompanied by three tenders of progressively diminishing proportions. Needless to say, the commander of a junk was a very important functionary. Often more than one junk would be owned by a single Chinaman. But then, "truly the Chinese are the wealthiest people on earth."

Our ambassador sent his servants, slave-girls and baggage on board; but the cabin was too small to hold both concubines and luggage; so the skipper advised him to hire a *kakam* or junk of the third size. This he did on a Thursday, the *kakam* took in its cargo, and he remained on shore the next day for public worship.

During the night, the terror of the sea fell on them all. A violent storm came on, and the waters shook the land. Some of the junks contrived to get away from the perilous neighbourhood of the shore to more open water; but one of them was wrecked, and only a few swimmers managed to escape. The *kakam*, with all his wordly goods and slave-concubines in it, had disappeared; but it had been seen making for the open. The body of an envoy was washed ashore, with the skull smashed in. A guardian Eunuch was also cast up, a nail driven right through the brain from temple to temple. Down came the Zamorin to the scene of disaster, Comedy attendant on Tragedy, for he braved the tempest clad with a loin-cloth, the scantiest of headgear, and a necklace of jewels, but the insignium of royalty, the umbrella, was somehow held up over his sacred head. Batûta cast himself on his prostration-carpet, which was all that was left to him, excepting ten pieces of gold and his servant, a freed slave, who immediately made off. Some pious people gave him small coin, which he kept as treasure, for it would bring blessing with it.

We are told of the noble deed of a simple Moslem sailor during this great storm. "There was a girl on board who was the favourite of a merchant. The merchant offered ten pieces of gold to anyone who should save her. A sailor, hailing from Hormuz, did save her; but he refused the reward, saying, 'I did it for the love of God.'"

The junk which held the precious gifts for China was seen to go down outside the port; and Batûta heard that the little boat which held all his slave-concubines and worldly goods had contrived to gain the open sea, and might conceivably put in at Quilon. He set off at once, and arrived there after a ten days' journey. He found the Chinese Embassy there. They had suffered shipwreck, but their junk had not broken up and was being refitted.

It did not require the advice proferred him by his co-religionists to deter him from returning to the capricious, passionate lord of Delhi. He bethought him of Jamâl Oddîn, ruler of Honowar, a man of sense and understanding, whom he had visited on his way to Calicut. It casts a pleasant ray on the Mohammedan occupation of India, that there were no fewer than 44 schools set up in the busy little capital of a small State, and that of these no fewer than 11 were for girls. Now Jamâl Oddîn knew the uncertain temper of the Lord of India quite as well as Batûta, and did not give him too hearty a welcome. So to appease offended Heaven, or to rehabilitate himself by an evidence of piety, he repaired to a mosque and read the Koran from end to end once, and ultimately twice, a day. Now, there were 52 ships being fitted out to attack the island of Sindâbûr; and Jamâl evidently thought that Batûta might prove useful, for he commanded him to accompany him on this expedition. Batûta tried to read the future by a time-honoured method of divination. He opened the Koran at random, and his eye fell on a promise of Allah to aid his servant. This was satisfactory to Jamâl Oddîn as well as to himself.

After strenuous resistance Sindâbûr was carried by assault, and Batûta, who was something of a warrior, received a slave-girl, clothing and other presents from his patron. He remained on the island with Jamâl Oddîn for some months, and then got permission to go to Calicut. For the Chinese fleet would be returning to India by this time, and he might get news of his little junk. At Calicut, he learned that his *kakam* had reached China, that his property had been divided up, and that his pretty concubine had died on the voyage. "I felt very much grief for her." He went back to the island to find the city besieged by Hindus.

Now he had heard marvellous things concerning the Maldives, an archipelago of small islands lying S.S.E. of India, near the equator. The inhabitants, under British rule to-day, had accepted Islam. He found that before he or anyone was allowed to land he must show himself on deck; "for although the islands are multitudinous, each lies close to its neighbour, and folk knew one another by sight." He speaks of the inhabitants as "pious, peaceable, and chaste. They never wage war. Prayers are their only weapons. Indian pirates do not alarm them; nor do they punish robbers; for they have learned that sudden and grievous ill will come to evil-doers. When any of the pirate-ships of infidel Hindus pass by these islands, whatsoever is found is taken, nor will anyone stand out." But, in spite of the moral reflection indulged in by the islanders, Batûta traces their policy of non-resistance to physical feebleness. And "there is one exception to it. Should a single lemon be taken woe befals the offender. He is punished and forced to listen to a homily. The natives delight in perfumes and in bathing twice a day, which the heat forces them to do; yet trees give delicious shade. Their trade is in ropes, which they make of hemp, and which are used for sewing together the timbers of ships of India and Yemen; for if a ship strike against a rock, the hemp allows of its yielding, and so saves it from going to pieces, which is not the case when iron nails are used. Shells are used for coin, and palm-leaves are used for all writing, except for copying out the Koran; and the instrument used has a sharp point."

Batûta sailed among these islands during ten days, and took up his abode on one, the sovereign of which was a woman. For the lady's husband had died, leaving no male issue; so she married her vizier who, in reality, ruled. Batûta took the full license accorded in Islam.

He married the four legal wives permitted, and took to himself some concubines also, " all pleasant in conversation and of great beauty." He must have divorced his previous wives before being able to do this. Marriage in the Maldive Islands was facile and cheap. Only a small dowry was demanded for a handsome woman ; but it was required that the stranger should divorce the wife on leaving the land, and by no means take her with him. But, should he not desire to marry, there was no difficulty in getting a woman to cook for him at a very small wage. Wives were less companionable here than in most parts of the world, since women and men took their meals apart ; nor could Batûta get his women-folk to break the custom of their country—a custom which Varthema speaks of, nearly two centuries later, as obtaining in South West India. Batûta had been appointed judge, and another thing that troubled him was the irregular attendance of the lax Moslems of his island at the mosque. He was very eager that such flagrant non-observance of religious duty should be duly punished ; and he urged that the best way would be literally to whip the recalcitrants to attend on public worship.

Now Batûta's wives had powerful relatives. The sister of one of his wives at Delhi was wife to the Emir of Mobar ; to whom, therefore, Batûta was doubly related. He had become a power in his island, and the vizier grew jealous and suspicious. Might not the stranger conspire to bring an army over from the coast of Coromandel ? When Batûta saw what was going on, he acted at once. " I divorced all my wives," he says, " save one, who had a young child, and I went on to other islands of that great multitude of them." From one of these, he shipped for Mobar ; but the wind changed, and he was driven to the coast of Ceylon and in no small danger of drowning. The governor of the port came sailing by, and refused a landing ; for he was no friend to Moslem skippers. Batûta won him over by telling him that he was on his way to visit the Sovereign of Mobar, that he was related to him by marriage, and that the whole cargo of the ship was intended as a present for that potentate. The Ceylonese Râja of the district was on good terms with his Moslem brother of Mobar, so Batûta was allowed to land. He found, like Marco Polo, that Ceylon was divided among four kinglets. He of the district soon sent for him, and gave him hospitality. He admired the famous herds of elephants, the troups of chattering monkeys, the pool of precious stones, and the luxuriant vegetation and glorious scenery of Ceylon. He scaled that iron chain, which still exists, to reach the top of Adam's peak, and gives us the measure of the print of Adam's foot, on hard rock ; for in Ceylon, as elsewhere, supernatural vestiges are to be found. He visited Colombo and several other places in the island, and then set sail for the coast of Coromandel.

But, while crossing the strait, " the wind blew strong, and the ship was nearly swamped. Our skipper was a lubber. We were driven near perilous rocks, and barely escaped going to pieces ; and then we got into shallow water. Our ship grated against the bottom, and we were face to face with death. Those on board threw all that they had into the sea, and bade farewell to one another. We cut down the mast and cast it onto the sea, and the sailors made a raft. The beach was eight miles off. I wanted to get down to the raft. I had two concubines and two friends with me. These latter exclaimed : 'would you get down and leave us ? ' I had more regard to their safety than to my own ; so I answered : 'Get down, both of you, and the young girl whom I love with you.' My other young girl said : 'I can swim. I will fix ropes to the raft and swim alongside these people.' My two comrades got down, one of the young girls being with them ; and the other swam. The sailors tied ropes to the raft, and so helped her to swim. I gave them whatever of value I had in the way of jewels, amber, and other goods. They got to shore safe and sound, for the wind was in their favour. But I stayed aboard the ship. The skipper got to shore on a plank. The sailors took the building of four rafts in hand; but night came on before they had finished, and the ship was filling. I got up on the poop, and remained there until morning. Then several idolaters came to us in their barque. And we got safe to land."

His connexion, the Emir, received him warmly. This potentate was about to attack a Hindu Power; and, while he was away on this expedition, Batûta travelled about. He tells us that he came across a fakir with long hair, who sat and ate in the society of seven foxes, and who kept a "happy family"—a gazelle and a lion together. The Emir was a ruthless tyrant, butchering women and children. Yet Batûta had no scruple in proposing a scheme to him for the conquest of the Maldives, where he had received so much kindness, and where he had left wives and paramours. But pestilence came and swept away most of the inhabitants of the district, including the Emir. The new ruler wanted to carry out the scheme for occupying the Maldives; but Batûta got fever badly, and very nearly died. When sufficiently recovered, he received permission to recuperate his energies by taking the long voyage round Cape Comorin to Honawar, where he wished to meet his old friend, Jamâl Oddîn, again. But, from time immemorial, the sea had been a no-mans province, infested by pirates; and the calling, continuous or accidental, of sea-thief was then as honourable as it was ancient. His ship was attacked by twelve Hindu craft, and taken after a severe battle. Batûta was stripped of his jewels and all his belongings, and set on shore with a pair of breeches on. He lost the notes of his travels with his other belongings. Out of the way of direct business, the robbers could be merciful, and there was no reason why they should take his life. He made his painful way to Calicut, and put up at a mosque—always the asylum of the indigent. Some of the lawyers and traders here had known him at Delhi. They clothed, fed, and housed him. What was he to do? He dared not return to Delhi. A son had been borne to him by a Maldive wife. He had a desire to see the child. The vizier was dead; but the queen had married again, and he wondered what sort of reception he should get. Paternal tenderness prevailed: "I went there on account of my little son; but when I had seen him, I left him with his mother, out of kindness to her." He was hospitably entertained, but stayed a very few days. The new vizier furnished him with those provisions which every traveller by sea must purchase for himself and carry with him in the fourteenth century; and he set sail for Bengal, where he arrived after 43 days at sea (A.D. 1341).

CHAPTER VIII

OFF TO MALAYSIA AND CATHAY

BATUTA speaks of Bengal as the land of plenty. Everything was cheaper there than anywhere else in the wide world. He picked up a very beautiful slave-girl for a trifle. But the muggy climate made Bengal "a hell full of good things." The Sultan was in revolt against his lord-paramount at Delhi; and as Batûta was a prudent person, held Mohammed Tughlak in wholesome awe, and could not predict the issue of the contest, he did not visit the Bengalese Court. He went up to the hill-country, half-way to the Himalayan giants, instead; for he desired to see an aged holy man who dwelt there, one who was reported to take no food excepting a little milk, and that only every ten days, and to sit upright all night. This old sheik was a seer, and foretold events which should befall his guest and which he declares really happened. Batûta was proud to be justly hailed as "the greatest traveller of all the Arabs." He returned from the hills to visit a city not far from modern Dacca.

We next find him on the Indian Ocean, standing off the Nicobar Islands, probably because his ship needed a fresh supply of water. The inhabitants were fearful of strangers, would not allow any ship to sail in front of their houses, had the fresh water required brought down to the shore by elephants, and traded by signs; for nobody could speak their language. The men went about naked, and the women wore a girdle of leaves only. All were remarkable for the ugliness of their dog-like faces. Batûta was told that a man might be the husband of 30 or more of these beauties. Adultery was severely punished, the male offender being hanged, unless he could find a friend or a slave willing to suffer in his place; the woman being trampled to death and her body cast into the sea. The king came down to the beach with an escort of his relatives, all mounted on elephants. He wore a coloured silk turban and a goat-skin tunic, with the hair turned outwards, and he bore a short silver spear in his hand. The usual gifts were presented in dumb-show. "These folk work magic on any ship that withholds presents; and it is wrecked."

Moslem traders called any part of the Malaysian Archipelago, Java; but the port to which our traveller next came was really in Sumatra. The Emir of the Mohammedan sovereign received the visitors with customary Eastern munificence and gave them rich dresses. Our traveller speaks highly of the Sultan as being a cultivated man who loved the society of the learned and enjoyed discussion with them. A modern writer says that the humblest man he ever knew was a duke, and Batûta might have said the same of some rulers. The humility of the Sultan of Sumatra was so great that he walked to prayers every Friday! Batûta took a long journey inland, and tells us of frankincense, clove, nutmeg, mace, and other products of Sumatra, and of how a man is sacrificed by the natives at the foot of the camphor-tree to ensure its good bearing.

He was eager to reach China—that land of strange ways and peculiar civilization in Farthest East. The complaisant Sultan gave him passage in one of his own junks, provided him with stores for the voyage, and ordered a guide-interpreter to attend on him. In three and a half weeks, he came to a place which he calls Kakula, and which may have been on the mainland. Here he was well received by the pagan king, and chanced to be present at a curious proof of devotion to royalty. "One day, a man made a long speech, not one word of which I understood. He held a knife in his hand, which he grasped firmly, and cut off his own head, and it fell to the ground." This sounds incredible; but it is a fact. The feat was done by means of apparatus. A sickle-shaped knife was attached to a stirrup. The suicide placed his foot in the latter, gave it a sharp jerk, and the knife shore off his head. Our traveller was told that the deed was done to make manifest the great loyalty of the victim, and that his father and grandfather had made the same praiseworthy exit from life in honour of the king's father and grandfather. Their families received compensation from the kings. A similar case of self-execution was authentically recorded in the last century.

The Eastern Ocean was so calm that the junk had to be towed by boats. Marco Polo had the same experience in these seas. Batûta touched at Kailiki, a port of Tawalisi, probably Tonquin ; but no one is quite sure where this land lay. Even the Sulu Islands have been suggested ! The king was as powerful as the Emperor of China. His people were idolaters after the manner of the Turks, and Batûta reports a conversation with his Amazonian daughter, introducing a few words of their language. This princess could write, but not speak Arabic. Some discredit has been thrown on this part of his narrative, mainly on the ground of language, but also because what he has to say about her recalls very ancient classical stories. But we must recollect that Batûta is relying on his memory at a time when the events belonged to a far-distant past ; that his work was dictated ; and that it was edited by the Secretary to the Sultan of Fez. He confesses that he did not understand very well what the princess said to him. And the language she spoke may have struck him as like Turkish in sound, and hence is given in some sort of imitation of that tongue. The more one studies ancient travellers and pilgrims the more assured one becomes of their essential sincerity and the general accuracy of their observation. We know very little indeed about the Nomadic penetration of the Far East. That this princess was able to write a little Arabic, would seem to show that there was considerable Arab trade with Tawalisi.

This lady was governor of the port, a post which her father had given her as the reward of her powers in battle. For, once, when her father's army was on the point of defeat, she routed the enemy, and brought back the head of their leader. She commanded an army. whereof one regiment was of women. Neighbouring princes had wished to marry her, but had withdrawn their pretensions; for she insisted that first they should overcome her in the lists; and they were afraid of the ignominy of being vanquished by a woman. She was amazed at the wealth of India, and said to Batûta: "I must conquer it for myself."

Favourable winds and strenuous use of the oar brought the junk to China. He found that he had to pass through a stringent customs-house; and that a register was taken of all who left or arrived at a Chinese port. The captain was held responsible for his crew and passengers, and to this end an official list was essential. Should the traveller elect to stay with some other trader, his host took care of his money and goods, but was bound to return them at the close of the visit, with a deduction for necessary expenditure. Any deficiency must be made good. But the trader might, if he chose, put up at an inn. Batûta was surprised to find paper-currency. He admired the big poultry; but not the dirty cotton-clothes of the Chinese, nor their relish for the flesh of dogs and swine. As in Hiuen-Tsiang's time, they burned their dead. A portrait of every traveller was taken without his knowing it, and thus, should an evil-doer try to escape from justice from one province to another, he was readily discovered. There were many Moslem traders in China; most of these had settled there; and Jews had found a home in China for eleven centuries.

Travelling in China was "safer and more agreeable than in any other land on earth. Although it takes nine months to cross this country, one need have no fear on the journey, even though one should have wealth in one's care. There is an official with troops, both horse and foot, at each hostelry to keep matters in order. This official, accompanied by his scribe, comes to the hostelry every evening; and the scribe writes down the name of every guest, seals up the list, and locks the door. They come again in the morning and go over the list and the inmates; and a man goes with the travellers to the next hostelry and returns to the officer with proof that they have arrived. . . . The traveller can buy all he needs at these inns."

Batûta visited the great port of Zaitun (Touen-chow), whence, among other manufactures, "clothes of gold and *satyns* riche of hewe"[1] were shipped. Perhaps there was no port in the world with so big a trade as Zaitun. Batûta thought so: "The harbour is one of the greatest on the earth—I err—it is the greatest. There I have seen an hundred junks of the biggest size at one time, and more smaller ones than could be numbered. . . . Here, as in every Chinese city, every citizen has a garden and a field, and his house stands in the middle of the land he owns. For this reason, the cities of China are very much spread out." At Zaitun, he had the good fortune to meet, in the Moslem quarter, the ambassador who had been sent to Delhi; and now great folk began to make his acquaintance. Among his visitors was "one of the merchants to whom I owed money when I ran into debt on my arrival in India, and who had shown more breeding than the rest of my creditors." The Head Mandarin wrote to the Emperor to ask permission for the traveller to visit him at his capital; and, while awaiting a reply, allowed him to travel by water-way far inland from Canton, and provided him with an escort. At Canton, he found temple-hospitals for widows and orphans, the blind, crippled, and infirm.

He tells how the sailors stood up amidship to row, and the passengers sat fore and aft. He visited one of those

[1] Chaucer, *Man of Lawe's Tale. Part I., st. i, l.* 4. The derivation of Satin is obvious.

wonderful saints who claimed incredible years. The holy man told him that he was one of the saints whom he had visited in India. This man had the reputation of being able to induce visions. Possibly he united the qualifications of skilled hypnotist and skilled liar.

When our traveller returned to Canton he received permission to visit the capital. He journeyed many days by land and along the Imperial Canal. He speaks rapturously of the fertility and charm of the country he passed through. Everywhere he was treated with the deepest respect. But there was a drawback: everywhere Paganism was flourishing. He met a fellow-believer, the brother of one of the seers of Egypt, a man greatly esteemed by the Chinese, and later on one particular prophesy was completely fulfilled, for he came across another brother, whom it was also foretold he should meet, on the borders of Sahara.

While attending the court of the viceroy at Hang-chow, he was eye-witness to a remarkable feat, of which he gives as circumstantial an account as one would expect to get from a man of the fourteenth century. "It was in the hot season, and we were in the courtyard outside the palace. A juggler, a slave of the Khân, came in, and the Emir commanded him to show some of his marvels. Thereupon the juggler took a wooden bowl with several holes made in it, and through these holes long thongs were passed. He laid hold of these thongs, and threw the bowl up into the air. It went so high that we could no longer see it. There was only a little of the end of the thong left in the juggler's hand. He ordered one of his boy helpers to lay hold of it and mount. The boy climbed up the thong, and he also went out of sight. The juggler called him three times; but no reply came; so he seemed to get into a great rage, snatched up a knife, and laid hold of the thong; and he also was no longer to be seen. After a time, down came one of the boy's hands, then a foot, than the other hand, then the other foot, then the trunk, and, lastly, the head. And now, down came the juggler, panting, and his clothes in a bloody state. He kissed the ground in front of the Emir and said something to him in Chinese. The Emir gave him some order, and he then took up the severed parts, laid them together properly, gave a kick, and behold ! the boy got up and was before us again. I was so astounded that my heart beat violently, as it did when the Sultan of India had a similar trick done before me. A drug was given me, which set me right again. The Khazi Alfkaouddîn was next to me. 'By Allah !' said he, 'as for me I believe there has been neither going up nor coming down, nor cutting to pieces, nor making the boy whole again. It is nothing but trickery.'"

We must not forget that Batûta was more than inclined to superstition, that he was very perturbed by what he saw, or thought he saw, that the "magician" had boys with him, who probably assisted in this trick, and that it is part of the conjurer's art to divert the attention of spectators while in the actual performance of his feats. And the event was reduced to writing years after it was observed. Moreover, one of the earlier investigations of the Society for Psychical Research shewed that, on an occasion when a clever amateur conjurer, not known to be such, invited highly educated and observant witnesses to a supposed spiritualistic séance, and received their accounts of what they believed themselves to have seen, written independently of each other and immediately after the event, "not one of the detailed reports is accurate throughout, and scarcely one of them is accurate in even all the points of importance."[1] But we have it on the authority of the Professor of Chinese at Cambridge that P'u Sung-ling, the author of the Liao Chai, relates having seen the complete trick, as Batûta describes it,

[1] Proceedings of the Society for Psychical Research, vol. iv. p. 405.

in the seventeenth century,[1] except that, in this case, the boy came out of a box. These are, perhaps, the most remarkable of many similar mystifications, some of them related by quite respectable witnesses, from the 13th century down to our own time.[2]

He tells us of the excellent workmanship of Chinese artisans, and how they worked in chains for a period of ten years. At the end of that time, they were free to go about in China, but not to leave the frontiers. At 50, they became absolutely free men, and were maintained at the public cost, old age pensioners, in fact, in this early fourteenth century. And the pension was not merely given to these slave-workers, but to nearly all Chinese.

He admired the gay life on the canal, crowded with

[1] P'u Sung-ling finished his work A.D. 1679, and saw the trick when he was a boy.

[2] Part of the illusion described by Ibn Batûta, known as the Indian Rope Trick, was seen by the late Professor Middleton, of the South Kensington Museum, in Morocco, and is fully described by Wilfred Scawen Blount's *Diaries*, 1888-1900, p. 86, sqq. The trick has been much discussed during the last few years, and conjurers confess that it perplexes them. ("*Baffled magicians,*" *Times*, Feb. 6th, 1919). Mr. C. R. Sanderson, Librarian to the National Liberal Club, kindly drew my attention to certain articles and correspondence in popular journals (*Strand Magazine*, April, 1919; *Daily Mail*, Jan. 7th, 1913, and a discussion in the same newspaper, beginning Jan. 8th, 1919, and ending Feb. 19th, 1919). It is a common belief among English residents in India that some of these illusions are due to hypnotism; but, as a rule, only people who are capable of great concentration of mind, or who are in the habit of obeying commands are readily hypnotized, and then only by direct suggestion, and not, so say the best authorities, by will-power. Cases of hypnosis at a distance have been recorded; but the subjects had already been hypnotized by the operator; and, if these accounts should be proved veridical, telepathy might possibly explain them. The instance photographed by Lieut. F. W. Holmes, V.C., is a degenerate form of the trick. If a cinematograph record of a really fine exhibition of this illusion could be taken, probably the problem would be solved conclusively.

the boat-houses of the people—a teeming happy population, dressed in bright colours, and pelting one another in pure fun with oranges and lemons. Hang-chow had within its great encircling wall six towns, each guarded by walls. At Khaniku or Khanbalik (Pekin ?) he was present at the obsequies of a great dignitary, whom he believed to be the Tartar Emperor ; but that was not so, for the Emperor, who had ascended the throne 14 years before Batûta's arrival, reigned 21 years after his departure. But he certainly was present at the funeral of some great Tartar ; for his account of the interment of the Tartar dignitaries of China is confirmed by at least one other early traveller. He tells us of how the dead man's concubines and horses were buried with him, alive, in the same grave. He relates, not very correctly, the ceremonies observed at the court of the Emperor. Apparently his recollection becomes confused with that of the court-usage at Delhi and Yemen. In any case, it is possible that he only had an interview with some viceroy, concerning whom he was misinformed or somehow mistook him for the supreme Khân.

A revolt against Tartar rule took place about this time, so Batûta thought it prudent to leave China. He embarked on a junk which belonged to the King of Sumatra, whom he had visited on his way out, and " whose servants are Mohammedans." On the voyage the junk laboured through a terrific storm. The mirage of a big mountain was also seen. The sailors took this for the fabled roc, with which the *Arabian Nights Entertainment* made our Childhood acquainted.

He remained in Sumatra three months, the guest of the monarch who had before entertained him ; and was fortunate in witnessing the nuptials of the heir-apparent. First came dancers and merry minstrelsy ; then the bride, conducted from the apartments of the women by forty richly adorned ladies, who carried her train. For this high occasion, they had removed their veils. The bride went up on a platform; and the bridegroom rode up, in all the pride of armour, of a stately elephant, and of his own self-importance. One hundred youths of quality, beardless like himself, attended him on horseback. They were clad in white, their caps being a glitter of gold and jewels. Largess was scattered among the crowd. The prince now went up to his father, kissed his foot, and ascended the platform. Then the bride rose and kissed her groom's hand; he sat beside her, and he and she put betel and fawfel into one another's mouth. Then the covering of the platform was let down, and the whole structure, with bride and bridegroom on it, was carried into the palace. Finally, a feast was given to the crowd.

From Sumatra, Batûta voyaged in a junk to the Malabar coast of Southern India, and thence sailed to Arabian Zafar (A.D. 1347), both well-remembered places, coasted to Hormuz, wandered over the Two Iraks (Persia and Mesopotamia) once again; made across Asia Minor to Tadmor and as far north as Aleppo. At Damascus he got the first news of home he had received during his wanderings; his father had lain fourteen years in his quiet grave at Tangier. The Black Death was raging at Damascus. It slew twenty-four hundred of the inhabitants in a single day. So Batûta made his way to Egypt through Syria and Palestine, and went on to Mecca by way of the Red Sea and Jidda. This was the fourth of his pilgrimages. On his return to Cairo, he found the Black Death wasting the population. Mocking, lethal, invisible, this awful plague was rapidly sweeping westward and destroying whole families. Agnolo da Tura of Siena tells us that he had to bury five of his sons in the same grave with his own hands, and that his was no exceptional case. Batûta left Cairo for Jerusalem and returned from Palestine to Egypt by sea. He now felt a desire to see his native land again. He took ship to Sardinia, and, wishing to see the island, let the vessel he had voyaged in go to Tunis. He was lucky, for it was taken by

Christians. He managed to reach Tunis in another ship, and got to Fez overland on Nov. 8th, 1349; having been on his travels nearly a quarter of a century. He presented himself before the Sultan, and was received as was befitting so pious a pilgrim and distinguished a traveller.

CHAPTER IX

MOORS OF SPAIN AND NEGROES OF TIMBUKTU

But Batûta's travels were by no means at an end. He made a filial visit to the place where earth that "makes all sweet" had closed on his father's history. Once at Tangier, the temptation was strong to cross the Straits and visit the shrinking Moslem dominion in Spain. He landed where his compatriots had landed to conquer the Peninsula—at Gibraltar (Jabal Tarik, the Hill of Victory). He saw a cousin by his mother's side, who had settled here; ran all over Moorish Andalusia, visiting renowned cities that still remained in Mohammedan hands; and came to lordly Grenada, where the Alhambra must have been nearing its completion. He returned to Fez by way of Ceuta.

His energy was unabated; his thirst for travel unquenched; he could not settle down. In February, 1352, he is off again; this time for Central Africa. At Tafilelt, on the borders of Sahara, he meets another brother of the Sheik at Alexandria; and so another prophecy is fulfilled. In mid-Sahara, he finds an oasis with a "village on it where there is nothing good. The mosque and the houses are built of blocks of salt and are covered with camel hide. There is no tree, for the soil is pure sand; but there are mines of salt." He had dropped on those dwellings of rock-salt of which Herodotus wrote seventeen hundred years before him. But only the underlings of traders abode there; and dates and camel's flesh were their fare. Here was the salt-supply for the wild tribes of Sahara. They cut the blocks of it into a certain shape and used this as money. The caravan with which Batûta travelled suffered severely here from the vileness of the water.

When Tashala was reached, the caravan rested three

days to make ready for a vast and solitary tract of desert "where there is no water, nor is bird or tree to be seen, only sand and hills of sand, blown about by the wind in such wise that not the smallest vestige of a track remains. Wherefore, no one can travel without guides from among the traders; but of these there are many. The sunlight there is blinding. . . . Evil spirits have their will of that man who shall travel by himself. They enchant him, so that he wanders wide of his path, and there he comes to his end."

A long journey across this great waste of sand brought the caravan to another oasis, where pits had been dug to fill with water, and where negroes took care of a store of goods out in the open. These negroes did not show the deep respect due to the superior white race; but Batûta had a fancy to learn all about them, so he stayed on, and put up with their want of manners for two whole months. Traces, at least, of polyandry were to be found here; for a sister's son succeeded to property, and everybody took the name of a maternal uncle. The women were good looking, but, alas! they were far from shy; they did not even wear a veil, notwithstanding their accompanying the men to the mosque. Traders might take them for their wives; but must leave them behind on their departure. Our zealous Moslem, experienced in matrimony as he was and so excellent a judge of concubines—all of them sacred property and his very own—was greatly shocked at yet another instance of the freedom in manners of women and absence of jealousy in the husbands among certain Mohammedan peoples. A man might have a woman visit him, even with her husband there, and in the presence of his own wife; and a man might go home to find one of his male friends sitting alone with the wife of his bosom. But what would perturb an ordinary man causes no flutter in this degenerate breast. "He quietly takes a seat apart from them until the visitor goes away." Batûta's sense of delicacy was much offended when, calling on a former host of his, who was a judge moreover, he found that a handsome young woman had also made a call and was still there. He upbraided his friend roundly, and the only reply he got was that it was the custom of the country. This was too much : he broke with the judge.

A long, difficult, but quite safe journey brought him and three companions to Malli. Here he was seriously ill, and the sickness lasted many weeks; "but Allah brought me back to health." A few white people dwelt at Malli, of whom the judge was his host. "'Arise,'" said the judge to him one day when the Sultan had given a feast, "'the Sultan hath sent thee a gift.' I fully looked for a rich dress, some horses and other valuable gifts; and lo! there were but three crusts of bread, a piece of dried fish, and a dish of sour milk. I smiled at people so simple and the value they gave to such rubbish." Experience of spendthrift Oriental Courts and the lavish munificence of princes in other parts of the Mohammedan world had spoiled him for the simplicity of Central Africa. He often saw the Sultan after this incident; but sorely as his self-love was wounded by such a contrast to the honour always paid to him hitherto, he held himself in until his fury reached fever-heat and it became impossible to keep a bridle on his tongue any longer. Then he rose to his feet: "I have travelled the world over," said he; "I have visited the rulers thereof; I have stayed four months in thy dominions; but no gift, no suitable food has come to me from thee. What shall I say about thee when men shall question me concerning thee?" A horse and good provisions, and a supply of gold now came from this "greedy and worthless man"; before whom the negroes presented themselves in the worst of their beggarly garments, probably as a sign of their humility; for they "crawled to his presence, beating the ground with their elbows and throwing dust on their heads." However the "greedy and worthless" Sultan is allowed at least one small virtue: he kept the land in order; the traveller there had no fear of robbers, and if any one chanced to die, his property was handed over to his lawful successors. And the people had a great virtue also; they were constant in their attendance at the mosque; and if a son did not learn the whole of the Koran by heart, his father kept him shut up until he had done so. Yet, in spite of such praiseworthy piety, they let their little daughters and slaves whether male or female, go about quite naked. Batûta remarks that here cowries were used as coin. Travellers in the Niger District during the third decade of the last century found that many of the habits and customs described by Batûta still obtained there.

From Malli, our traveller journeyed on to the banks of the Niger, and saw, with surprise, its great herds of hippopotami. He visited Timbuktu, and believed he was journeying along the banks of the Nile; a pardonable mistake; for the Niger takes a general direction towards the North-East in this part of its course. He now returned to Fez by a different and more easterly route (A.D. 1355).

He had traversed the entire Mohammedan world, and beyond it to wherever a Mohammedan was to be found. He had visited several far-separated places several times, and had obeyed the obligation to visit Mecca oftener than the most zealous Moslem was wont to do. The Sultan commanded that an account of his travels should be recorded. The Sultan's Secretary edited the work, and thought to embellish a plain tale by overloading it with literary pinchbeck and by dragging in irrevelant quotations from the poets. The last words of the work are: "Here ends what I have put into form of the words of Sheik Ibn Abdulla Mohammed, whom may Allah honour! There is no reader of intelligence but must grant that this Sheik is the greatest traveller of our days; and should any one dub him the greatest traveller of all Islam, it were no lie."[1]

[1] A translation of an abbreviated copy of Batûta's travels was

Ibn Batûta was 51 at the end of his recorded journeyings. In spite of the racket of thirty years, spent in unceasing travel, of shipwreck and battle, of privation and fevers and much suffering of many kinds, all of which he brushes lightly aside as matter of small moment, his natural vigour remained such that he lived three years beyond the alloted span. The " fitful fever " of his life ceased in the year 1377.

made by the Revd. S. Lee, and published by the Oriental Translation Fund in 1829. Since that date the French advance in Algeria led to the discovery of several copiesof the unabridged work; and the " *Voyages d'Ibn Batoutah,*" translated into French by C. Defrémery and Dr. B. R. Sanguinette, with the original Arabic text under the translation, appeared in Paris in 1853, at the hands of the *Société Asiatique.* There are several examples of the original MS. extant, which slightly vary from each other, and often differ considerably from the abbreviation as to matter of fact.

IV.—LUDOVICO VARTHEMA OF BOLOGNA,

RENEGADE PILGRIM TO MECCA. FOREMOST OF ITALIAN TRAVELLERS.

CHAPTER I. THE GREAT AGE OF THE RENAISSANCE AND OF DISCOVERY.

By the close of the Fifteenth Century, the relative stability of society and of its convictions during the Middle Ages was undone. The Italian, at least, had cast off the restraints of that rigid and traditional world, and was in reaction against it. For, social bonds were loosened, and the corporate life of guild and city was in decay. With the revival of letters, society became imbued once again with the Greek and Roman conception of man as a progressive creature, and was awakened to the richness of thought and feeling to be enjoyed in vigorous passionate life. Self-sufficiency, self-assertion, and force of will were admired above all other qualities, and it was the ambition of most men to achieve them. Each man strove to fulfil his own nature in his own way. Religion rapidly degenerated into an indispensable observance of formalities, a traditional habit, a customary cloak. The rigorous men of the Renaissance sought to live fully, freely, and with diversity; they thirsted for new and refreshing springs; they quaffed delightful and refreshing draughts; they boldly winged their way to unfamiliar spheres, or gratified sense and passion to the full. The age was a-glow with all manner of ideality. On the whole its passions were unrestrained, save by prudence; unchecked by any moral curb, which it had counted foolishness. The religious rapture of Savonarola was an ephemeral phenomenon, and almost unique. Even in the gentle grace of Perugino's Madonnas and the sweet innocence with which he invests the Child, we may mark the substitution of religious affectation for religious sincerity. The age loved pomp and magnificence; and these appear in the frescoes of Pinturicchio. It was a field for the development of a deep-seated, incalculable, yet persuasive force of Will: the spirit is portrayed in the subtle eye and inscrutable smile of Monna Lisa.

It was when the Renaissance was in full flood, but before Ariosto, " with his tongue in his cheek," had achieved his cantoes of romantic chivalry; before Raphael plied his brush with too perfect and serene a finish; before Michael Angelo cast aside charm and beauty for the expression of strength and power, that the energy of the age found a new field for activity. The Turk swept the Ægean Sea and ruled the Western Roman Empire. But the great drama of History unfolds tragic irony surpassing the invention of poets. When the vast spaces of the great Church of Justinian rang with the shout of the victors, the knell of Moslem predominance sounded unheard. The Turk had captured the gateways of the East only to force the European, in adventures beyond the seas, to the domination of the world. Pioneers set out from Portugal and Spain, and tried to cut out the Moslem middleman; they steered to find a sea-way to the fabulous wealth of India. They coasted along amazing lands, peopled by strange races, and entered novel and unsuspected seas. Columbus found a new world beyond " wandering fields of barren foam "; Vasco di Gama was forcing his way round Africa. Many a narrow, ancient illusion was dispelled; and the minds of men were excited to a rapture of expectation. The hearts of pious Portuguese and Spaniards beat high at the hope of combining the salvation of heathen souls with the profitable enslavement of heathen bodies. All men were allured by the prospect of acquiring new markets, priceless gems, and the gold dust of El Dorado. The modern world of aggressive commerce was engendered in the very bosom of the High Renaissance.

CHAPTER II.—FROM VENICE TO DAMASCUS.

No commercial arithmetic called a certain Ludovico di Varthema to adventure. Like Dante's Ulysees, "nothing could quench his inward burning to have full witness of the world." "Ungifted," so he tells us, "with that far-casting wit for which the earth in not enough, and which ranges through the loftiest regions of the firmament with careful watch and survey; but possessed of slender parts merely," he fixed his mind on beholding with his own eyes some unknown part of the world and on marking "where places are, what is curious in their peoples, their different animals, and what fruit-bearing and scented trees grow there. . . . keeping before me that the thing which a single eye-witness may set forth shall outweigh what ten may declare on hearsay.' It is as if a cavalier of Boiardo or Ariosto had forsaken fairy land and sought novel adventure in the kingdom of knowledge. Varthema set out to see and know; and, although obviously a man of no great fortune, he would seem to have neglected remarkable opportunities of trading and growing rich.

That he was a Bolognese, we learn from the title-page of his volume—the *Itinerario.* As a citizen of Bologna, the Pope was his overlord; and we find him calling himself, by a pardonable license, a Roman. Whether eager curiosity was the only motive which impelled him to travel, we know not. He lets drop in the middle of his volume that he left a wife and children at home. Marriage in Italy was a matter of family arrangement, with a view to the increase of family wealth and power; and children could readily be left under the care of kinsmen. "The Italians make little difference between children and nephews or near kinsfolk," wrote Bacon, "but, so they be of the lump, they care not, though they pass not through their own body." And the family council has parental force in Italy, even to-day. The unsettled condition of every Italian State in the days of that "Most holy Lord the Pope Alexander Borgia," his crafty, treacherous son, and hardly less crafty and treacherous native statesmen and foreign invaders, often made swift change of residence highly desirable. Of that affectation of the men of the Renaissance—excessive and trumpeted desire of fame, which was a mere imitation of the classics,—there is not a trace in Varthema: he cared as little for bubbles as for baubles. Whatever other motives may have incited him, lust of travel was his predominant passion. What his occupation had been is unknown. On an occasion when it was helpful to him to pose as a physician he did so; and his close observation of the structure and habits of animals and the qualities of plants, suggests the kind of educative discipline which a physician would receive. But since he confesses to having ordered a cold astringent preparation when a warm laxative was required, his knowledge of physic was limited or readily forgotten. Again, since, on one occasion, he takes military service as a Mameluke; professes himself, on another occasion, to be an adept in the manufacture of mortars; and we find him fighting with the intrepidity and skill of a proved warrior against Arabs in India, he may very well have been a soldier before setting out on his travels. In that age of confusion, when the successes of the French in Lombardy broke the balance of power among the Italian States, there was ample opportunity of martial employment. There is not a trace of the accomplished haunter of courts, no love of literature or of art apparent in the *Itinerario.* Varthema's birth, upbringing, and "the fate of his bones" are secrets which lie securely hidden in the ruins of time. But his narrative endures—an imperishable monument. It reveals him as a true man of his period. His skill in dissembling, and his insensitiveness at the call of expediency to any obligation of truth or gratitude, contrast with his scrupulous pursuit of truth for its own sake and the accuracy of his observation. His record of travel is one which displays the coolness of his courage no less than its intrepid dash; it reveals a man constant of purpose, and endowed with ingenuity, resourcefulness, self-restraint, prudence, sagacity, and a sense of humour. Here indeed is a rare man!

In the year 1502 there was peace in the Levant. Lucrative trade between Venice and Egypt went on, unmolested by Turkish fleets. At the close of that year, Varthema took sail for Alexandria; the wind was favourable, and he reached the great port on one of the early days of 1503. Alexandria was the chief mart for the interchange of the wares of East and West, and therefore well known to Europeans; "Wherefore," says Varthema, "yearning after new things as a thirsty man doth for fresh water, I entered the Nile and arrived at Cairo." "Babylon," as Europeans called Cairo, was reputed to be one of the most marvellous of cities; but our traveller was disappointed to find it far smaller than he had thought. He declines to discuss the government established there, or the arrogance of its Mameluke rulers; "for my fellow-countrymen well wot of such matters." Close upon two centuries had passed since a Circassian slave clothed the Imam with a royal robe, usurped his mundane powers, reduced him to a nonentity, founded a dynasty, and ruled by military force from the Taurus and Euphrates to the Nile. This dynasty delegated authority to Emirs and Sheiks. It ruled by means of a soldiery, like itself, of slave origin, cruel, insolent and unbending. Children of Christian descent, brought mainly from the region which lies to the south of Caucasus, were instructed in the faith of the Moslem and trained to physical endurance, boldness, skill in warfare, and contempt of all men save their masters and themselves. These Mamelukes, as they were called, received liberal payment; they were allowed to keep a harem and to rear a family. The land lay crushed and impotent beneath this military caste. Military slaves, they exhibited the vices of slaves in office. As in the time of Ibn Batûta, the Sultan of Cairo ruled; but now ruled over delegates who were frequently rebellious to his authority; yet he and they and all, even to the terrible ottoman Turk at Constantinople, who now held Eastern Europe in bondage from the Danube to Cape Matapan, acknowledged the headship of the Imam at Cairo as legitimate Caliph of the great Abbaside line.

Leaving Cairo, Varthema took ship for Beyrout. Here, he saw nothing noteworthy, save the ruins of an ancient palace, " which, *so they say*," was once the residence of the princess whom St. George rescued from the dragon. We find a novel scepticism in this man of the new age. " So they say." is a phrase of frequent recurrence in the *Itinerario*. The sceptic's ears are as open as his brain is active; he repeats all the information given to him, however extavagant and however healthy his doubt; but he is careful to let the reader know that it is mere hearsay; he gives a hint of his own disbelief, and leaves the matter open to sane judgment: the piping times of a merchant in marvels have passed away. When Varthema has his own ends to serve, we shall find him telling a lie with as little scruple as any diplomatist of his generation; but he records faithfully and exactly what he went out to see and the incidents which befell him. We have the testimony of the precise Burton that " all things well considered, Ludovico [1]Bartema, for correctness of observation and readiness of wit, stands in the foremost rank of oriental travellers "; and that great authority writes thus although he only quotes from Richard Eden's imperfect and interpolated translation of a Latin deformation of the *Itinerario*; and probably knew of no other copy.

[1] B and V are to be found controvertible both in old Italian and in old Spanish. Bartema instead of Varthema is on the title page of more than one edition of the *Itinerario*.

Occasionally Varthema falls into a not uncommon blunder: he exaggerates numbers; but he is always hard-headed, incredulous of tradition, and not at all given to romancing.

A short voyage of two days brought our Italian from Beyrout to Tripoli, whence he took the caravan-route to Hamath, a large city on the Orontes, once an outpost of Judah, retaken by Israel in the wars between the two kingdoms. At Menin, a land of luscious fruits and the serviceable cotton-plant, he found a population of Christian-subjects of the Emir of Damascus and two beautiful churches, "said to have been built by Helena, mother of Constantine." He went on to Aleppo, and thence eight days of easy travel brought him to a city so ancient that its foundation is lost in unfathomed time. He writes of Damascus that "to set it forth is beyond my power." Here he remained some months, in order to learn Arabic—a task quite indispensable for farther travel in Mohammedan lands. He tells us of the fortress, built by a Florentine renegade, a man skilled in physic, who cured a Sultan suffering from the effects of poison, and is venerated as a holy man. This transformation of the physician into the saint may have suggested some serviceable play-acting in India, of which we shall become spectators later on.

The military Empire of Cairo was in decay, and had become very corrupt. A vivid picture is set before us of delegated despotism and its concomitants; greed graft, outrage and squeeze. Whenever a new Sultan succeeded to power, very large sums would be offered him for the rule of such a wealthy city as Damascus. Of course the gold would have to be wrung out of the resident merchants. If a good instalment of the promised "present" were not speedily forthcoming, the Sultan would find means to remove the dilatory Emir at the sword's point, "or in some other way; but, let him make the present aforesaid, and he shall retain his rule." "The traders of the city are not dealt with justly. The rulers vie with each other in oppressing them, by robbery or by dealing death. . . . The Moors are subject to the Mamelukes after the fashion of the lamb to the wolf. . . . The Sultan will send two missives to the governor of the citadel, one of which will command him to call together there such lords or traders as he may choose. And when they are gathered together in the citadel, the second letter is read to them, whereof that which is its purpose, is gotten without delay. Thus doth the lord aforesaid set about getting money." We are told of the curious way in which strict guard is enforced at the citadel: throughout the night at intervals each sentinel signals to his next neighbour by beating a drum; he who fails to pass on a responsive rat-tat has to spend a twelvemonth in prison.

Varthema found the houses dirty outside—(they are still built of a sort of cob), but the interiors splendid, with fountains and mosaics and carvings and columns of marble and porphyry. He visited the Great Mosque "where, so it is said," the head of St. Zechariah is kept; and was shown the exact spot where, "so it is given out," Saul, breathing out threatenings and slaughter, saw a great light and heard the voice of Jesus; also the house "where (so they say) Cain slew Abel, his brother."

"But let us now return to the liberty which the Mamelukes aforesaid enjoy in Damascus. . . . They go about in twos and threes, since it is counted for dishonour to go alone. And, should they chance to meet two or three ladies, license is granted to them, or they take it. They lie in wait for these ladies in certain great hostelries, which are called Khans; and, as ladies pass by the doorway each Mameluke will lay hold of the hand of one of them, draw her inside, and abuse her. The lady resists having her face seen; for women go about with face covered in such wise that while they know us, we do not know who they are. . . . And sometimes it chances that the Mamelukes, thinking to take some lord's daughter, take their own wives; a thing which happened whilst I was there. . . .

When Moor meeteth Mameluke, he must make obeisance and give place, or he is bastinadoed, even should he be the chief merchant of the city."

We are told that rich Christian traders in every kind of merchandise dwelt in Damascus, but were "ill-treated." Long-eared goats were brought up three flights of stairs to be milked for your meal. A detailed description is given of the productions of the city and the dress and customs of its people.

CHAPTER III

OVER THE DESERT TO MECCA

Now, the yearly caravan from Damascus to the Holy Cities of Arabia was in preparation—a journey which the pious Moslem makes by rail to-day. For, as has been truly remarked, "the unchanging East" is a venerable catchword : the Orient moves on, but slowly. No "unbelieving dog" might plant his foot on Arabian soil; no European Christian had ever seen its sacred fanes. Here was a golden opportunity for one "longing for novelty." Varthema had learned to speak Arabic. That insinuating smile, persuasive accent, and ingratiating address, so characteristically Italian, were surely his, for we find that he never fails to secure the firm friendship of utter strangers whenever he may require it—nay, he exerts some exceptional fascination on all men, some dæmonic force, as Goethe calls it. He says: "I formed a great friendship with the Captain of the Mamelukes" who were to accompany and protect the caravan. Doubtless, Varthema's look and bearing were martial; and, as has been said, he may have acquired experience in the Italian wars. To his credentials he added the persuasive argument of a bribe. His new friend accepted him as one of the escort. True, he must profess conversion to the Mohammedan Faith. This was no great strain on the conscience in days when Borgia and Julius della Rovere and the Medici sat in the chair of St. Peter, and when most Christians contented themselves with a half-sceptical observance of habitual forms. Like Henry of Navarre, Varthema thought an apple off another tree than his own a matter of small moment in the fulfilment of his purpose. He repeated the necessary formula and became a Moslem. He had to take a new name. Might it be because he was committed to an unparalleled adventure that he took the name of the son of Amittei? He called himself Jonah.

This bold step was worthy of the Italian Renaissance, when a man had thought it shame not to fashion his own life to his own ends; when he might brush weak scruples aside, and overcome obstacles as the oar turns the wave, converting hindrance into help. Behold our unflinching traveller mounted on a spirited steed, armed to the teeth; ready to encounter all chances of battle, desert-thirst, and unknown peril—one fulfilling old Malory's test: "he that is gentle will draw him unto gentle tatches."

The caravan, of pilgrims and merchants, women, children and slaves (about 40,000 souls) and 30,000 camels, was guarded by only 60 Mamelukes, 20 being in the van, 20 midmost, and 20 bringing up the rear. Damascus was left on April 8th 1503, and on the third day El Mezarib was reached, a place on the high land east of the Jordan and about 30 or 40 miles from it. Here the caravan rested 3 days to give the merchants time to buy Arabian steeds. Doughty, that intrepid English traveller and writer of unique English, tells us that, not many years ago, El Mezarib remained the appointed place for gathering up the pilgrim multitude. In Varthema's time the sheik of the district was both powerful and predatory. He is said to have owned 300,000 camels (50 times the number accorded to Job in the day of recompense), 40,000 horses and 10,000 mares. The number may be exaggerated; but the sheik was able to pounce down on the granaries of Egypt, Syria or Palestine when he was least expected—even believed to be a hundred miles away. "Truly, these folk do not run, but fly, swift as falcons; and they keep close together like a flock of starlings," Varthema tells us. Their fleet spirited Arabian mares would run a whole day and night without stopping, and be fresh again after a draught of camels' milk. He describes the marauding Arab very correctly as of dark complexion, small make, effeminate voice, and with long, stiff, black hair.

From El Mezarib, the caravan pursued its ancient course through Syrian and Arabian deserts; but more to the east than in later days. The scheme of travel was to march for about 20 hours; then to halt at a given signal and unload the camels; after resting for a day and night, a signal was again given, and, in a trice all was made ready, and cavalcade and "ships of the desert" were off again over rocky wastes and pathless seas of sand. Then as now, camels were fed on balls of barley-meal and watered every three days. Every eighth day, if no well was found, the ground was dug deeply for water, and the caravan halted a day or two. But it was invariably attacked by Bedouins when this happened. It was their amiable custom to lie in wait for the caravan and carry off women, children or any other unconsidered trifle which might fall within their grasp. Unhappy Joseph Pitts of Exeter (who was captured by Algerine pirates, professed Mohammedanism to escape cruelty, and accompanied his third master on a pilgrimage to Mecca in 1680) describes how, between Mecca and Medina, "the skulking thievish Arabs do much mischief to some of the Hagges (pilgrims to Meccah). For in the night-time they steal upon them . . . . loose a camel before and behind, and one of the thieves leads away the camel with the Hagge upon his back asleep." And, thirty years ago, Charles Montagu Doughty told us how the Bedouin youth would emulate Spartan boyhood and strain every power to rob a Hadji, for the glory of the feat.

There are many ruins to be found in Edom and Arabia Petrea. Like most men of sceptical turn, Varthema tempered a spirit of free enquiry with a little credulity. He saw distant rocks of red sandstone, fantastically shaped; they were "like blood on red wax mingled with soil." He was told that these were the ruins of the cities of the plain, and writes, probably from conviction, certainly with commendable prudence, seeing that he had posed as an apostate: "Verily, Holy Writ doth not lie, for one beholds how the cities perished by miracle of God. Of a truth, I believe from the witness of my own eyes that these men were evil; for all around the land is wholly dry and barren. The earth may bear no single thing, and of water there is none. . . . and, by a miracle the whole ruin is there to be seen even yet. That valley was full twenty miles long; and thirty-three of our company died there from thirst, and divers others, not being quite dead, were buried in the sand, their faces being left uncovered."

One day, when traversing what the Bible calls "the wilderness of Edom," "we came to a little mountain, and near to it was a cistern; whereat we were well pleased and encamped on the said hill. The next day, early in the morning, 24,000 Arabs rode up to us and demanded payment for their water"—a time-honoured exaction of the Bedouin Arab, which in our own days is said to have supported one third of Arabia.—"We refused, saying that the water was the gift of God. Thereupon they opened battle with us, saying that we had robbed them of their water. We set the camels as a protecting rampart all round us and put the merchants in the midst thereof and we stood siege during two nights and two days; and a constant skirmish went on. By that time both we and our foes had come to an end of our water. The mountain was wholly encompassed by Arabs, and they averred that they would break through our defence. Our leader, finding himself unable to hold on, took counsel with the Moslem traders; and we gave the Arabs 1,200 ducats of gold. But, when they had gotten the money, they said that not even 10,000 ducats of gold should be satisfaction for their water; whereby we perceived what they sought more than money. So our sagacious leader agreed with the caravan that all men capable of battle should not mount on their camels, but look to their arms. In the morning we put the whole caravan forward, and we Mamelukes stayed behind. We made a strength of 300 fighting men; and we had not to wait long for the fray. We lost but one man and one woman, and we killed 600 of them."

This statement evokes from a French author the ironic wit of his race: he thinks that the two who were slain may be pitied for their remarkably bad luck. Burton, who more than once accuses Varthema of exaggerating numbers, thinks that his statement here may confirm Strabo's account of Ælius Gallus having lost two soldiers only in a battle with 10,000 Arabs. We must not forget that the Arab's body was bare and wholly unprotected; he rode his steed bare-back, carried no fire-arms, and his only weapons were lance and bow. He attacked in dense formation. No wonder therefore that Arabs fell in masses as they came on, and that the carnage was still more terrible when they fled, helter-skelter "Come le rane innanzi alla nimica Biscia" as "frogs before their enemy the snake."[1] And the Mamelukes, few as they were, rode saddled steeds, were disciplined, protected by armour, possessed of fire-arms, and almost unerring of aim. Once Varthema saw one of the Mamelukes perform a feat which recalls the legend of William Tell: At a second attempt, he shot off from the bow a pomegranate poised on the head of a slave at a distance of about twelve or fifteen paces. And they were as expert horsemen as the Arabs. A Mameluke removed his saddle, put it on his head and replaced it while at full gallop.

Thirty days were spent in absolute desert, and the caravan was always attacked when it encamped by a water supply; but the only loss which the foe caused during about six weeks of journeying was in the big battle in which the man and woman were killed. A little later on and up to our own time, the water-cisterns were defended by fortifications. Leaving arid and rocky hills,

"Boundless and bare
The lone and level sands stretched far away."

[1] Dante, Inferno, ix, 76, 77.

"Through these," says Varthema, "we travelled five days and five nights. Now you should understand all about it. It is a great level stretch of white sand, fine as flour, and if by mischance the wind blow from the south, all may be reckoned as dead; even with the wind in our favour we could not see each other ten paces off. Wherefore there are wooden boxes set on the camels, and in these the travellers sleep and eat. The guides go on in front with compasses, even as if they were at sea. Many died here from thirst; and very many, having dug for water and found it, drank it until they burst; and here are mummies made."

It is interesting to know that, up to 1908, when the railway for the conveyance of pilgrims from Damascus to Mecca was completed, those of the richer sort still used the wooden protection which our author describes. Possibly the mummies of which he speaks were merely corpses dried in the sun; but the preservation of the dead body by embalming was a very ancient practice in these parts. Doughty found no actual mummies in the Nabatean temples; but he collected and brought back, from the funeral chambers at El Khreby, resinous matters of the same character as those found in Egyptian sarcophagi. Presently, Varthema shall see powders for the mummification of the dead sold outside the Mosque at Mecca. Dried human flesh was an important part of the stock in trade of an Arabian physician whom Burton came across. But faith in the efficacy of pulverised mummy has been by no means confined to Arabia. In the Seventeenth Century, Sir Thomas Browne, tells us in his "Urn Burial" that: "Mummy is become merchandise, Miriam cures wounds and Pharaoh is sold for Balsams"; and even within the last few years Harry de Wint found the repulsive drug on sale as a cure for cancer at Serajevo in Bosnia.

It so happened that the usual discomposing sounds, made by the movements of unstable sand-hills, broke the silence of the desert just where the Prophet had once stopped to pray. The superstitious Moslems must have been wholly dismayed and demoralized, for even the iron nerve of Varthema was strained; he tells us that he "passed on with great danger, and never thought to escape." At last, a thorn bush or two broke the monotony of this "sea of sand," and the travellers knew that Medina was now only three days off. Even more pleasing than the sight of vegetation to those pilgrims, who had "seen neither beast, bird, reptile, no, nor insect, for fifteen days," was the pair of turtledoves that lodged in the branches of the thorn bush. And, most delightful of all was the well of water which gave being to this miniature oasis. The water-skins were refilled; and, so copious was the supply that sixteen thousand camels were re-laden with the precious burden. Hard by, on a mountain, dwelt a curious colony, who depended on the well for their water. Varthema could see them in the far distance, "leaping about the rocks like wild goats." And one does not wonder at their excitement; for the cistern would not fill up again until the rains should come. Varthema learned that these people were Jews, who burned with hatred of all Mohammedans, probably not without very just cause. "If they catch a Moor, they flay him alive." They had the shrill voice of a woman, were swarthy, and went about naked. Probably their "nakedness" really amounted to their wearing a simple loose robe or a loin-cloth only. That they lived on goats' flesh is not remarkable; for it is the staple food of the Bedouin Arab. Probably they were of small stature; but Varthema dwarfs then into comicality: he gives them but five or six spans of height. But he only saw them from afar. That they were Jews is no fable. In spite of the general expulsion of Jews from Arabia with the first successes of Islam, the existence of a remnant of the Chosen People in this district has been well authenticated by Arabian writers; they were to be found there nearly three centuries after Varthema saw them, and towards the close of the past century Doughty heard tradition of them. By some accident Varthema, or more likely, his printer, places them between Medina and Mecca; but he came across them before he reached Medina. It is hard to account for their presence in this isolated and desolate district; and many are the explanations which have been offered, and varied are the legends which have grown up. Badger thought "that their immigration occurred after the devastation of Judea by the armies of Nebuchadnezzar, and that the colony was enlarged by successive bands of refugees down to the destruction of Jerusalem by Titus and the persecutions to which they were subjected under the Emperor Hadrian." Here is one of the many problems of History which are "beyond conjecture and hopeful expectation."

Two days after this event, the pilgrims came up to another cistern of water; they were now only four miles from Medina. Everyone thoroughly cleansed himself thereat from all the grime and sweat of the hot, dusty desert, and put on fresh linen, in order that he might present himself purified before the sepulchre of the Prophet on the morrow. All around, the land "lay barren and under the curse of God"; but, two stones' cast from the city there was a grove of date-trees and a refreshing conduit.

Our traveller found Medina to be but a poor place of about 300 hearths. Food was brought thither from Arabia Felix, Cairo and Ethiopia; first, to a port on the Red Sea, and thence overland by caravan—a journey which occupied four days. He found the inhabitants "scum"; a character which all travellers of all ages agree in giving them, and which they shared with the people of Rome and of all places whither pilgrims and the folk of many nations were wont to congregate. The Sunnites and Shiites there, the two great sects which divide the Moslem world "kill each other like beasts anent their heresies." And Varthema, the pretended proselyte, suddenly remembers that he is writing for a Christian world, and is careful to assure it of his own conviction that " these (beliefs) are false—all of them."

" One wished to see everything," he says, so the pilgrims passed three days at Medina, " Some guide took each pilgrim by the hand and led him to the place where Mohammed was buried." Varthema gives a description of the Mosque, than which, says Burton, nothing could be more correct. " It is surmounted," writes the English traveller, " by a large gilt crescent, springing from a series of globes. The glowing imagination of the Moslems crown this gem of the building with a pillar of heavenly light, which directs, from three days' distance, the pilgrim's steps towards El Medinah." Varthema avers that the marvellous light had a real matter of fact basis, being due to a cunning deception. Whether due to trickery, or to the suggestive efficacy of faith and expectant attention, the miracle once had a rival in the more ancient supernatural outburst, every Eastertide, of the holy fire at the altar of the Holy Sepulchre in Jerusalem. Neither Varthema nor his friend the Captain of the Mamelukes was a man easy to dupe, or given to the conjuring up of visions. " At the third hour of the night," we read, " ten or twelve greybeards came to our camp, which was pitched two stones' throw from the gate, crying, some here, some there, ' There is no God but God ! Mohammed is the Prophet of God ! O Prophet ! Do obeisance to God ! Do obeisance to the Prophet ! We implore forgiveness of sin.' Our captain and we ran out at this clamour ; for we thought the Arabs were on us to rob the caravan. We demanded why they were crying out ; for they made the same sort of din which may be heard among us Christians when a saint works a miracle." (Varthema cannot conceal his sceptical temper!) " These elders answered : ' Do ye not see the splendour coming forth from the tomb of the Prophet ? ' Our Captain replied that, for his part, he could see nothing, and asked us if anyone had seen anything; but we all said, 'No.' Then one of the old men demanded: 'Are you slaves?' Which is to say, Mamelukes. Our Captain replied, 'Yes, we are slaves.' To which the old man responded: 'O, sirs, it is not given to you to see these heavenly things; for you are not yet well grounded in the faith,'" Now, in the morning of the same day, the Captain had offered the Sherîf of the Mosque 3,000 ducats to see the body of the Prophet, telling him that he had neither father nor mother, brothers nor sisters, wife nor children, and had come thither to save his soul. Whereupon the Sherîf had fallen into a rage and demanded how he dared desire to behold him for whom God made the heavens and the earth. Since the body was entombed within closed-up, solid walls, such an audacious request marks the sceptical irreverence and haughty insolence of the Mameluke, even before one of the most sacred temples of Islam. The Mamaluke had declared himself ready to pluck out his own unholy eyes for love of the Prophet, if only he might see his body first. The Sherîf, probably in order to silence him, then said that Mohammed had been translated to Heaven by angels. So now, the Captain shouted contemptuously to the reverend greybeard who had told him that it was denied him to see the vision by reason of imperfect faith: 'You fool! Shall I give thee three thousand ducats? By God, I will not. You dog, son a dog!'.... The Captain thought that enough; and said so; and, turning round to his comrades, exclaimed: 'See where I wanted to throw away 3,000 seraphim!'" And he mulcted the Mosque by forbidding any of his men to visit it again.

Varthema dispels the popular belief that Mohammed's coffin was suspended in mid-air by the attraction of a magnet. "I tell you truth when I affirm that there is no coffin of iron or steel, or any loadstone, or any loadstone mountain within four miles."

The journey from Medina to Mecca was at this particular

time beset with more than usual difficulty and peril. The Hejaz was nominally a vassaldom of Cairo; really, it was under the almost absolute rule of its own despot; and we learn from Arabian Chroniclers that the despotism was being fought for by rival brethren. Indeed, throughout Eastern lands, war between sons for succession to the throne rendered vacant by the death of a father was the rule. And, in the long run, this bloody business usually ended in the success of the most capable competitor; so that, however horrible, it did not work out badly; for what can be more fatal to a weak, subservient people than an incompetent ruler? "There was a very great war," says Varthema, "one brother being against another; four brethren contended for the lordship of Mecca; so that we travelled for the space of ten days; and twice on our way we fought with 50,000 Arabs." Probably Varthema habitually over-estimated numbers; but there is no doubt that he had cause for alarm before he reached the second of the two sacred goals.

Our traveller descended one of the two passes cut through the hills which girdle and defend Mecca, and found himself in a "very famous, fair and well-peopled" city. The caravan from Cairo had arrived eight days before. Joseph Pitts, the Exeter sailor, also tells us how the "caravans do even jump all into Mecca together." "Verily," says Varthema, "never did I see such a multitude gathered together in one place as during the twenty days I stayed thereat." He writes us at some length, though not so minutely or correctly as Burckhardt, of the great house of Allah and of the Ka'abah within it—a building which conserves the form of the old heathen temple and which was a place of pilgrimage for ages before Mohammed; but this he did not know. He speaks of the sacred pigeons of the precincts; of the seven circuits made by the pilgrims; of the sacred well Zemzem, in whose brackish waters the Moslem cleanse themselves both spiritually and physically; for did not Hagar quench the dying

Ishmael's thirst therewith? of the sacrifice of sheep, and how the flesh was cooked over a fire made of camels' dung; of elaborate rituals; of the gift of what was superfluous in the feast to the many famished poor among the pilgrims; of the ascent to Arafat, where Gabriel taught Adam to erect an altar; and of that strange, ancient relic of heathen times, the casting of stones at the devil. But he says not one word of the "Black Stone" of the Ka'abah, once the fetish of ancient Arabian worship, and kissed to-day by the Hadji (pilgrim). We learn that Mecca, like Medina, was fed from Arabia Felix and Africa. It was a mart as well as a place of pilgrimage.

Now for a marvel. In an enclosure of the Mosque were two unicorns! They were presents from an Ethiopian monarch to the Sultan of Mecca as "the finest thing that could be found in the world . . . the richest treasure ever sent. "Now, I will tell you of their make," writes our author; "the elder is shaped like a colt of 30 months, and he has a horn on his forehead of about 3 arm lengths. The other is like a colt of one year, and his horn is the length of 3 hands. The colour is dark bay; the head like a hart's, but no long neck; a thin short mane hangs over one side; the legs are slender and lean, like a goat's; the foot, a little cloven, long, and much like a goat's, with some hair at the back of the legs. Truly, this monster must be a very fierce and rare animal."

Whatever our interpretation, this is no "traveller's tale" of Varthema's making. His painstaking veracity, except in the "practical politics" of life, has been confirmed a hundred times over. Later on in his book, we come across a description of the structure and habits of the elephant which is a triumph of sharp prose-vision and detailed matter of fact. One cannot doubt that he saw a beast at Mecca which resembled, not remotely, the Unicorn supporter of our Royal Coat of Arms. It is remarkable that Pliny describes a similar animal, and that Ctesias, Aristotle and Strabo speak of the Unicorn. The name occurs nine times in the Bible; but it is commonly supposed to refer to the Rhinoceros. Varthema's strange beast was a very different animal, aparently resembling the horse-like creature with a solitary central horn which Niebuhr found repeatedly sculptured on the ruins of Persepolis. Similar beasts have been reported from Abyssinia and Cape Colony; and at one time the unicorn was believed in India to inhabit that refuge of the rare, inaccessible Thibet. Yet a generation that is still with us regarded the gorillas and pygmy men of Hanno as Carthaginian fables, until Du Chaillu brought back carcasses of the one and Stanley gave authentic word of the other. But scientists leave us no hope that some happy traveller shall come across a unicorn dead or alive. For the stumpy protuberance of the rhinoceros is an epidermal tissue, and the true bony horns of the deer tribe are developments which grow from, or correspond to, two frontal bones; and it would be impossible for a bony outgrowth to proceed from the mesian line. Varthema's statement must be deemed by all who know anything of comparative anatomy to be incorrect. The great Owen thought that one of the two horns of the animal must have been broken off or remained undeveloped. Mr. Dollman, of South Kensington Museum, whose opinion the author sought through the kind agency of Mr. S. le Marchant Moore, thinks the creature was an onyx, with one of its horns suppressed and both gentlemen suggest "that Varthema saw the creature in profile, and having ascertained as well as he could under the circumstances, the existence of one horn, did not trouble himself much further about it: possibly the horn might have become more or less incurved." We must leave the question there, until someone shall give us ocular evidence that Varthema made not the slightest blunder: truly *his* "horn shall be exalted!"

Varthema had now been signally successful in gratifying the passion to penetrate unknown and mysterious regions which Spanish and Portuguese discovery had aroused in him. So far as is known, he was the first European Christian to reach the holy cities of Arabia ; and since his day no traveller ventured on the long and perilous route which he took. At least six Europeans managed to visit Mecca in the last century ; but they all took the short route from the Red Sea.

CHAPTER IV.

THE ESCAPE FROM THE CARAVAN

AND now, in the spirit of Alexander sighing for new worlds to conquer, he looked forward with dismay to the return-journey of the caravan. A perilous surprise awaited him which, with wonted adroitness, he turned to his purpose. "Having charge from my Captain to buy certain things, a Moor looked me in the face, knew me and asked me 'Where are you from ?' I answered : 'I am a Moslem.' His reply was : 'You lie.' 'By the head of the Prophet,' I said, 'I am a Moslem'; whereto he answered : 'Come to my house'; and I followed him thither. Then he spake to me in Italian, telling me whence I had come that he knew me to be no Moslem ; and that he had been in Genoa and Venice ; whereof he gave me proof. When I understood this, I told him that I was a Roman, and had become a Mameluke at Cairo (!) Whereat he rejoiced greatly, and treated me with much honour." Varthema now began to ask questions of his host ; craftily affecting ignorance of recent events and pretending to be very hostile to Christians and greatly indignant at hearing of the appearance of the Portuguese in Eastern Seas. "At this, he showed me yet greater honour, and told me everything, point by point. So, when I was well instructed, I said to him : 'O friend, I beseech you in the name of the Prophet to tell me of some way to escape from the Caravan ; for I would go to those who are the Christians' bitterest foes. Take my word that, if they knew what I can do, they would search me out, even as far as Mecca.' Then he : 'By the faith of our Prophet, tell me, what can you do ?' I replied that I was the most skilful artificer in large mortars in the world. Hearing this, he exclaimed : 'Mohammed be praised for ever, who has sent such an one to the Moslem and God.'"

Whereupon, a bargain was struck. The Moor was ready to hide Varthema in his house, if Varthema could induce the Captain of the Caravan to pass fifteen camels, laden with spices, duty free. Varthema was so confident of having thoroughly ingratiated himself with the Captain that he was ready to negotiate for the free passage of a hundred camels, if the Moor owned so many. "And, when he heard this, he was greatly pleased," and gave full information as to how to get to India. There was no difficulty about bribing the Captain ; and the day before the departure of the caravan, Varthema stole to the Moor's house and lay there in concealment.

Next morning, two hours before daybreak, bands of men, as was the usage, went through the city, sounding trumpets and other instruments, and proclaiming death to all Mamelukes who should not mount for the journey to Syria. "At this," says Varthema, "my breast was mightily troubled, and I pleaded with tears to the merchant's wife, and I besought God to save me." Soon he had the relief of knowing that the caravan was gone, and the Moorish merchant with it. He had left instructions with his wife to send Varthema on to Jidda, on the Red Sea, with the caravan returning to India. It was to start later than the Syrian caravan. Varthema was a man of winning ways, and he found no difficulty in fascinating man or woman. He was far from being as vain as, say, Lord Herbert of Cherbury, but, like that ingenuous gentleman, he does not neglect to inform us when he has pleased the fair. "I cannot tell how much kindness I received from this lady, and, in particular, from her niece of fifteen years. They promised to make me rich if I would stay on. But I declined their offer by reason of the pressing peril. I set out at noontide of the following day, with the caravan, to the no small sorrow of these ladies, who made much lament."

In due time the caravan arrived at Jidda, which was then a very important mart and harbour. Varthema immediately made for a mosque, with thousands of indigent pilgrims, and stayed there a whole fortnight.

"All day long, I lay on the ground, covered up in my garments, and groaning as if I suffered great pain in my bowels and body. The merchants would ask: 'Who is that, groaning so?' Whereto the poor people about me would reply: 'He is a poor Moslem who is dying.' But when night came I would leave the mosque to buy food. Judge of what my appetite became when I could only get food (and that bad) once a day."

When the caravan had left the port, he contrived to see the master of a ship bound for Persia who agreed to take him as a passenger; and on the seventeenth day of hiding at Jidda, the ship put forth on the Red Sea. To a true Moslem, the whole Eastern world as far as China was barely more perilous than the Mediterranean was to a Christian. Those were days when the seas teemed with pirates; but, on land, property was better safeguarded by the despotic rulers of Asia than it was in Europe. But the line between Eastern and Western traffic was rigidly drawn at certain marts of exchange. Such were Aleppo and Beyrout for commodities forwarded by way of the Persian Gulf; and still more important were Cairo and Alexandria, the marts of Mediterranean and Red Sea commerce. The Eastern trade was mainly in the hands of Arabs; but it was pursued by certain Greeks, Albanians and Circassians also, who, or their forefathers, had renounced Christianity for gain; and these were not few. Jidda and other ports of the Red Sea, as well as those of Somaliland, were crowded with ships, great and small, bearing spices, drugs, dyes and other Eastern goods for the markets of Western Asia and Europe. The Arabian coast of the Red Sea was hugged, and often, for days together, no progress could be made at night; for the multitude of rocks and sunken reefs rendered navigation perilous enough, even by day, and a look-out was always kept at the mast-head.

Varthema's ship visited and made some stay at several ports which are now decayed. At one place, "coming in sight of dwellings on the shore, fourteen of us landed to buy victuals. But they were the folk called Bedouin; there was more than a hundred of them to our fourteen; and they greeted us with slings and stones. We fought for about an hour; and then they fled, leaving twenty-four of their number lying slain on the ground; for they were unclad, and the sling was their only weapon. We took all we could find, that is to say fowls, calves, oxen and other things for eating. But, in two or three hours time, the turmoil increased, and so did the natives of the land—to more than six hundred, in fact—and we were compelled to draw back to our ships."

CHAPTER V. CERTAIN ADVENTURES IN ARABIA THE HAPPY.

On arriving at Aden ; which was a place of call for every ship trading with India, Persia, and Ethiopia, custom-house officers at once came on board the ship, ascertained whence and when it had sailed, the nature of its freight, and how many were on board. Then the masts, sails, rudders and anchors were removed to ensure the payment of dues. On the second day after Varthema's arrival, a passenger or sailor on board called him a "Christian dog, son of a dog," the usual polished address of the proud Moslem to one who, albeit a co-believer, had not the good fortune to be born in the faith. This exclamation aroused a suspicion that he was a spy; for, a year before, Portuguese had appeared for the first time in the Arabian Sea, had captured certain vessels, and killed many of their crews. He was seized at once and violently carried off to the deputy of the Sultan of Yemen. Now this Sultan was an unusually merciful man, who rarely (Varthema says never) put anyone to death ; so he was merely clapped into gaol, and his legs fettered with eighteen pounds weight of iron. On the third day of imprisonment, some Moslem sailors who had escaped in the warfare with the Portuguese, attacked the prison with the intention of slaying him ; and the inhabitants were divided as to what they should do. The Emir's deputy decided to spare the prisoners (another suspected person would seem to have been incarcerated with Varthema) ; and they languished sixty-five days in gaol. Then a message came from the Sultan, demanding that they should be brought before himself. So, instead of voyaging to Persia, Varthema, still in irons, was put on a camel and taken an eight days' journey inland to Radâä. Ibn Abd-el Wahâb, Sultan of Yemen, was busy marshalling a large army. In it, were three thousand horsemen, born of Christian parents, but sold, while still children, by "Prester John," as the Portuguese called the King of Abyssinia. These slaves formed the bodyguard of the Sultan. At this moment the rule of Yemen was disputed among petty despots, and the Sultan was bent on reducing the turbulent, rebellious tribes to his sole sway.

Varthema is brought in to the Sultan's presence; his life hangs on a hair; it is as if the sharp edge of the scimitar were already at his neck; yet he does not lose his presence of mind. "I am of the country of Rûm, my lord," he began; and he began with a "parliamentary expression" for, to an Arab, Rûm meant Asia Minor, recently the possession of *New* Rome, *i.e.*, of the Byzantine Empire. "I became a Mohammedan at Cairo (another trifling inexactitude). I came to Medina of the Prophet, to Mecca, and then to your country. Everyone says, sir, that you are a sheik" (a Mohammedan priest) "Sir, I am your slave. Sir, do you not know that I am a Moslem?" The Sultan called upon him to repeat the formula: "'There is no God but the God: Mohammed is the Prophet of God.' But, whether it was the will of God, or by reason of fear which gat hold of me, I could not pronounce these words." Our hero was indeed lucky, for the merciful Sultan only ordered him to be taken to prison and kept there under strict guard while he should be away. For he was about to attack Sanäa, the ancient capital of Yemen, And so, "they guarded me for three months, supplying me with a loaf of millet each morning, and another in the evening; yet six such loaves had not satisfied my hunger for a single day; nevertheless, if I might have had my fill of water, I had thought myself happy."

In the East, the body of an insane person is believed to be occupied by some spirit; and mad folk are therefore treated as irresponsible. Varthema knew this, and he, two fellow-prisoners, one of whom he twice speaks of as "my companion," and yet another, "a Moor," arranged that one of the number should pretend to be mad in order to help the others. The trick is time-honoured in the East; thereby David escaped the hands of Achish, King of Gath. Lots were cast, and the lot fell to Varthema. We can see him, like the Israelite King, "changing his behaviour, scrabbling at the doors of the gate, and letting the spittle fall down upon his beard"; he was allowed to go out, crowds of children following him and shying stones at him. In self-defence he had to store up a plentiful supply of like missiles in his garment and give a sharp return. "Truly," says he, "I never was so tired with labour and worn out as during the first three days of my feigning."

Now, the prison adjoined the palace; and there remained in the palace one of the Sultan's three wives with her "twelve or thirteen very comely maidens, rather more than inclining to black. This queen" (so Varthema dubs her) "was very tender-hearted to me. She was for ever at her lattice with her damsels, staying there throughout the day to see me and to talk with me; and I, while many men and merchants were jeering at me, went naked before the queen; for she took very great pleasure in seeing me. I might not go from her sight; and she gave me right good food to eat; so that I gained my point."

One of the most striking characteristics of the men of the Renaissance is the combination of great intellectual power and lofty enthusiasm with mediæval brutality. Now, the Sultana, in whose veins the warm blood of the East flowed freely, suffered from the dull monotony of the harem. She wanted excitement. She suggested to the supposed madman that he should slay and spare not; for the fault would not be imputed to him. He took the hint at once. He called on a fat sheep to declare its religion, repeating the very words which the Sultan had addressed to him: "Prove yourself a Moslem." "The patient beast making no reply, I took a staff and brake its legs. The queen looked on laughing, and fed me with the flesh thereof during three days; nor do I remember to have eaten better. Three days later, I killed an ass, which was bringing water to the palace, in the same way; because that he would not become a Moslem. And, in like manner, I cudgelled a Jew, so that I left him for dead." One of the gaolers, whom he declares to have been more mad than he, called him "Christian dog, son of a dog." This was enough: a fierce battle by lapidation began—Varthema alone, on the one side; the gaoler and children on the other. Varthema allowed himself to be badly hit by two stones, "which I could have avoided easily; but I wanted to give colour to my madness. So I went back to my prison, and blocked the door up with large stones, and there I lived for the space of two days without meat or drink. The queen and others thought I might be dead, and caused the door to be broken open. Then these dogs brought me pieces of marble saying, 'eat; this is sugar;' and others gave me grapes filled with earth, and called it salt; but I ate the marble and grapes and everything, all mixed up."

It was an enlightened custom in Mohammedan countries to examine into the mental condition of insane people at regular intervals. Rabbi Benjamin of Tudela, the Spanish Jew, tells us that, in the sixth decade of the Twelfth Century, he found Commissioners in lunacy at Baghdad; although he also speaks of that barbarous practice of chaining the madman which obtained in England until some centuries later. Two Mohammedan Ascetics, who dwelt in the mountains as hermits, were brought to the prison to determine whether Varthema might be a person bereft of mere mundane reason through his exceptional sanctity, or only ordinarily mad. The hermits took opposite views on this knotty question, and spent an hour in violently contradicting one another. The prisoner lost all patience and, anxious to be quit of them, put a stop to the discussion by the simple device which Gulliver employed to extinguish the conflagration at Lilliput. "Whereupon," says he, "they ran off crying 'he is mad; he is no saint.' The queen and her maidens saw all this, for they were looking on from their casement, and burst into laughter, vowing that 'by God, by the head of the Prophet, there is no one in the world like this man.'"

Next day Varthema followed this up by laying hold of the gaoler by those two horns or tufts of hair which were then, as now, fashionable in Arabia, kneeling on his stomach, and so belabouring him that he "left him for dead," like the Jew. The queen was again vastly entertained, and called out: "Kill those beasts."

But it was discovered that, all this time, Varthema's fellow-prisoners had been digging a hole through the prison-wall, and, moreover, had contrived to get free from their shackles. The Sultan's deputy was fully aware of the favour with which the Sultana regarded Varthema; and the lady knew him to be ready to carry out her commands. She ordered the prisoner to be kept in irons, but to be removed into a doorless lower chamber of the palace, and to be provided with a good bed, good food and perfumed baths. For, as the reader will guess, she had fallen in love with the captive. Sexual love among Arabians is anything but a refined or spiritual passion; and the harem has not been found precisely a temple of chastity anywhere,—mainly, perhaps, because it is a harem. And this lady possessed a temperament as sanguine and scandalous as any Messalina or Faustina or Empress of all the Russias. Alas! Fate doomed her to bloom unseen in Arabia, and waste her sweetness on its desert air. At the end of a few days, she started by bringing Varthema some dainty dish in the dead of night. He tells us how, "coming into my chamber, she called 'Jonah! Come. Are you hungry?' 'Yes, by Allah!' I replied; and I rose to my feet and went to her in my shirt. And she said: 'No, no, not with your shirt on.'

I answered: 'O Lady, I am not mad now'; whereto she: 'By Allah, I know you never were mad. In the world there is no man like you.' So, to please her, I took off my shirt, holding it before me for the sake of decency; and thus did she keep me for a space of two hours, gazing at me as if I had been a nymph, and making her plaint to God in this wise: 'O Allah! Thou hast made this man white as the sun. Me, Thou hast made black. O Allah! O Prophet! my husband is black; my son is black; this man is white. Would that this man might become my husband! And while speaking thus, she wept and sighed continuously, and kept passing her hands over me all the time, and promising that she would make the Sultan remove my irons when he returned.

"Next night the queen came with two of her damsels, and said, 'Come hither, Jonah.' I replied that I would come. 'Would you like me to come and stay a little while with you,' she asked. I answered, 'no, lady. I am in chains; and that is enough. Then she said, 'Have no fear. I take it all on my own head. If you do not want me, I will call Gazelle, or Tajiah, or Gulzerana to come instead. She spoke thus because she was working to come herself. But I never gave way; for I had thought it all out."

Varthema had no desire to remain in Yemen, even should he mount its throne,—a far less likely event than discovery and a horrible death. "I did not wish to lose both my soul and my body," he writes. "I wept all night, commending myself to God.

"Three days after this the Sultan returned, and straightway the queen sent to tell me that, if I would stay with her, she would make me rich."

Sufficient unto the day is the evil thereof. Varthema is the man to mould circumstances to his will: no web, however cunningly woven shall hold him prisoner; his keen wit is ready to comply with the Sultana's request, if she will have his fetters struck off.

The lady fell into the trap. She manifests the clever, feminine guile of the harem in her dealings with Ibn Abd-el-Wahâb, but she is no match for Varthema. The Sultan is a strong man and a mighty man of valour; but he is uxorious, and as wax in her hands. She ordered the prisoner to be brought at once before the Sultan and herself. Ibn Abd-el-Wahâb, good easy man, asked Varthema whither he desired to go if he should choose to release him. The mendacious Italian replied: "'O Lord, I have neither father nor mother; wife nor child; brother nor sister; only Allah, the Prophet, and you. You give me food, and I am your slave.' And I wept without ceasing." Then the artful Sultana reminded the Sultan that he would have to account to God, of whose anger he should beware, for having kept an innocent man so long time in prison. Abd-el-Wahâb proved as unsuspicious and benevolent as history declares him to have been; yet he was as firm and able as a ruler as he was bold and experienced in arms. His Sultana knew how to play on his merits and convert them into defects. He at once granted Varthema liberty to go whithersoever he chose. "And, immediately, he had my irons struck off; and I knelt before him; and kissed his feet and the hands of the queen. She took me by the hand, saying: 'Come with me, poor wight, for I know thou art dying of hunger.' When I was with her in her chamber, she kissed me more than a hundred times; and then she gave me excellent food. But I had seen her speak privily to the Sultan, and I thought she had begged me from him for a slave. Wherefore, I said: 'I will not eat, unless you promise me my freedom.' She replied: 'Be silent, madman. You know not what Allah will bestow. If you are good, you shall be an Emir.' Now, I knew what kind of lordship she desired to bestow on me; so I answered that she should let me get into fitter condition; for fear filled me with other than amorous thoughts. She replied: 'By Allah, you say well. I will give you eggs, fowls, pigeons, pepper, cinnamon, cloves and cocoa-nuts every day.'[1] So, at these good words and promises, I plucked up heart a bit. To restore me to health, I stayed fifteen or twenty days in the palace. One day, she sent for me and asked if I would go a-hunting with her ; which offer I refused not ; and, at our return, feigned me to fall sick by reason of weakness ; and so continued for the space of eight days ; during which time she was unceasing in sending persons to visit me. One day, I sent to tell her that I had vowed to God and Mohammed to visit a holy man at Aden, who was reputed to work miracles."

We may not count meanness among the *petits défauts* of this lady of spacious passions. She was " well pleased " with Varthema's suggestion, and provided him with a camel and twenty-five golden ducats—a sum which would go a long way in Arabia. We shall see presently to what use he applied it. Eight days' journeying brought him to the holy man of Aden ; and the second day after his arrival, he professed that he was cured. He wrote to the Sultana that, since Allah had been so merciful, he wished to see the whole of her kingdom. " This I did because the fleet which was there could not set sail again for a month. I spoke with a skipper in secret, and told him I wished to go to India, and would give him a handsome present if he would take me. He replied that he wished to touch at Persia first." Nothing better could have fallen in with Varthema's wishes. Meanwhile he would explore Arabia Felix.

So, having adroitly contrived to reject the love of the Light of the Harem without exciting her fury, and even coming by her purse, he turns the opportune gift to account, and fills up the month of waiting by a zig-zag camel-ride through Southern Yemen—the first and boldest European traveller in the district, and the one who has penetrated

[1] Varthema gives all the words of the queen in Arabic, phonetically written, followed by a rendering in Italian. He had learned to speak Arabic, none too perfectly, but not to write it.

it must thoroughly. With the intention of doing this in his mind, he ends his chapters on "How the women of Arabia Felix are partial to White Men," and on "The liberalty of the Queen."

His record of Southern Yemen bears witness to a shrewd observant eye and a tenacious memory. Probably he travelled mostly with caravans. He gives an account of the natural features of the land, its curious domesticated animals, its wild beasts, its vegetable productions, its trade, the colour, manners and dress of its strange natives—all borne out by a variety of independent testimony. He visited many cities. One, he found barbarous and poor; another, renowned for its attar of roses. Several of these towns were flourishing centres of trade. He even got to Sanäa, the walls whereof were so wide that "eight horses might go abreast on the top of them." Apparently Abd-el-Wahâb had not yet conquered the petty chieftain, El Mansûr, who reigned there; so Varthema found himself in the domain of the Sultan's bitter foe. We hear that rumour gave this ruler a mad son who would bite, and slay, and then feed on his human victims. Varthema again tells us of other madmen, Shiites and Sunnites, the rival sects of the Mohammedan world, who kill each other like dogs for Religion's sake. At Yerim, he talked with many who asserted that they had reached their hundred and twenty-fifth year; but, since there was no registration of birth, we may venture to entertain our doubts. He tells us how it was the fashion throughout Arabia to twist the hair into horns, and how the women wore loose trousers. He came to El-Makrana, where "the Sultan keeps more gold than a hundred camels might bear; and I say this because I have seen it." What became of that mighty bulk of gold? The Arabian chroniclers tell us the firm, merciful and increasing rule of Abd-el-Wahâb in Yemen had a tragic end: Turkish invaders captured him and put him to death, not in the heat of warfare, but in cold blood.

Varthema "ran some risk from the multitude of apes" (of which Niebuhr also speaks), and from "animals like lions (hyenas?). We passed on in very great danger from the said animals, and with no little hunting of them. However, we killed very many with bows and slings and dogs; and thereby passed in safety."

On reaching Aden he repeated the trick which had proved so successful at Jidda. "I took shelter in a mosque," he says, "feigning to be sick, and there I lurked all day long; but, at night, I went forth to find the skipper of the ship; and he smuggled me aboard."

CHAPTER VI. EASTWARD HO!

For six days the wind was favourable; but it was now December of the year 1503; and on the seventh day out, the North Eastern monsoon drove the vessel back "with 25 others, laden with madder for the dying of clothes. By dint of very great labour, we made the port of Zeila" (on the African Coast, opposite to Aden); "and tarried there five days both to see it and to wait for better weather." Zeila was a great place for traffic in gold and ivory, the law was well administered; but the cruel slave-trade prevailed there then as, in a different form, it did up to our own times. The Christian dominions of Abyssinian "Prester John" were raided by Arabs; his subjects captured; and sold in Egypt, Arabia, Persia and India. The merchants here would seem to have found a profitable trade in beasts left with but a single horn; for Varthema saw some, which, however, were quite different from those wonderful unicorns at Mecca. He gives a faithful description of the black and white Berbera sheep of Zeila.

The weather having improved, the ship touched at Berbera, and then sailed up the Gulf of Aden and across the Arabian Sea. Twelve days saw her at Diu, an island to the south of the Indian Peninsula of Kathiawar and subject to the Sultan of Gujarat. Varthema calls it the "port of the Turks"; but by Turks we must understand Mohammedan inhabitants of the Levant who had settled at Diu. It was an important halt for ships trading between India and Arabia and Persia. The vessel which bore Varthema must have been a tramp, picking up what cargo offered, and altering her course from time to time, to dispose of it; for, after spending two days at Diu, we find her taking a three days run up the Gulf of Cambay to Gogo, a place "of great traffic, fat, and rich; where all are Mohammedans." She now recrossed the ocean to Eastern Arabia, and put in at Julfar, on the shores of

Oman. Once again she reversed her course ; and a favourable wind bore her to Muscat, a port which is still of some importance, and which, at that time, was one of the small independent States of Arabia. Then she tacked back, and came to New Ormuz, a port on the island of Jeruan.

Old Ormuz was a city on the mainland, which Marco Polo visited in the eighth decade of the Thirteenth Century, but, shortly after his time, almost all the population deserted the old city for the island. As in the days of Ibn Batûta it was famous for its pearl-fisheries. "Here," writes Varthema, "are found the largest pearls in the world"; and hence it is that Milton couples the wealth of Ormuz with that of India.[1] "At three days' voyage from this island, fishers pay out ropes, one from either end of their little boats. To each rope, a big stone is tied, so as to keep the boat moored ; and they pay out yet another rope to the bottom, with a stone to it, from the middle of the boat, whereby one of these fishermen, having hung two bags round his neck and tied a big stone to his feet, goes down fifteen paces into the water, and stays there as long as he is able, to find those oysters wherein are pearls. These he puts into the bag, and gets quit of the stone at his feet, and comes up by one of the ropes aforesaid." The pearl-diver is not given the wholly impossible time under water which Ibn Batûta credited him with. With customary caution our Italian is content to say that he "stays there as long as he is able."

This trade and the city of Ormuz were in the hands of Arabs, who paid tribute to the King of Persia, and were dependent for food on the mainland. Ormuz was one of the great centres along that trade-route between the East and the Levant, which traversed the Persian Gulf,

[1] "High on a throne of royal state, which far
Outshone the wealth of Ormus and of Ind,
Or where the gorgeous East with richest hand
Showers on her kings barbaric pearl and gold,
Satan exalted sat." —*Paradise Lost*, ii. 1–5.

and made its way by Bagdad, and the Euphrates Valley and Aleppo to the Mediterranean; just as Aden was one of the great centres of the other route through the Red Sea and Egypt to Cairo and Alexandria. Our traveller would pass along streets crowded with men from many nations.

From Ormuz comes a tale of cold-blooded parricide, fratricide, and subtle perfidy very characteristic of the dynastic families of Asia. "At the time when I visited this land, there happened that which you shall hear." The Sultan of Ormuz had eleven sons, of whom the youngest was judged to lack half his wits, and the eldest was, beyond doubt, "a devil unchained." This Sultan had purchased two Abyssinian children, and brought them up as carefully as if they had been his own sons; for it was a practice in Arabia and India to rely on the valour and sagacity of Abyssinian slaves, to entrust them with the most important military commands, and to consult them as closest advisers. One of these men was named Caim; the other Mohammed. One night, when, all was dark and silent in the palace, that "devil unchained," the eldest son found an opportunity to put out the eyes of his father, his mother and all his brethren excepting those of his youngest brother; for he supposed him to be incapable of aspiring to the throne. Not satisfied with blinding his victims, he caused them to be burned alive within the palace-enclosure. Next morning he proclaimed himself Sultan; and the supposed fool fled to a mosque; for the rights of sanctuary were to be found there, if anywhere. At first, the city was in tumult; but the bloody deed was over and done with; and a city of trade is soon glad to quiet down and resume business. The problem now before the new Sultan was: how to get rid of Caim and Mohammed. Both men were in high position: that were a small matter; but they held command of fortresses. Somehow, he managed to get Mohammed to venture into his presence, and, after making much of him, breathed into his ear that, if he would slay Caim, he should be rewarded with the command of five fortresses. Mohammed protested: "'O Sidi, I have shared bread with him from our childhood; for thirty years. By Allah, I cannot bring my mind to do this thing.' Then said the Sultan: 'Well, let it alone.'" Having failed in the attempt to induce Mohammed to murder Caim, the Sultan now tried to induce Caim to murder Mohammed. Caim made not the least demur, and straightway sought out his old friend and companion. Mohammed at once read what had happened written in the face of his false friend, and charged him with the fact. Caim, guilt-stricken, cast his dagger at the feet of Mohammed, fell on his knees, and implored forgiveness of the meditated crime. Mohammed reproached Caim in the mildest way, and then either from magnanimity or from policy, or from both, he passed over his treachery; but made him vow to go to the Sultan and pretend that he had done the deed.

"When the Sultan saw him, he demanded: 'Hast thou slain thy friend?' Caim answered: 'I have, Sidi, by Allah!' Then the Sultan: 'Come here'; and Caim went close up to him; whereupon, the Sultan seized him and did him to death with his dagger." Three days passed, and then Mohammed stole stealthily into the Sultan's chamber, "who, when he saw him, was greatly perturbed, and exclaimed: 'O dog, son of a dog, are thou still alive?' Mohammed replied 'Yea, I live, in spite of thee, and thee will I slay, thou worse than dog or devil! Both men being armed, they fought together for a space of time; but in the end, Mohammed killed the Sultan, and put the palace into a state of defence. But, because he was much beloved, the populace ran thither with shouts of 'Long live Sultan Mohammed.'"

Mohammed was a man as prudent and experienced as he was ready and resolute: he saw a way to do the state good service and to preserve for himself the reality of power while maintaining the shows of legality and removing the occasions of envy. At the end of twenty days, he call the chief citizens together, "and spake to them in this wise: That what he had done had been of strong necessity; that he knew he had no right to the throne; and that he begged them to allow him to transfer his power to the son who was supposed to be crazy. And thus the son became Sultan; but, nevertheless Mohammed rules. The whole city said, 'of a surety, this man is the friend of Allah.' For which reason, he was made Governor of the City and of the Sultan; the Sultan being in the state aforesaid."

A very narrow little strait lies between Ormuz and the mainland of Persia. Varthema left his "tramp," and crossed over. His itinerary through the ancient and renowned Empire is by no means clear; but we find him at Herat, 600 miles in a bee-line from Ormuz, and at that time the capital of Khôrasân and the residence of its able ruler—Sultan Hosein Mirza, a man who boasted his descent from Timour the Tartar. Varthema speaks of Herat as being a great market for stuffs, especially silk stuffs, and for rhubarb. Badger, commenting on this statement, suggests that Herat lay on the direct route along which rhubarb was conveyed between Thibet, Mongolia, and the West. Certainly exports and imports of Persia, India, Turkestan and Afghanistan passed through Herat.

It strikes one as singular that, although Varthema would seem to have journeyed some 1,500 miles in Persia, he says very little about the country. This may be because the Venetians were directly acquainted with that fascinating Empire; and consequent on this, a general knowledge of it would spread throughout Italy. For, when the great blow was struck at Venetian trade by the Turkish capture of Constantinople and Negroponte, and the "Queen of the Adriatic" no longer held "the gorgeous East in fee," she sent three separate embassies on a bold and perilous mission. She sought to secure the alliance of Persia against their common foe, the Ottoman Turk. Few records of travel and adventure are more animating or fuller of interest than those of the Venetian Ambassadors, Barbaro and Contarini.[1] Varthema must have made a bold journey. The "Adventures of Hadji Baba of Ispahan" probably furnish as true and vivid a picture of what life and travel in Persia were like in the early years of the sixteenth century as they do of that which was to be experienced in the early years of the nineteenth century, Persia has remained in the same case of what may be called immutable instability from the days when she was won for Islam down to the days of the immortal Morier and to our own times.

From Herat, he took the caravan-route back to Shiraz in Persia, a journey of fully 700 miles. Here was a great mart for the turquoises, rubies and other jewels of Khôrasân and Badakshan, as well as for musk and ultramarine; and he learned something of the business capacity of the Persian; he complains that "our musk"—that delight, with other overpowering scents of his nation and time—"is adulterated by these folk, who are master-hands for intellect, and misleaders beyond all other peoples."

It is a problem how Varthema contrived to cover such vast distances on what was probably a lean purse. He is silent as to his financial resources; as we have said it is unlikely that his private means were considerable, and it would seem that he did not trade. As a Mameluke he would receive payment which carried him to Aden; and the money which the enamoured Sultana furnished him with would partly, if not wholly, give him the means to reach Persia. But he employed his infinite power to charm; he was burthened with no weak scruple as to blinding a newly-captured friend and using him, with

[1] Giosafat Barbaro & A. Contarini. Travels to Tana and Persia. Tr. by W. Thomas, Clerk of the Council to Edward VI., and by S. A. Roy. 8o. 1873.

wise moderation, in the service of that central purpose which was the heart of all his being. And thus, as we shall presently see, like Iago, he made his fool his purse. But he is capable of appreciating the good qualities of the generous friend whom he made his dupe; and is careful to pay tribute to him. If he must deceive in order to use him, it is to realize his purpose of seeing the world at first-hand and recording its wonders.

After remarking on the tricks of Persian traders, he adds: "Yet I must also say they are the best companions and the most generous among men. I speak thus with knowledge; having had experience of a Persian merchant of Herat in Khôrasân, whom I met in this city of Shiraz. He had known me at Mecca two years before, and spoke to me thus: 'Jonah, what is your business here? Are you not the same man who went to Mecca some time back?' I replied that I was, and that to find out about the world was the quest I was on. Then said he: 'Allah be praised! for I shall have a companion to make discovery with me. Do not leave me.' We stayed on fifteen days in this same city of Shiraz." Varthema's magnetic charm was at work; and luck stood his friend in bringing him across this old acquaintance.

The twain set off together from Shiraz, bound for Samarkand in Turkestan; for the merchant, whose name was Cazazionor, insisted on keeping Varthema with him, and presumably payed all expenses. But they travelled through a land in turmoil. The struggle between the Ottoman Turks established in Europe and the Turcoman dynasty of the White Sheep established in Persia was happy indeed for the Christian world, since it diverted the forces of Constantinople to the East at a time when Europe lay divided and helpless, but it was disastrous for Persia and ended by throwing her into confusion. Just now Ismail-es-Sufi, a descendant from the Prophet, who had overthrown the forces of Bayazid, and laid the foundations of a great Persian dynasty, which endured more than two centuries, was consolidating a country which had been torn by internecine strife. As is so often the case, religious differences afforded the trumpet-call to the struggles of peoples. As in the days of Ibn Batûta the Sunnites of the West fought the Shiites of the East for domination ; but they fought in the name of Allah and under the banners of sectarian difference. In order to seat himself firmly on the throne, the Great Sofi, for so Europeans called the monarch of the new, able and powerful dynasty roused the enthusiasm of the native Shiites, and converted the less numerous native Sunnites to his own true faith by blood and iron. Varthema tells us that the Sofi was passing through the land with flame and slaughter.

Cazazionor, finding the country so disturbed, thought it wise to return towards Herat. So delighted was he with the personality and society of "Jonah" that he offered to give him his niece to wife. She was a beautiful girl named Sharus, a feminine noun in Persian as in other languages, although it signifies The Sun. Cazazionor took Varthema with him to his own home ; which was probably at Shiraz ; and presented the young lady to him. She could not have attained womanhood ; for he was allowed to see her. He feigned delight at her beauty ; but he says that his mind was "bent to other things" —probably less on wife and children at home than on his still insatiate desire for travel. After enjoying Cazazionor's hospitality for eight days, he returned with his host to Ormuz, and took ship for Scind. They were landed at Joah, a port on the delta of the Indus, and proceeded to Cambay, an important harbour in Gujarat, whence fifty ships, laden with cotton, sailed yearly to different lands.

CHAPTER VII.

THE PAGANS OF NARSINGA.

BEFORE Batûta reached India, and therefore long before Varthema's time, Afghan chiefs had swooped down on the fertile plains of India with the war cry of "Allah and the Prophet," and Northern India, with the exception of its southern and western districts, where the Rajpoots maintained their independence, was now under the rule of various Moslem despots. The Deccan was under the sway of a powerful Moslem dynasty—the Brahmany Sultans; but what is now the presidency of Madras and Mysore was divided into a number of petty kingdoms, subject to the Hindu Râja of Narsinga. A full century of conflict had resulted in a partial triumph of the Moslem: the sovereigns of Narsinga paid a certain tribute to be left at peace, although the western coast was, in a measure, protected by a wall of mountains. But Portuguese traders had just sailed into the Arabian Sea and had established themselves here and there at trading stations on the Malabar coast; and these they had fortified. On his outward journey, Varthema, for obvious reasons, showed no disposition to cultivate the acquaintance of these Christian Europeans.

Gujarat was under the rule of Fath Khân, whom Varthema calls Sultan Machamuth. "You shall now hear of the manner of his life. He and all his people are Mohammedans; and he keeps twenty thousand horsemen always with him. When he arises in the morning, fifty elephants, each with a man atop, come to the palace and do him reverence; and this is all the labour they are put to . . . When he eats, fifty or sixty different kinds of music discourse; such as trumpets, different sorts of drums, recorders and fifes, and many others; and the elephants again do him reverence. . . . The Sultan's moustachios are so long that he ties them up over his head, as a woman doth tie her tresses; and his beard, which is white, comes down to his girdle." Fath Khân was greatly dreaded by his subjects; and they believed strange things concerning him; stories which are worthy of the Arabian Nights. These Varthema heard and set down, as did Barbosa, who travelled in the East a few years after the Sultan's death. Machamuth was reputed to eat poison daily, so that, while he himself had become poison-proof, he had only to spit at a foe and death followed within half an hour. "Every night that he shall sleep with one of his three or four thousand women, they shall take her up dead in the morning."

The Sultan was continually at war with a neighbouring Hindu Râja; and his Kingdom of Gujarat had been taken from the Jains—"a race which eats of nothing wherein courseth blood, and will kill nothing that hath life. They are neither Moors nor heathens; and I believe that, if they should be baptised, they would all be saved by their good works; for they never do unto others what they would not that others should do unto them. For dress, some wear a shirt; some, only a cloth round their middle and a large red cloth on their head; and their colour is tawny. And the aforesaid Sultan took their kingdom from them because of their goodness."

These Jains, who at first, mainly differed from Buddhists in believing that the purification of the soul resulted in a Heaven and not in Nirvana, and the relation of whose creed to Buddhism is far from being clear, had built some of their remote and mysterious temples on the heights of Gujarat, where through clouds of incense, female figures, clothed in scarlet and gold might be seen, weaving strange figures and chanting monotonous psalms. But these, Varthema, posing as a pious Mohammedan, might not see; and he makes no reference to the famous temples of Gujarat.

From Cambay, the Persian and our Italian sailed along

the coast to Chaul; thence to a port which has disappeared but which was near Ratnagiri, on the Concan coast; and thence to the island of Goa. "On this island there is a fortress by the sea, kept by a Mameluke with four hundred other Mamelukes. If the captain shall come across any white man he gives him much wage; but first he sends for two jerkins, made of leather, one for him and one for him that wishes to take service; each puts on a jerkin, and they fall to. If he prove himself a strong man, he is put among the able men; but if not, he is set to other task than that of fighting. The captain wages great battle with the Râja of Narsinga" (Bijayanagar the capital of the Carnatic).

From Goa, seven days of land-travel brought the pair to "the city of Decan" (Bîjapûr), a Mohammedan place where "the King lives in great pride and pomp. Many of them that serve him have their very shoes adorned with rubies, diamonds, and other jewels; so you may judge how many garnish their fingers and ears. They wear robes or shirts of silk, shoes and breeches after the style of sailors; and ladies go quite veiled, as in Damascus."

Thence they returned to the coast, and visited ports, many of which have decayed or disappeared. These were subject, but not always friendly, to the Râja of Narsinga; and the Kinglet of Honawar was friendly to the Portuguese. But in spite of incessant warfare, life and property were respected. The journey now lies along the Malabar coast to Cannanore: "the port to which steeds are brought from Persia, and you must know that the levy for each horse is twenty-five ducats. . . . . Here we began to meet with spices." Here, also, were Portuguese established.

They now turned their steps to Narsinga, where Heemrâj held his court. Varthema calls him "King," and indeed he ruled, for like the Frank "Mayors of the palace," he had gradually usurped the powers of the real Râja, and held actual sway in the place of an ancient race which boasted an uninterrupted succession lasting seven centuries.

The city was great and grand; the court, splendid; the revenue, enormous; the army boasted 40,000 horsemen and 400 elephants, and was constantly doing battle with the Moslem and neighbouring Pagan States. "The elephant wears armour; in particular, head and trunk are armed. To the trunk a sword of two arms' length is fastened, and as broad as a man's hand." "Seven armed men go upon the said elephant," shielded by a sort of castle, "And in that manner they fight." "The King wears a cap of cloth of gold; and a quilted garment of cotton when he goes to the wars; over this a garment beset with gold coins; and all manner of jewels are at the border thereof. His horse wears jewels which are of more value than are some of our cities. When he journeys for pleasure, three or four kings and five or six thousand horsemen attend him. Wherefore, one may account him a most powerful prince. The common people go naked save for a loin-cloth. . . . In this realm you may go where you list in safety; but it behoves you to beware of lions on the way."

Varthema was very much impressed by the singular structure and equally singular habits of the elephant, and he speaks admiringly of its sagacity and strength. He devotes a considerable space to this noble beast; gives us the most accurate details; and recurs to the subject over and over again.

The Persian jewel-merchant and he left Narsinga after two days' stay, and visited places which were of much importance then, but which have disappeared from the modern map. At last, they arrive at Calicut.

"Having come to the place where the greatest fame of India is gathered up" our traveller devotes the whole of his second book concerning India to Calicut and the manners and customs of its people, as being those of all the inhabitants of that part of the peninsula which lies between the Malabar and Coromandel coasts. From time out of mind Calicut had been a famous emporium;

to it calico owes its name. When Islam arose, the spread of the Mohammedan faith stimulated the enterprise of the intrepid Arab sailor and merchant and of the renegade from Eastern Europe and Western Asia. The activity of the hardy Arab found scope by reason of the natural indolence of the Hindu and his dislike of the sea. A rich and well organized traffic sprang up between Persia and Arabia on the one side and China and the Spice Islands on the other. Even in China, the Arab contrived to settle; and Calicut remained the chief centre of the Eastern trade. Here, in the season of calm, might be seen the leviathan junks of China; and, at all times, the ships of every civilized Eastern people. But, by the time Varthema reached Calicut, the Arab had found Malacca to be a more convenient mart for the trade of the far-East; and Calicut, a little fallen from her high estate, had become mainly a market for the products of Southern India and Ceylon, and a port of call. And yet greater change was at hand. One of those new routes had been opened up which from time to time, abase the pride of commercial nations and transfer their wealth: the Portuguese rounded the Cape, reached East Africa, broke across the Ocean, and, in 1498, Vasco di Gama anchored off Calicut. The jealous Arabs burned down the factory which the native ruler had allowed the Portuguese to erect, and fierce sea-fights ensued, which were accompanied by much brutality. The contest was between the best sailors of Europe and the huge, but ill-built and ill-navigated fleets of the Arab traders. The latter were unable to expel or even to discourage the invaders, who, incensed at opposition, shewed no mercy, and suffered from severe reprisal. While Varthema was at Calicut, the Zamorin (as its ruler was called by those English travellers who arrived a little later) "agreed that the Moors should slay forty-eight Portuguese, whom I saw put to death. And for this reason the King of Portugal is always at war, and daily kills very many; and thereby the city is ruined, for in every way it is at war." Our traveller arrived at Calicut at the precise time when India, cast into a welter by Mohammedan aggression in its lust for wealth and dominion, was confronted with the yet more insatiate greed of European adventures for fabled gold and direct markets. The competitors vied with one another in all the arts of treachery, cruelty and fraud.

Calicut was a city of mean appearance, occupying an area of about a mile; but the "compounds" were spread over a space of six miles. It was crowded with traders from Ethiopia, Arabia and Persia, Syria and the Levant, Bengal and Sumatra. Varthema calculates that no less than fifteen thousand Moors were domiciled there. He visited the palace of the Zamorin, which was divided into chambers by wooden partitions, on which supernatural beings were carved—beings named dêvas in the Indian Scriptures, and taken by our Italian for devils. The flooring was a preparation of cow-dung, used then, as it is to-day, for its antiseptic properties. Ramna and Krishna and a demon-goddess called Mariamma were the chief objects of worship; so we are not surprised when we read that, in the "chapel" of the palace, the oil-lamps were set on tripods, "on each side whereof are three devils, *in relievo*, very fearful to behold. Such are the squires that bear lights to the King." The chapel was small, but its wooden door was elaborately "carven with devils. In the middle of it is a devil seated, all in bronze; and the devil wears a threefold crown, like unto that of the Papacy. He has four horns and four teeth, a huge mouth and nose, and his eyes strike terror into him that looketh thereon. Devils are figured around the said chapel; and on each side thereof a Satan is seated, in flaming fire, wherein are a great number of souls. And, the said Satan has a soul to his mouth with his right hand and with his left hand he grips a soul by its middle." Perchance the chapel recalled memories of pictured hells on the walls of the Pisan Campo Santo, or of certain other mediæval frescoes at Florence.

He went to a great religious festival near Calicut. "Truly," he says, "never did I see so many gathered together save at Mecca. From fifteen days' journey round about came all the Nairs and Brâhmans to sacrifice." Passing through trees which bore lights innumerable, one came to a tank, wherein the worshippers first bathed before entering the temple, which stood up from the middle of the tank. It had "two rows of columns, like San Giovanni in Fonte at Rome." The head Brâhmans first annointed the heads of the worshippers with oil, and then burned incense, with elaborate ritual, and offered the sacrifice of a cock at an altar laden with flowers. "At one end of the altar is a Satan, which all go up to worship, and then depart, each on his own way."

Early in the morning, it is the duty of the Brâhman to bathe in a tank of still water, and then to wash the idols with perfumed water ; after which he burns incense before them ; nor does the Zamorin eat of food that has not first been presented to the god. "Then the Brâhmans lie flat on the ground, but in a secret manner, and they do roll their eyes in a devilish way, and twist their mouths horribly for the space of a quarter of an hour ; and then the time to eat is come. And men eat of food which has been cooked by men ; but the women cook for themselves."

Varthema's account of the manners and habits of Southern India is neither so wholly accurate nor arranged with such lucidity as Hiuen-Tsiang's record of the region of Ganges and Jumna, written nine centuries before. Nor does Southern India present us with such a high civilization as does the empire of Sîlâditya. But Varthema makes few statements that are not confirmed by other early travellers, and his record bears ample witness to a shrewd, observant eye and honest enquiry. He describes the Brâhmans ; the Nairs, or warrior-caste ; the artizans and other castes of the Malabar Coast. We learn that no one of the two lowest castes may approach a Brâhman within fifty paces "unless he bid him do so"; wherefore they shout a warning as they pass along, and take private paths through the marshes," for, should they not cry aloud, and should any of the Nairs meet them, they may be killed by him, and no punishment follow thereupon."

The Nairs "eat no flesh without sanction from the Brâhmans; but other castes eat all manner of flesh, saving that of the cow." The lower castes "eat mice and fish dried in the sun." All sit on the ground at meals; and the upper castes use the leaf of a tree to scoop up their food from metal bowls; while the lower castes make balls of rice and take it by the hand from a pipkin. All castes and both sexes wear a cotton loin-cloth only. The lowest sort of people suckle their children for three months only, and then feed them on milk night and morning. "And when they have stuffed them therewith, they do not wash them, but cast them into the sand, where they lie until evening. As they are nearly black, one cannot tell whether they be little bears or buffaloes; and they look as if they were fed by the Devil."

Justice was admirably administered—a characteristic of Hîndustân noticed and praised by Greeks, Romans, Arabians, and all travellers. In fact, life and property were fairly safe throughout all civilized Asia. Creditors, on proof of claim, drew a circle round their debtor with a green bough, and within this he must remain until he pay or perish. Should he leave the circle, his life was forfeit to the Zamorin. Murder was punished by impalement; wilful injury to another by fine. Traders transacted business by secret negotiation under a coverlet, certain signs being made with the fingers.

When a man is sick, he is visited by a dozen men, "dressed like devils," who are accompanied by players on divers instruments. "These physicians carry fire in their mouths," and go about on stilts fixed to their hands and feet; and so they go shouting and sounding the music; so that truly they would make a hale man fall to the ground for fear at the sight of these ugly beasts." They force ginger juice on the sick; and, in three days, he is well again—cured in the main, one may surmise, by workings of belief on his expectant imagination. Abracadabra is a useful and time honoured ally to the learned professions. The spirits which preside over the fertility of rice are propitiated in a similar manner by the same men. "When the Nairs die, their bodies are burned with much pomp, and some among them keep the ashes; but common folk are buried within the house or garden."

Varthema tells us of certain social customs which persist to this day in Southern India. The caste or tribe of Nairs who preponderate there, maintain to-day the institutions of their ancestors before history began. Marriage is acknowledged to be the least stable and most diversified of all human institutions; but the Nairs retain more than a trace of the matriarchate and of the polyandry which was associated with the matriarchate. They count descent through the children of sisters only; and marriage is with them the loosest of ties; it involves no responsibility towards the woman or her child. Again the worship of the snake, and, for obvious reasons, of the cobra in particular, throughout India is a remnant of phallic worship. Let us hear what Varthema has to tell us of a state of society which exhibits a stage in the slow and fluctuating course of moral development from primitive promiscuity to the high moral standard extolled, if not completely attained, by the Christian West. There was a habit which is still regarded in many parts of the world as the seal of amity and the highest possible honour which a man can bestow on a friend. "The Pagans exchange their wives." Indeed, they bestowed them on a friend with all the ready generosity of Cato the Censor to Hortensius. "And when the King takes to himself a wife, he chooses among the most worthy and honourable of the Brâhmans" him to whom shall be accorded the *jus primae noctis*. The Brâhman affects unwillingness "and the king must pay him four or five hundred ducats." Here, almost for certain, we have a vestige of old phallic worship. When the king is journeying, he passes on his matrimonial privileges to a Brâhman. Among the inferior castes, "one woman has five, six, and seven husbands, and even eight. . . .The children go according to the word of the woman." "The son of one of the sisters of the late king follows him on the throne." As to serpent-worship, "you must know that, when the King of Calicut has word as to the place where a nest of any of these vile animals is to be found, he has a little house builded over it for water.[1] And, if anyone should kill one of these animals or a cow, he would be put to death. They say that these serpents are divine spirits; and that, if they were not spirits, God would not have bestowed on them so great power that, by biting a man but a little, he shall fall headlong and straightway die." "And when these Pagans go a journeying, it is held for good luck to meet one of these creatures . . . . There are however, great enchanters: we have seen them grasp deadly serpents."

The Zamorin "wore so many jewels in his ears and on his hands, arms, legs and feet, that here was a marvel to behold." His treasury held the immense collection of many previous reigns, stored up for time of need. But that recent scourge of mankind, which spread so rapidly over the world, and which every nation called by the name of a neighbouring nation, had already reached India; this magnificent monarch had "the French disease in the throat."

When the King eats, Brâhmans, stand around him, at a space of three or four steps distant, bending the back, and holding the hands before the month. When the King speaks, there is silence, and much reverence is paid to his words."

[1] Should not Varthema have written milk?

In the warfare between the States of Southern India, an economy of bloodshed was observed which would have done credit to those Italian warriors of whom Machiavelli tells how the condottiere captain was circumspect to save his men, and the foughten field remained almost as bloodless as a chessboard. The Princes went forth to battle with great armies of foot-soldiery and elephants (but no cavalry), armed with swords, lances, bows and arrows, and furnished with shields. But when battle was joined, and the armies were distant from one another as far as two cross-bows' shots might carry, Brâhmans were ordered by one King to go to his royal foe, and ask that a hundred Nairs should fight on either side. Then the selected Nairs would meet midway between the two armies and fight by established rule—" two strokes to the head and one at the legs; and this though they should fight for three days. And when from four to six on either side are slain, the Brâhmans go straightway into their midst, and make both sides return to their encampments." Then the kings were wont to employ the Brâhmans again to bear messages, one to another, asking if that were enough, or more were wished for. " The Brahman says 'no.' And the enemy says the same. Thus do they do battle together; an hundred set against an hundred."

Varthema tells us of the habit of betel-chewing and gives us many other details of the life and manners of the people; of their skill as workmen; of their wretched shipping and of their poor navigation. He had the naturalist's eye, and tells us much of the animals and plants of the district. He describes the crocodile as a " kind of reptile, as big as a boar, but with a greater head; it has four feet, and is four cubits long. It is engendered in certain marshes. The natives say it is without venom; but an evil beast; doing evil to folk by its bite."

The Persian merchant had avowed that his desire was to travel, and not to trade, for he had enough; but all the same, he was sufficiently eager to find good markets.

"My comrade," whose name is now spelled somewhat differently—Cazazionor becomes Cogiazenor—"being unable to sell his wares for that the trade of Calicut was ruined at the hands of the King of Portugal; for the merchants that were wont to hie thither were not there, nor did they come; we set forth, taking the way of a river, which is the most beautiful I have ever seen, and came to a city called Cacolon, fifty leagues distant." This "river"-way was by the Backwater of Cochin.

Cacolon, like so many places visited by our traveller is not to be found on a modern map, but was a mart of some importance in its day, "because of pepper of the best which grows in these parts." Here dwelt a few native Christians "of St. Thomas, some of whom were merchants, believing in Christ." A little later on Varthema's journey, he is told of the tomb of the Apostle, "guarded by Christians." That St. Thomas was the first missionary to India, and that he was martyred there is an ancient tradition. William of Malmesbury tells us in his "Chronicles of the Kings of England" how "Alfred sent many presents over sea to Rome and St. Thomas in India. Sighelm, bishop of Sherborne, sent ambassadors for this purpose, who penetrated successfully into India: a matter of astonishment even in the present time." The legend concerning St. Thomas is however not earlier than the Fourth Century. Earlier tradition makes him the evangelist of Parthia; and St. Thomas was probably confused with one Thomas, a bishop, who arrived on the Malabar coast in the middle of the Fourth Century. The shrine of the saint is in a suburb of Madras. Indian Christianity was an offshoot of Syrian Gnosticism, and Indian Christians were subject to the authority of the Nestorian Patriarch at Mesopotamia. "These Christians say," writes Varthema, "that a priest comes from Babylon every three years to baptize them."

The next place reached by the travellers was Quilon in Travancore, the port of a powerful little kingdom "for ever at war with others. . . . At that time the king of this city was the friend of the King of Portugal, but we did not think it well to remain there, for he was fighting others." The contentions of these petty sovereigns with each other gave the Portuguese the opportunity which has always offered itself to the invaders of India, and which they have never been slow to seize.

From Quilon, they sailed to the south, touched at a place where there was a pearl fishery, rounded the "head of India," and arrived at a port of the Carnatic, which Varthema calls Coromandel. The King of Coromandel was also at war with a neighbour, so Cazazionor and other merchants hired a "sampan," or flat-bottomed boat, and, "at great peril, by reason of many rocks and shoals," sailed from the Coromandel coast and reached Ceylon.

CHAPTER VIII.

FARTHER INDIA, MALAYSIA AND THE BANDA ISLANDS.

ALAS ! the visit was of little profit. As in Ibn Batûta's time, nearly two centuries before, the island was divided between four kings, and " for that they were waging fierce war with each other, we could not tarry long time there." Another reason for the short stay made in Ceylon was that Cazazionor got alarmed at false information concerning the good faith of one of the Kings to whom he was to carry his corals and saffron. This was given him by one of the Moorish traders who were settled in the ports of the island. This gentleman had the same kind of goods to dispose of as Cazazionor, and contrived to hoodwink the Persian with a commercial astuteness and subtlety worthy of a later age. Afraid that one of the kings would contrive to " convey " his merchandise he departed in haste, and Varthema with him.

The latter made marvellous use of eye and ear during his few days' stay in Ceylon. He draws an admirable picture of the people, the climate, the cinnamon, the rich fruits and other vegetable produce, the roses and other flowers, the immense herds of elephants and the big rubies of the island. He was told of the impression of Adam's foot on a high peak, but had no time to visit it, even had the fighting then going on allowed of it. It shows how feeble was the authority of an Indian overlord, and how little supreme sovereignty was concerned with matters other than tribute, that the warring Râjas were the subjects of the Râja of Narsinga, " because of rice, which is brought from the mainland." " Some have lances of cane and swords, and they fight together with these ; but they do not slaughter each other over much ; for they are cowards."

Three days rowing brought them to Pulicat, a town a little north of Madras. They abode with a Moorish trader, who eagerly bought the large store of corals, saffron, figured velvet and knives Cazazionor had with him. "As this land was waging fierce war with the King of Tarnassari, we were not able to stay very long. After a few days we set sail for the city of Tarnassari, which is at a thousand miles distance from here. And we arrived there in fourteen days" In fact, they sailed across the Bay of Bengal to Tenasserim, a fertile province of the Malay Peninsula, at that time tributary to Siam. We find that the Râja "is a most powerful lord and is for ever at war with the King of Narsinga and the King of Bengal. He has an hundred elephants in armour, which are the largest I have ever seen. He keeps an army of 100,000 men, part on foot, part on horse, ready for war. They are armed with small swords and shields, some of which are made of the shell of the tortoise and some are like those used in Calicut; and they have store of bows and of lances, some of which are of cane and some of wood. When they go to war they wear a garment much stuffed with cotton. . . . Much silk is made there." As usual, the domesticated and wild animals are described. Varthema was much surprised at the size of the cocks and hens. "In this land we took great pleasure from some of the things which we saw, and, in particular, at the Moorish traders making some cocks fight every day in the streets where they dwell; and the owners will wage even to a hundred ducats as to which will prove to fight best. And we saw two which fought five hours on end, so that, when it was over, both of them lay dead."

Tenasserim retained traces of phallic worship to an even greater degree than Calicut did. The extreme mark of friendship, so far as the *jus primae noctis* was concerned, was extended to every visitor, preference being given to white men from all lands; "for," says Varthema of the natives, "they are a most liberal and agreeable people." Yet, this obligation fulfilled, the husbands were most jealous of their wives, and whosoever should attempt to maintain relations with them would "put his life in jeopardy."

At dead of night, the corpses "of every Brâhman and of the king are burned, with solemn sacrifice to the devil. And they keep the ashes in vessels of earth, baked into a kind of glass, with narrow mouths. Such a vessel, with the ashes therein, is buried within the house. The sacrifice is made under trees, as at Calicut. And the fire is fed with all the perfumes that can be gotten . . . together with coral. And while the body is burning, all the music in the city is sounded; and fifteen or twenty men, who are dressed as devils, stand there, with much rejoicing. And the wife is there, making very great lamentation; but no other woman." Here Varthema saw the horrible practice of Suttee. He tells us of another custom which strangely recalls the Romantic Service of Love in the days of Provençal minstrelsy. A passionate youth will burn his naked arm severely to prove to his mistress "that he loves her and that he is ready to do any great deed for her."

"As to the manner of refection in this city, the Pagans eat all flesh, saving that of the ox, and eat on the ground from very beautiful vessels of wood, without a coverlet. They drink water, sweetened if it may be. They sleep on high beds of good cotton, with coverlets of silk or cotton. They wear a robe, with a quilt of cotton or silk. . . . Their ears are full of jewels; but of these the fingers are bare."

We find that the son of the King succeeded to his father's throne here; and not the sister's son, as in Southern India. Deeds conveying property were written on paper instead of palm leaves. The bodies of Moorish traders who were unhappy enough to die here were first embalmed, and then buried, with the head turned towards Mecca. We are told of the flat bottomed boat, the double canoe, and the junk; the latter carried small boats to Malacca, where they were unshipped and sailed on to the Spice Islands.

Cazazionor was able to dispose of some of his goods at Tenasserim; and then he and Varthema took ship for Bengal. Eleven days of fair wind bore them across the Bay of Bengal to a city which the ever whirling wheel of change has borne away, and the very site of which is indicated only on some ancient and imperfect map. Banghella was one of the first ports and one of the first cities of the age, situate on one of the mouths of the treacherous Ganges—a river of shifting currents and disappearing shores. Its Sultan was a Mohammedan, for ever at war with the Hindu Râja of Narsinga. "Here," says our traveller, "are the richest traders I have ever met with. Every year, fifty ships are laden with stuffs of cotton or silk . . . and these goods go throughout Turkey, Syria, Persia, Arabia Felix, Ethiopia, and India. Here also are many merchants of jewels from other lands. . . The stuffs aforesaid are woven, not by women, but by men." Like Ibn Batûta, he found Bengal the cheapest place to live in of the whole world.

The records of old pilgrims and travellers are a riot of surprise. Not one of the least unsuspected of Varthema's adventures is his dropping here on Christian traders, who came from a Chinese city, which probably lay north of Pekin. "They had brought silken stuffs, aloes-wood, benzoin, and musk; and said that in their land were many Christian lords, subject to the great Khân of Cathay"—that is to say, to the Emperor of China. The reader will remember that the Chinese Government pronounced Christianity to be a satisfactory faith in Hiuen-Tsiang's time. Fra Oderico tells us of the considerable number of Christians in China during the early years of the Fourteenth Century. Probably the Christian Chinese whom Varthema came across were Nestorians; strange products of the wasted subtlety of the Greek mind during its theological degeneracy; followers of the heretic Nestorius, who upheld that two natures, the human and divine, were in Christ's body, but separate from one another. We may hope that, after so many centuries, such problems had ceased to perplex the good Christians of far-off Cathay. They said that their home was at Sarnau, a place probably identical with the Sanay or Sandoy of Fra Oderico. They wore their native silken breeches and red-cloth caps studded with jewels—a proof of the safety of the city-street and of the highways from land to land under Eastern despotism.

Men are not wont to carry the bitterness of religious prejudice into the market, where mundane profit is at stake; and Cazazionor, the Moslem; Varthema, the Catholic renegade; and the Nestorian heretics seem to have hobnobbed together very amicably. The latter were on their way to Burma, and told Cazazionor that there he might exchange some very fine branches of coral he had for rubies which would sell in Turkey for ten times as much. They proposed that our travellers should go on with them. So Cazazionor sold off all his merchandise, with the exception of "corals, saffron, and two pieces of cloth of Florence of a rose colour. . . . We departed from that place with the aforesaid Christians, and voyaged towards a city which is called Pego (Pegu), distant from Banghella some thousand miles."

Now the King of Burma, being at war with the King of Ava, was away with his army. The party chartered a long dug-out canoe, and followed him; hoping to induce him to purchase. But they were forced to return, owing to the war; and five days afterwards the King of Burma, having gained a victory, returned to Pegu.

The very next day, the Chinamen, who, it would seem, had had previous dealings with the King, visited him, and were told to return two days later, "for that, the next day, he must sacrifice to the devil for having triumphed. When the time named had passed, directly the King had eaten, he sent for the aforenamed Christians and for my companion to bring the merchandise before him." They found the Râja magnificently set in jewels: his head, limbs, fingers, and even all his toes sparkled with precious stones; jewelled ear-rings dragged down the lobes of his ears to the length of half a palm, and the rubies on him "were more than the value of a very great city. . . At night-time he shone like the sun." Yet this resplendent monarch was "so entirely human and homely that a child might speak to him."

Then Cazazionor and other merchants who would seem to have become his partners in this business of the corals, uncovered them. The monarch was so unbusinesslike, or allowed himself to behave so indiscretely, as to show enthusiasm at the sight of such magnificent coral-branches; "and truly there were two of these the like of which had never come to India before." Now begins an Oriental comedy, wherein the trader shall simulate munificence, and extract tenfold from the monarch by craftily working on his natural generosity or regal pride.

The King asked if the corals were for sale. The reply was that they were at his service. The King sighed that war had emptied his treasury; but he was willing to barter rubies for the corals. "We made him learn through these Christians that all we desired was his friendship: let him take the goods and do as pleased him. He answered: 'I know that Persians are a free-handed people; yet did I never see one so free-handed as this man'; and he swore by God and the Devil that he would see which should excel in generosity, he or a Persian." So he ordered a casket of rubies to be brought in, and commanded Cazazionor to choose those he would like to have. "My companion answered: 'O sire, you show me so much benevolence that, by my faith in Mohammed, all these things are a present, which I offer you. And understand, sire, that I journey about the world not to gather merchandise, but merely to see the different races of men and their ways.' The King replied: 'I cannot overcome you in generosity, but take this which I give you.' And so he took a large handful of rubies from each of the (six) divisions of the casket aforesaid, and gave them, saying, 'Take these for the generosity which you have shown towards me.' And in like manner, he gave two rubies each to the Christians aforesaid. . . . which were worth about 1,000 ducats; and those of my companion were given a value of 100,000 ducats." The Chinamen were apparently content with a commission of one per cent., for nothing is said of the vendor paying any. "Wherefore," Varthema continues, "by this, the King may be judged to be the most free-handed ruler in the world; and his income is of about a million a year in gold," derived from lac, cotton, silk, and valuable woods; and this he spent on his army.

The King gave the travellers free quarters which they occupied five days; when there came news that war had again broken out with Ava. So, having seen the burning of two widows, and other sights of Pegu, and found the Burmese "very fleshly," the Chinamen, Cazazionor and Varthema embarked for Malacca.

It is possible that Varthema was not the very first European to visit the city which had become the most important port in Eastern waters; but it is certain that he was the very first European to describe it. It had taken the place of Calicut; it was nearer the sources of supply; the enterprising Arab had settled there and ruled the city, subject to the payment of a tribute to the King of Siam; and the recent descent of the Portuguese on the coast of Malabar had increased its importance. Here were to be found the huge, unwieldy junks of China—those floating towns, with gardens blossoming on their decks—for there was no longer need for them to creep through the straits and take the perils of the Indian Ocean; and the most halcyon of summer seas is never to be quite trusted. Malacca was a cheaper market than Calicut; and hither were sent the drugs, dyes, perfumes, and spices, the precious woods and other productions of China, Banda, the Phillipines, Siam, the Moluccas, Borneo, Java, and Sumatra. "Verily," writes Varthema, "I believe that more ships sail hither than to any other port in the world." He remarks on the infertility of the soil; but speaks of the wealth of Malacca in sandal-wood and tin. The travellers were presented to the Moorish Sultan, who had appointed a Governor to do justice; but the inhabitants at that time were Javanese. "They take the law into their own hands; and are the vilest race ever created on earth. When the Sultan shall hinder, they say that they will no longer dwell on land, for that they are sea-farers"—that is to say they were quite able and ready to make a new settlement. "One may not go about here when it grows dark; for folk are killed as if they were so many dogs; and all the traders who come here sleep in their ships." There was no market for jewels here; and the Chinamen, who still acted as guides to our travellers, advised them to be off. So a junk was hired, and the whole party turned back through the Straits for Pider, on the northern coast of Sumatra.

We are told that the natives of Sumatra were far from being a bellicose race. They were eager traders, very friendly to foreigners, excellent swimmers, and skilful in filigree work. "There were three crowned Pagan Kings; and their religion, way of life, dress, and habits are the same as at Tenasserim; moreover, the wives also are burned alive." The houses were roofed with the shells of gigantic sea-turtles; and the ships were three-masted, with a prow fore and aft. Here were huge herds of elephants, finer than any he had seen; and the land was productive of long-pepper, benzoin, different kinds of perfumed wood and the silk-worm.

The Chinamen now became anxious to return to their own country; but Cazazionor wanted to see the land of nutmeg and clove: could they get there in safety? The Christians replied that they need fear no robbers; but there remained the chances of the sea; the island could not be reached in a large ship; a sampan must be bought. Two sampans were purchased, manned, and provisioned; and then the wily Persian who wished to keep the Christians as guides, began to work on them. "'O dearest friends,' said he, "although we be not of your race, we are all sons of Adam. Will you leave me and this other man, my companion, one who was born in your faith?' 'In our faith? Is not your companion a Persian?' 'He is a Persian now, because he was bought at Jerusalem.'" Whether this statement was a convenient lie, told by Varthema to Cazazionor, or was the calculated fabrication of the latter is not apparent; but it was effective; for "the Christians, hearing the name of Jerusalem, at once lifted up their hands towards Heaven; and kissed the ground thrice, and asked when I was sold at Jerusalem. We answered: 'When I was fifteen years old.'" The Chinamen thought that Varthema must remember his native land, and Cazazionor at once saw his opportunity and used it. Quoth he: "'He does indeed remember it. For months my sole delight has been in listening to the things he told me thereof; and he has taught me the words for the parts of the body and for different sorts of food.'" This settled the matter. The Christians consented to go on with them; and if Varthema would return to China with them, he might remain a Mohommedan, and they would make a rich man of him. "'Nay,' said Cazazionor, 'I am much pleased to have your company; but he may not remain with you: for, out of the love I bear to him, I have given my niece to be his wife.'" A money-bargain settled the question; in two days, the Sampan was ready. "We put many kinds of food on board; and, in particular, the most toothsome fruits I ever tasted; and took our course to the island of Banda."

Not even Marco Polo or Fra Oderico had ventured so far towards the rising sun. Varthema was the very first of European travellers to reach the Spice Islands.

One of those who "cannot rest from travel, but must drink life to the lees," he might, had he been a better lettered man, have quoted the lines of his own great countryman :

> "Ma misi me per l'alto mare aperto
> Sol con un legno e con quella compagna
> Picciola dalla qual non fui deserto."

("I put forth on the deep open sea, in but a single ship, and with that little band that had not deserted me." But if Varthema is no scholar, is he not for ever revealing himself as a single-minded, enthusiastic traveller; an excellent actor, and quite able to live up to his part, a man of sound judgment, native wit, sly humour, and pronouncedly brave; direct and unflinching of purpose; a little vainglorious, yet discrete?

The comrades traversed the landlocked straits of Malacca and the Java and Banda seas, and after fifteen days found themselves on an ugly, gloomy, and flat island, where dwelt "a beastly kind of men, without king or even governor. . . . The administration of justice is not needed; for the natives are so stupid that they could not do evil if they would. They are pagans." Such was this specimen of the Nutmeg Islands. Two days spent here was more than enough for our travellers; so they set sail for the Moluccas—the Clove Islands—and found "the people even viler than those of Banda, but whiter; and the air is a little cooler." We have a full description of the clove tree and are told that cloves were sold by measure, "for they understood not weights. We were now wishful to change to another land, in order to learn new things and all about them." So Borneo was steered for; and, on the voyage, the Chinamen took delight in questioning Varthema concerning Christians and their faith. "And when I told them of the impress of our Saviour's face, which is in St. Peter's, and of the heads of St. Peter and St. Paul and many other saints, they advised me in secret that if I would go with them, I should be a very great lord, because I had seen these things. But I doubted if, after I had been led thither I should ever come to my own land again; and therefore I kept me back from going." Varthema does not think of his indebtedness to his generous Persian host; he has no use for the inconvenient fidelities of friendship or the costly coercion of gratitude; such altruistic weakness did not afflict the men of the Renaissance; "ma per sè foro"—"they were for themselves."

The temptation to visit China must have been strong for a man of Varthema's spirit. A few missionary friars had reached Mongolia in the thirteenth century, a very few bold spirits had penetrated Asia as far as China at the end of that and the beginning of the next century; and Tartars kept up some commercial intercourse between Europe and China a little later. But when the great Tartar Empire fell into decay, and the Moslem recovered his grip of Central Asia, intercourse between West and Farthest East became impossible. The few missionaries who set forth for the Celestial Empire never returned, and China became a shadow and a name to Christian Europe. But it would be no easy matter for Varthema to slip away from the Persian just here and now; the difficulty of ever returning from China, even should he reach it, would indeed prove a formidable problem; and we may suspect, too, that the hardships of the voyage and the heat and discomforts of the climate were beginning to tell on Varthema's iron nerve.

He found the natives of Borneo to be "Pagans, and good folk. . . . Every year much camphor is shipped; which they say is the gum of a tree that grows there. I have not seen it; and therefore I do not affirm it to be so. Here my companion hired a ship. . . . We directed our course to the very beautiful island called Java; and came there, always sailing southward, in five days." On the voyage, the skipper pointed out the Southern Cross; and "told us that, to the south, beyond the island aforesaid

(Java) dwell sundry other sorts of men, who steer by these stars which are set over against ours; and, further, they made known to us that the daylight stays but four hours in those parts, and that it is colder there than elsewhere in the world. Whereat we were much solaced and gratified."

Now, there is no inhabited land to the south of Java where the shortest day is of four hours only; but the assertion of the Malay captain reads as if he had visited Australia, or had gotten some true information concerning that continent; and bold navigators of Malaysia *may* have ventured or been driven much farther over the Southern Ocean to a very high latitude; or, the statement as to shortened hours of sunlight and cold *may* have been a mere inference from the progressive diminution of the day and of heat in sailing south. It is said that indications of the discovery of Australia a very little after Varthema's time are to be found on manuscript maps of unknown authorship. It is interesting to find that the skipper steered by means of a compass, which was not of Chinese make, for the magnet pointed to the north; and that he was provided with a chart intersected by perpendicular and horizontal lines.

Java was under the rule of several kings: "some adore idols as at Calicut; some worship the sun; others, the moon; many, an ox; very many, the first thing they shall meet of a morning; yet others, the devil." Nonetheless, "I believe the natives to be the most true dealers in the world. . . . Some use pipes, from which they blow poisoned arrows from the mouth; which bear death however little blood they may draw. . . Some eat bread made of corn; and some eat flesh of sheep or deer or wild pigs; and some eat fish and fruits. Among the flesh-eaters, when their fathers become so old as to be past labour, their children or relatives put them up for sale in the market-place; and those that buy them kill and eat them cooked. Likewise if any young man shall fall into any dire sickness; and if those that have knowledge deem that he shall die thereof, the father or brother of the sick one shall slay him ; and they do not wait for him to die. And, having killed him, they sell him to be eaten of others. We, marvelling at such a business, some traders of this land, to us : 'O you dull Persians, why do you leave such toothsome flesh to the worms ?' Whereupon, my companion cried out 'Quick, quick, to the ship ; for never again shall these folk come near me on land.'" This is a strange statement ; but there is abundant evidence as to the prevalence of cannibalism throughout Malaysia at this period to confirm it. Yet, says Varthema, "justice was well administered" ; the natives clothed themselves in silk, camelot and cotton garments ; and traded wth the gold and copper which their island furnished abundantly, as well as the finest emeralds in the world. They were a maritime people and fought their battles at sea.

Varthema had lost count of time. It was now the month of June. He was south of the equator, and had crossed the ecliptic ; and, directed by the Chinamen, he found the sun casting a shadow in a direction the reverse of that of northern latitudes. "And thereby we learned how far we had come from our country, and stood amazed. . . . Having seen the manners of the island, we saw no great reason for remaining there ; for we had to keep watch all night, lest some scoundrel should steal up to us, and bear us away, and eat us. Wherefore, having called the Christians, we told them that, as soon as they were ready, we would return to our land. Before we set off, however, my comrade bought two emeralds. . . and two little male children with their private parts wholly cut away ; for in this island there is a sort of merchants who follow no other calling than that of buying little children, from whom they cut all away, so that they are left as if women."

It is obvious that different communities, at varying stages of civilization, inhabited Java ; from "the truest dealers in the world," and those who administered justice well, down to bestial savages. Tales, and perhaps evidence, of the cruel brutality of the Aborigines, affected the imagination of Cazazionor and Varthema strongly; they were not sure that the cannibals, finding themselves in the close neighbourhood of "Persians," and therefore quite unusual visitors to Java, might not be tempted to try the flavour of a novelty; their Chinese guides, moreover, had taken them to most of the parts of Malaysia with which they were acquainted; the softening effect of an equatorial climate relaxed their desire to push on into that cold and gloomy region to the south, of which the Malay skipper had told them; and it would seem that, out of commercial jealousy or from rude humour, "merchants of the country" took a pleasure or sought a profit in playing upon their fears. So they hired a junk, and sailed boldly over the more open water, along the south-east coast of Sumatra, rounded the northern extremity of that great island, and saw Malacca again on the fifteenth day of voyage.

Here they stayed three days, while Cazazionor made up a cargo of spice, perfumes and silk; and here "our Christian companions stayed on. It were not possible to make a short history of how they wailed and lamented; so that, verily, had I not had a wife and children, I had gone with them" (this is the first and last time that Varthema mentions the relatively unimportant fact of his being a yoke-mate and father off the chain). "And likewise, they said they would have come with us, had they known how to travel safely. . . . . So they stayed behind, saying that they would return to Sarnau; and we went on in our ship to Ciromandel" (Negropotam). Probably the Chinese would take passage in some junk of the fleet which came to Malacca every year.

CHAPTER IX.

SOME CUNNING MANŒUVRES.

HAVING unloaded the junk, our travellers chartered a sampan and sailed to Quilon. Now Varthema was very silent about the Portuguese at Cochin and Cannanore when he was on his outward voyage, and indeed he discreetly avoided them, lest discovery of his nationality should wreck his purpose. They must have been at Quilon, too, when he was there before; for the Râja of the district had welcomed Pedro Alvarez Cabal in 1503, and permitted the building of a Portuguese factory. There were now 22 Portuguese settlers in this factory, which was fortified, of course; and a wave of home-sickness swept over the traveller: "I greatly desired to escape," he says; "but I held on, because they were few in number, and I was afraid of the Moors; for there were merchants with us who knew that I had been to Mecca and to the tomb of the Prophet; and I feared lest they should take it into their heads that I would uncover their deceits; so I held me back from running away." The gist of this statement is that Varthema feared the Portuguese garrison was too feeble to undertake the protection of a false hadji from the fierce resentment which Cazazionor and the Arab traders would evince. The excuse as to the uncovering of Mohammedan frauds is but a poor sop to whatever Christian prejudice might remain in Italy. His work done, he was on the look out for a really favourable opportunity of returning to Europe. He had small dread of failure. He had not lost his nerve in the least, this son of the Renaissance of so infinite resource, of such invincible self-confidence and of ability to match; unshakably resolute when confronted with any peril that was unavoidable, and deterred by no feeble scruple when by any means it was possible to evade it ; one wholly sincere in gaining his end—a man of "*virtu,*" a manful man, as the Italians of his day termed it.

After a stay of twelve days at Quilon, the pair voyaged along the Backwater of Cochin to Calicut, and arrived there in ten days. There he found two Milanese refugees who had deserted from the Portuguese ships in which they had arrived at Cochin. It at once occurred to his quick brain that he might use these fellow countrymen of his. "Never had I more joy than in beholding these two Christians. They and I were going about naked" (i.e. girt with a loin-cloth only) "after the manner of the country. I asked them if they were Christians. Joan Maria answered: 'Yea, verily.' Then Piero Antonio asked me if I were a Christian. I answered: 'Yea, praise be to God.' Then he took me by the hand and led me to his house. And when we had come thither, we began to embrace and to kiss each other and to shed tears. In sooth, I could not speak like a Christian; my tongue seemed to be unwieldy and hampered; for I had been four years without speaking to (European) Christians. I spent the night following with them; and neither they nor I could eat or sleep, because of our great joy. You may think how we wished the night were a whole year, that we might talk together of diverse matters." Varthema ascertained that these Milanese were skilled in the making of ordnance, and had instructed the natives in their art, which had brought them the favour of the Zamorin. Hence they feared to return to a Portuguese settlement and, indeed to attempt to escape by land. Experience had sharpened Varthema's inborn ability at stratagem; and when he returned to Cazazionor in the morning and was asked where he had spent the night, he replied: "at the mosque, rendering thanks to Allah and to Mohammed for the blessing of a safe return; whereat he (Cazazionor) was much pleased. And, so that I might learn what was going on in the land,

I told him I meant to keep on sleeping at the mosque, and that I did not hanker after riches, and that I wished to remain poor. And, wishing to make my escape, I saw no way but by deceit; for the Mohammedans being the most stupid of all folk, he was satisfied. And this I did to be able to talk often with the Christians; for they had daily word of everything from the court of the King. I began to act out my deceit, and put on the Moorish saint, and never would partake of flesh, excepting at the house of Joan Maria; but there we eat two brace of fowls together every night. And I would no longer mix with the merchants; nor did any man see me to smile; and I kept in the mosque all day, save when he (Cazazionor) sent for me that I should go eat with him; and he rebuked me for not eating flesh. Quoth I: 'Eating overmuch leads man to sin greatly.' And so I began to be a Moorish saint; and the man was happy who might kiss my hand, and some my knees.'"

Luck was, as usual, on Varthema's side. A merchant, a great friend of the Persian, falls sick, and our new *Santon* (holy man) is asked to visit him. He and Cazazionor go to the sick man's house together; and Varthema assumes the air of a skilled physician, and puts various medical questions in the most approved manner. "Then my companion turned to me and asked: 'O Jonah, knowest thou of any medicine for this my friend?' I answered: 'My father was a physician in my land, and what I know is by that practice which he taught me.'" Then the Persian asked "Jonah" to do his utmost. "'Then' quoth I: 'In the name of Allah, the Pitiful, the Compassionate One!' and felt his pulse, and found him to be very feverish.'" Questioning the patient in true professional style "Jonah" found that he was suffering from some intestinal obstruction. So our physician administered a series of clysters "which did more harm than good"; for by a singular blunder he had used astringent herbs in their preparation, and forgot to warm the last clyster, which put the patient into agony. Then a scene ensued which is told with Rabelaisan directness and is as coarsely comical as that pursuit of Monsieur de Porceaunac by the apothecaries, which delighted the court of the *Grande Monarque.* Jonah is a man of resource and unconquerable force of will; he has his man hoisted by the heels, and keeps him suspended, hands and head only touching the ground. The unhappy patient roars for mercy: "Stop, stop; I am killed, I am killed"; and Cazazionor exclaims: "O Jonah, is it your practice to do thus in your land?" Varthema preserves the assurance of the orthodox physician who cannot err; he asserts that it is no error, and goes on when the sick man is at the point of death. This last remedy is efficacious, however, though it leaves the patient in a painful condition; and Jonah, who was by no means without some grains of human compassion, ordered him some excellent remedies and gave him still better advice. The story which is told with a strong sense of humour, ends with a prescription worthy of the famous Abernethy. The patient is restricted to two meals a day; and is to take a mile of exercise before each of them; "for these folk eat eight or ten times a day. This order seemed to him to be without ruth. However, in the end he was wholly cured; and thus my hypocrisy gat me great reputation. They said that I was the friend of Allah. This merchant would have me to take ten ducats; but I would take nothing. I even gave three ducats which I had to the poor; and this I did openly, so that they might know that I had no desire for gold or gear. Henceforward, happy was the man who might give me to eat at his house; happy he who kissed my hands and feet; and, when anyone kissed my hands, I played my part, letting him know that, being a saint, he gave me my desert. But my companion gat me most credit; for he also had faith in me, and said that I eat no flesh, and that he had seen me at Mecca and before the body of Mohammed, that I had always journeyed with him, that he knew my ways, that I was in verity a saint, and that, knowing me to be holy and devout, he had given me one of his nieces to wife Thus, all men were my well wishers ; and every night I went in secret to the Christians."

At last, the Milanese told Varthema that there was word of twelve Portuguese vessels having arrived at Cannanore, and advised him to try to get there by land. He confesses that his courage failed him for an enterprise so hazardous ; "for I might be killed by the Moors, I being white and they black." The news was confirmed by two Persian traders who arrived from Cannanore, and who were immediately invited by the hospitable Cazazionor to sit down and eat with him and Varthema, who was with him at the time. The traders said that the Portuguese were building a strong fort at Cannanore : "What kind of people may these Portuguese be ?" asked Cazazionor of Jonah. "I answered : 'Do not speak of such a people; for they are robbers and sea-thieves one and all. Would I could see them all of our Mohammedan faith ! ' Whereat he became very filled with malice ; and, privily, I rejoiced."

Next day, the Mohammedan traders, fully alive to the fact that the firm establishment of the Portuguese in India meant the ruin of their trade, flocked to prayers at the Mosque, and took Varthema with them. None but so holy a man should be *imam* and lead the prayers on such a grave occasion. So we find him solemnly reciting the Koran.

During the next few days, he pretended to be very ill, and, in answer to Cazazionor's anxious enquiries, said he thought that the air of Calicut did not agree with him. The attachment of the Persian to Varthema was sincere and deep, and he was not in the least suspicious. He urged the new-found saint to go to Cannanore until they should be able to return to Persia together ; he had a friend there who would give him hospitality. Varthema affected to hesitate "because of those Christians." Cazazionor replied that there was no need to fear ; he should remain within the city. "In the end, having paid good heed to the fleet which was being made ready at Calicut, and the army which had been mustered against the Christians, I set out to give them word of it, and to save me from the hands of dogs."

But first he came to a final understanding with the Milanese. Then there were two dozen Persian, Syrian, and Turkish merchants with whom he was friendly at Calicut. Which would be the better course: to take leave of them, and so, possibly, to set them talking, and arouse suspicion; or to slip away, and so, if some ill-chance should stop him, to condemn himself by having observed secrecy? He decided to be off without speaking about it to any one except Cazazionor and his two friends who were about to return to Cannanore. So, early one morning, he set out in a boat with these two Persian merchants who kept silence about their journey because they were trying to evade the export-duties levied by the Zamorin. But their little bark had only got a bow-shot from the shore, when Nairs shouted to the skipper to return at once. They demanded by what right he was carrying Varthema off without sanction. "The Persians answered: 'this man is a Moorish saint; and we are going to Cannanore.' 'We know full well that he is a Moorish saint,' replied the Nairs; 'but he understands the tongue of the Portuguese, and will tell them of all that we are doing; for a great fleet is being made ready;' and they laid strict command on the captain of the ship that he should not give me passage; and he went by it. We stayed on the beach; and the Nairs went back to the King's house. One of the Persians said: 'Let us go to our lodging,' that is, to Calicut. I said 'Do not go back; for you will lose these fine pieces of cloth, seeing that you have not paid dues to the King.' The other Persian said, 'O sir, what shall we do?' I answered 'Let us go along the shore until we shall find a *prau,*' which is to say, a small bark; and they fell in with this; and we went twelve miles of march, laden with the goods aforesaid. You can figure to yourself how my heart beat at finding me in so great danger. At last, we found a *prau*, which bore us to Cannanore."

He immediately went to Cazazionor's friend with his letter of introduction, wherein was a request that "Jonah," who was a saint, and about to become a relation, should be entertained as if he were the writer, until such time as he should arrive. The merchant laid the letter on his head, and vowed that he would answer for his guest with that organ. A feast was prepared; but, alas! the ascetic saint, however resourceful and however hungry after the journey and its perils, must keep to his rôle, and could only look on—a Tantalus of the Sixteenth Century. The repast finished, the company took a little walk by the sea, and Varthema marked where the fortress of the Portuguese was a-building, and resolved to try for liberty the very next day.

He was up early in the morning, and expressed a desire to stroll about. The Persians said: "Go where you please"; but they went with him. He contrived to lead them in the direction of the fort and to get a little ahead of them. Happening to come across two Portuguese, he declared himself to be an escaped Christian; and one of them immediately hastened back to the fort, taking Varthema with him. Lorenzo de Almeyda, son of the Viceroy and Commandant of the fort was at breakfast. Varthema cast himself on his knees before him and besought protection. Just at this instant, the hubbub at Cannanore, which arose on the discovery of Varthema's escape, dinned in their ears. The artillerymen made ready; but everything quieted down; and Varthema revealed the preparations for war which were being made at Calicut. Lorenzo de Almeyda sent him to his father Don Francisco, the Viceroy, who was at Cochin, where the Portuguese had supported a revolting tributary, and made themselves masters of a little State.

The Viceroy, delighted at getting accurate word of

the designs in progress at Calicut, gave a very favourable audience to the refugee.

Varthema was quite sensible of the generous hospitality and sincere affection which Cazazionor had bestowed on him. He not merely mentions, but reiterates the fact. Yet he exhibits not the smallest compunction at having tricked and deserted him. All moral obligation was as a feather, when weighed against the achievement of personal freedom and that self-fulfilment which was the goal of the Italian of his period. One wonders what were the sentiments of that deluded and forsaken friend. As for Varthema, once more among Europeans, and those Europeans of a cognate race, he absorbs their prejudice against Orientals and "Moslem dogs"; and one realizes how deeper even than to-day, and how impassable, was the gulf which separated East from West. It is to his credit that he faithfully fulfilled his promise to Joan Maria and Piero Antonio; he obtained a pardon and safe-conduct for them from the Viceroy, and a promise as to their safety from all officials who might put an obstacle in the way. To induce the Viceroy to grant a pardon was easy; for that dign tary was aware that he was likely to deprive the foe of two artillerymen and add them to his own forces; moreover he would learn much from the intermediary messengers who were to be sent to them. On Varthema's return to Cannanore, he found a serviceable Hindu, whom he sent five times to the two Milanese, holding his wife and children as a pledge of faithful service. The Milanese were instructed to say not one single word to their wives, who were natives, or to their slaves; but to leave these behind them, and steal off, at dead of night, with what money and valuable jewels they could bring with them. All was arranged; but a slave had been stealthily watching his master's doings; he went to the Zamorin, and told his tale. The Zamorin refused to credit it; but put a guard over the Milanese. The slave, who probably was filled with a spirit of revenge, for which he may have had good cause, next went to the Moorish Cadi. The enraged traders, when the secret doings of the Milanese were made known to them, collected a hundred ducats and sent this to the " King of the Yogis," or ascetic Fakirs. Presently, the homes of the Christians were surrounded by a mob of Hindu devotees, sounding horns, and yelling for alms. " They want more than alms," said the unhappy men. The fanatics rushed the houses ; and, although the two Europeans fought desperately for their lives, they were slaughtered ; yet not before six Yogis lay dead at their feet, and forty were wounded. It was reported that the infuriated Hindus cut their throats when they had overwhelmed them and drank their blood.

Somehow, the native wife of Joan Maria contrived to escape from Calicut, and made her way to Cannanore, bringing her little son with her. Varthema, although he had left his Persian benefactor without a sigh, was touched at the condition of the little half-caste. He remembered the aid which the Milanese had given him and the pleasant nights they had spent together ; and the tragedy which had ensued on their intercourse pierced his feelings. He became the guardian of his friend's son, purchasing him for eight ducats in gold, and getting him duly baptized. But the little fellow was fatally infected with the new scourge, which it would seem the Portuguese had brought with them to the East, and he died exactly a year after baptism. " I have seen this scath three thousand miles beyond Calicut," says Varthema ; " and it is said that it began about seventeen years aforetime ; and that it is far worse than ours."

CHAPTER X.

WAR BY LAND AND SEA

ALBEIT sheltered by a cognate Latin people, our traveller had by no means found a haven of perfect safety. In a few days, we find him taking his part in a great sea-fight between the Portuguese fleet of eleven ships (of which two were galleons and one a brigantine), commanded by Don Francisco de Almeyda, and the great Indian fleet of two hundred and nine sail, which had gathered together from all those parts of the Malabar coast which remained in the hands of the Mohammedan traders. But only eighty-four ships of the Mohammedan fleet were large sail; the rest being *praus*, mainly propelled by the oar. Nor were they all meant to fight: many of them were traders under convoy. As they approached, "it was as if one looked on a very big wood." Varthema, restored to western civilization and Christianity, is borne away by the inexorable spirit of the Portuguese sea-dogs. Never saw he braver men and he is with them in their prayers to God "to confound the heathen faith." He tells us how the Admiral incited his men, by the passion of Christ, to thrust at these dogs; for this is the day which shall cleanse them from their sins; and how the Spiritual Father, crucifix in hand, exhorted them in language so beautiful that the graceless men shed tears. All received absolution, and then the Admiral sailed past two galleons of the foe, firing broadsides into them to find out of what mettle they were. Nothing further happened that day; and next morning, the Moorish Admiral made certain overtures to be allowed to pass by in peace. "Sail by if you can," was the reply of the Portuguese Admiral; "but first learn what manner of men we Christians be." "Mohammed is our trust against you Christians," retorted the Moors, and then they crowded all sail and plied the oar. Don Francisco de Almeyda let them come on until they were immediately off Cannanore; " 'for he wished the ruler of the city to see what stuff Christians were made of" . . . And when the time to eat had come, the wind freshened somewhat and our Captain said: 'now, up, my brothers; now is the time,' and sailed for the two biggest ships." The Moorish fleet struck up all kinds of weird, inspiriting music while the fleets met. Thrice did Almeyda's men cast their grappling-irons on the largest galleon, and thrice they failed; but the fourth attempt was a success. The retaliatory cruelties of the Moors at Calicut were remembered, and not one of the six hundred crew was suffered to escape. Another Moorish vessel was boarded, and five hundred Moors were slaughtered. But the enemy still fought desperately and well, and managed to divide the Portuguese fleet. The galley commanded by João Serrão, who had taken Varthema from Cannanore to Cochin was surrounded by fifty vessels, great and small; and the brigantine was boarded by fifteen Moors, who drove its crew to the poop. But the captain, one Simon Martin, called aloud to Jesus Christ for victory, smote off half a dozen Moorish heads with his own hands, and cast such fear into the surviving boarders, that they threw themselves into the sea for safety. Four other Moorish vessels now drew on; but Martin saved the situation by seizing an empty barrel and making as if it were a mortar; and seeing this, the attackers turned back. Don Francisco de Almeyda then sailed into the very midst of the convoyed traders, captured seven of them, laden with spice and other goods, and sank nine or ten more by gun-fire, amongst which was one with a cargo of elephants. The Moors fled, and the pursuit was kept up by ships' boats, to prevent any attempt at swimming ashore. About two hundred swam twenty miles and escaped; but cross-bow and lance put an end to most. Next morning all the corpses that could be recovered from the waves, or the shore, or from captured ships, were counted: they numbered three thousand six hundred; but, "by God's grace, no Christian was killed on galley or other ship; but many were wounded during the long day of battle." The Moors were a match for the Portuguese in battle, but not in artillery, ships or seamanship. This sea-fight took place in March, 1506, and three months later the Viceroy rewarded Varthema's services, by making him head-factor of the Portuguese warehouses. A man with so much knowledge of Mohammedan and Hindu customs and method, speaking Arabic, and with some smattering of the native tongue; a man, withal, with such experience of the ways of the world, so diplomatic, and so masterful, would be invaluable. A little later, he was sent from Cochin to Cannanore to get behind the curtain of certain frauds; for traders from Calicut had got safe-conducts there by passing themselves off as residents of Cannanore. About this time the Râja of Cannanore died; and the new sovereign was no friend to the Portuguese. He got artillery from the Zamorin, and, from the 27th April until the 17th August there was open war, begun by Moorish traders, who attacked the Christians when they were going to a well to draw water. The latter retired to the fort, in good order; and Varthema and 200 men held it, under the captaincy of a certain Lorenzo de Britto. They had nothing to eat but nuts, rice and sugar. Water they had to draw from a well a bow-shot off, after fighting for it all the way. The investing force had more than 140 cannon; but, although it consisted of thousands of men, they were mainly armed with bows and arrows, spears, swords and shields. This host would rush on with fury, inspired by musical instruments of many kinds and the splutter of fireworks; but they never got within two stones' cast of the fort; and every day half of a score of them were killed and the rest fled. "They said we kept the devil with us for our defence."

At last, up came the Portuguese fleet under Tristão

da Cunha, of unperished name, and his three hundred knights in shining steel, who were dissuaded with difficulty from burning Cannanore to the ground. The ocean, up to now the auxiliary and defence of the Peninsula and its Moorish traders, had become a highway for the enterprise of the armed fleets of Europe. On the arrival of this strong force, the Râja and the Moorish traders sued for peace, which the Viceroy had the foresight to grant. For, whatever victories the Portuguese might win, and at however small a cost, their position in the East was precarious. The Mohammedan world was weak as against Europe for the same reason that Europe was weak as against Constantinople: it was divided. Should the spirit of resistance once become so strong as to overcome local jealousies, with the whole Mohammedan world set aflame in Europe, Africa and Asia, and with the countless hosts of the Far East at the call of the Mohammedan trader, where had the Portuguese—nay where had Europe been?

Varthema, once again a devout Catholic, tells us how he spent leisure hours when there was peace with the natives, in trying to convert some of his old acquaintance among the traders of Cannanore to Christianity. He professes great disdain for the simplicity and ignorance of these Pagans! and the arguments he used were not precisely scrupulous, and were far from skilful.

In November, 1507, at the request of the Viceroy, Varthema accompanied him and Tristão da Cunha to the assault on Ponani, a port to the south of Calicut. He tells us how, after the customary prayers and spiritual monitions, "a little before break of day, we opened war to the death on these dogs, who were eight thousand; and we, about six hundred." Native troops have never had a chance against European arms and discipline. The disproportion of the opposing troops was about the same as at Plassey, two centuries and a half later; and if all De Almeyda's troops were Europeans, as Clive's were not, the latter were all led by European officers and trained in European methods. And if, opposed to Clive and the famous Thirty-ninth *primus in Indis* there were a few French auxiliaries, opposed to De Almeyda and Da Cunha were 64 Moors vowed to victory or death, "for each one of them was master of a ship." "But God gave us His help, so that none of our folk were slain here; yet we killed 140; and of these, with my own eyes, I saw Don Lorenzo slay six; and he got two wounds; and many others were wounded also. For a little while the battle was most fiercely fought. But our galleys neared the shore; and then these dogs began to give way: and for that the water (of the river at Ponani) began to fall, we followed them no farther. But these dogs began to swell their numbers; so we set fire to their ships, burning thirteen thereof, most of them newly builded and big. And then the Viceroy withdrew all his troops to the headland; and here he made some knights; and of these, of his grace he made me one; and that most valiant leader, Tristão da Cunha, was my sponsor." And then they all embarked for Cannanore.

CHAPTER XI.

THE NEW WAY ROUND THE CAPE.

THE home-bound fleet was now loading. Varthema had given the Portuguese a year and a half of faithful service; he tells us that he was anxious to return to Europe; he had had fully five years of perilous wanderings through Moslem and Pagan lands to where no European foot hitherto had pressed the soil; and he was urged "by the affection and kindly feeling I bore my country, and my desire to carry thither and place upon record news concerning a great part of the world." The grace demanded was freely given to one who had worked and fought so well; and on December 6th, 1506, a fortnight after the last great fight, he went on board, and the San Vicenzo and other great ships set sail.

A long voyage across the ocean brought the fleet to the coast of what is British East Africa to-day. Malinda, Mombasa and the island of Pemba were touched at during the voyage along the eastern coast; then, Kiloa, the extreme limit of Ibn Batûta's voyage, a German port not so long ago; then, the Comoro islands, together with several other trading-places which the Portuguese had seized and fortified. All this part of the "Dark Continent" had been long peacefully penetrated by Arab traders and had profited by commercial intercourse with them; and the natives were incited to expel the intruder. The appearance of a rival had infuriated the Moslem trader, and the natives caught something of his spirit in resisting the new comers. They were now beginning to experience the tender mercies of the Christian. The Portuguese spread their faith among the palm groves of the South after the fashion of the Teutonic knights over the heaths of Prussia. They used the sword mercilessly; they burned towns and wrought every horror that can be inflicted by the passions of men released from discipline and from the restraints of a long voyage—men stimulating each other to brutality by mutual example, and infected with that mad fury which is apt to possess any excited gang. But Varthema tells us of the pleasure he felt at the successes of the Portuguese and the spread of Catholic truth. He found Pagans were baptized daily in Africa, as in India. "From what I have seen of India and Ethiopia," he writes, "methinks the King of Portugal, should it please God, and his victories go on, will become the richest King on earth. . . he is the means whereby the Christian faith is spread daily; wherefore it may be credited that God hath given him victory and will continue to prosper him."

We must not accuse our whilom Mameluke of any grave insincerity in writing thus. No doubt he had an eye to the good will of Julius II., and the Catholic public; but every son of the church was expected to express himself in this way, and every son of the Renaissance was ready to do so. As has been said, the Italian of the age was not burthened by any undue sense of sin or over-vexed about religion. These high matters were the care of a special profession—the clergy—and of an organized institution—the Church. The direst lapses into iniquity were "bad shots," as sins were called by the Greeks—mere unfortunate glancings aside from the bull's eye—and absolution was easily obtained. The main thing was to aim at making life a full, rich, and splendid success. None the less, the Rock of St. Peter was at once the emblem of European Civilization and the foundation on which in theory it rested: The Church and European civilization must be spread, to put an end to Mohammedanism, that enduring peril, and the Paganism from which it drew its recruits and no small measure of its wealth and power. This is what lies at the bottom of Varthema's mind. The King of Portugal is destined to become the wealthiest and most powerful of rulers; and the possession of wealth and the unrestricted exercise of power of every kind, mental and moral and physical was the ideal of the age and the reward of its *virtu*.

At Moçambique, an island off what is still Portuguese East Africa, the fleet remained fifteen days to take in provisions, and Varthema crossed to the mainland. He tells us of the blackness of the natives; of their woolly hair, thick lips, and "teeth white as snow"; of how the men wore bark and the women leaves as a loin-cloth; and of the clicking of their speech, like the noises, made by tongue and palate, with which the muleteers of Sicily urge on their steeds. (So probably at some time Varthema had visited Sicily). Finding these negroes "few and vile," he and five or six others armed themselves, engaged a guide, and went on an excursion. They saw great herds of elephants roaming about; but by collecting dry wood, and setting fire to it, they scared the great beasts away. Yet, in the end, they were chased by three she-elephants who had their calves with them, and had to make for a hill in all haste. They escaped with difficulty, and doubtless had not done so but for the mothers of the herd being hampered by the calves they found themselves called upon to protect. The party crossed some ten miles over the ridge and came to cave-dwellers, of whom they purchased fifteen cows for a little rubbish of European manufacture. When on the way back to the ship, they heard a great uproar. It came from the caves, and greatly alarmed them, until they understood from the signs made by two negroes, who were driving the cows, that they need have no fear; and their guide assured them that these people were only quarrelling as to which of them should be the possessor of that rare treasure, a little bell.

Sailing from Moçambique between the mainland and San Lorenzo (as Madagascar was then called), our traveller remarks that in his belief "the King of Portugal will soon be lord thereof; for two places there have already been seized and put to fire and flame." After the Cape was rounded the fleet encountered terrific storms. The ships were dispersed by their violence, nor did they sight each other again during the remainder of the voyage.

Off St. Helena, the voyagers on Varthema's ship were scared by the appearance of whales. "We saw two fishes, each as great as a great house, which, when on the surface, raise a kind of vizor, I should say of the width of three strides, and let it down when they go under again. We were so alarmed at the power of these fishes in swimming that we let off all our artillery." He next describes the boobies of Ascension: birds "so simple and foolish that they let themselves be caught by the hand. . . . and, before they were caught, they looked on us as at a miracle. . . . . On this island are only water and fish and these birds." A few days later, they saw the North Star on the horizon. They touched at the Azores, and at last reached the beautiful estuary of the Tagus, and anchored off the "noble city of Lisbon."

And now we find our traveller, of whom it might, by the alteration of a pronoun be said as of the Egyptian Queen: "Nought could excel his infinite variety," turned courtier. Don Emanuel, "the Fortunate," was staying at his palace opposite the city, and Varthema crossed the Tagus to kiss the royal hand. So interesting a traveller with so much to relate was most graciously received and kept at court for some days. When he conceived himself to be sufficiently established there, he seized an opportune moment, presented the patent of Knighthood which the Viceroy had given him, and asked the monarch to confirm it. It was his majesty's pleasure to order a diploma of knighthood to be drawn up on parchment, and then to sign it with his august hand. This document was impressed with the royal seal, and Varthema having seen it registered, took his leave, returned to Italy, and "came to the city of Rome."

Julius II. sat on the throne of the Fisherman. That

old warrior was the very man to appreciate the resolution, the resourcefulness, and the exploit of Varthema. *Papa plusquam Papa*, he had been a mighty man of valour from his youth upwards; his will of iron was unbroken, and he retained in full the ardour of earlier years. A man of *virtu*, he aspired to control and guide the restive Powers of Europe to his own ends; and to make Rome the centre of the Arts, as well as the political Mistress of the Western World. If he was Head-bishop of the Western Church, claiming supreme authority over the Christian world, he was also a Temporal Prince, a patron of letters and enlightenment. At this very time, Michael Angelo was busy, by Papal command, adorning the Sistine Chapel with stupendous fresco and endowing sculpture with all his own redundant energy and life. Raphael was employed in painting delicate poems on the walls of the Papal *Stanze*. It was intended that Rome should become the world's magnificent capital—a temple to strike awe and submission into the beholder; its only defect, that perchance it might shelter an empty shrine. There was as yet little hint of the terrific revolt of priest and scholar, *lanzknecht* and trader, which was preparing beyond the Alps; a revolt which tore away half the Empire of the Papacy. Little did Theodosius dream of the overthrow of the, sacred city, "urbs æquæva polo," as Claudian sings by the barbarians of the North; and as little did Julius deem that it was destined soon to be sacked by the same rude race. It was nothing to Julius that Varthema had posed as a renegade: here was a man after his own heart. Nor were most of the Cardinals indifferent to the discovery of memorable matters. If an alien faith had been successfully professed for a laudable purpose so full of commercial possibilities, a few aves and paternosters, or a slight penance, made amends in that lax age. Julius gave mandate by word of mouth that Varthema's account of his adventures should be duly licensed, and Raphael, Cardinal of St. George, "Chamberlain of our

Most Holy Lord the Pope of the Holy Roman Church," "being advised thereto by many other Most Reverend Cardinals of the Apostolic See," gave the necessary licence. "Holding the work worthy, not only of commendation, but of ample reward," he granted that the author and his heirs should hold copyright for a space of ten years. The Cardinal did this on the ground, as he explicitly states that Varthema had, in his seven years of travel, corrected many of the errors of ancient geographers, and that the "public use and study" of his volume would be of service. Such a decision had been impossible after the Reformation, the Counter-Reformation, and the Council of Trent. It were hard, even in our days of more single purpose, severely to censure the sanction to publish the work of a Christian who had posed as a Mohammedan only to "promote," as the cardinal says, "such studies as have always been held in the highest honour." Varthema had fully described the products of the East and the localities whence they came; and such information was not only to the advancement of knowledge but to the commercial advantage of his time. Had the Papal Court decided otherwise, the world had lost a priceless record of virile purpose fulfilled and of remote regions hitherto hardly known or wholly unknown. The world is indebted to Julius II. and his Cardinals for their action, whether it be called broad-minded toleration or latitudinarian indifference. Probably the copyright was no unimportant matter to the returned wanderer. As has been remarked, we hear nothing of his having made money by trade in the countries he visited. He was no vulgar gainer of gold, but one who set out to behold the splendour of God on the earth and the amazing manners of that prodigy, man. He dedicated his *Itinerario* to Agnesina Colonna, a daughter of the illustrious house of Montefeltro, mother of that Vittoria Colonna whom Michael Angelo and her own pen have made famous, and the fourth of five distinguished women in whom learning and ability descended from mother to daughter. It appeared in 1510.[1] The Dedication informs us that I, Varthema, "having gone over some parts of the countries and islands of the east, south and west, am of fixed mind, should it please God, to make enquiry into those of the north. And so, since I do not perceive that I am fitted for any other undertaking, to employ what remains to me of my fleeting days in this honourable task." Clearly, seven years of peril by land and sea, the greater part of the time being spent in tropical heat, had not satiated the curiosity or abated the audacity of the born-traveller. But no new *Itinerario* came to tell us of Laps driving their teams of rein-deer, of the splendours of the Northern Lights, or of the marvel of the Midnight Sun.

The *Itinerario* of 1510 was re-printed more than once in Rome, Venice and Milan during the following fifty years. In 1515 it was translated into German; in 1520, it appeared in Spanish; in 1556, in French; and in 1563, in Dutch. In 1577, Richard Eden gave a truncated and corrupt form of the work, which he had translated from a Latin version into English. It was incorporated with his "History of Travayle in the West and East Indies," and reprinted for private circulation by the Aungerville Society in 1884. But twenty-one years before this last date, the Hakluyt Society had printed a translation from the original Italian edition by the Rev. Geo. Percy Badger. The modern translation is faithful and eminently readable; Mr. Badger's annotations are invaluable; and John Winter Jones supplied a preface which is a bibliography. But Richard Eden's imperfect work necessarily conveys more of the vigorous diction and quaint archaicisms of the original because the English style of Elizabeth's time more closely resembled that of ordinary Italian prose in the days of Julius II. Yet, readable and delightful as Mr. Badger's

[1] A copy, rebound in red velvet, is one of the treasures of the Library in the British Museum.

translation is, Varthema remains known only to the specialized student; to the general reader, together with many another ancient worthy of heroic mould, he is unknown, even by name.

THE END.

FOX, JONES & Co., High Street, Oxford, Great Britain.